Desert Wildflowers
OF NORTH AMERICA

Desert Wildflowers
OF NORTH AMERICA

Ronald J. Taylor

Mountain Press Publishing Company
Missoula, Montana
1998

Library of Congress Cataloging-in-Publication Data

Taylor, Ronald J., 1932-
     Desert wildflowers of North America / Ronald J. Taylor.
          p.   cm.
     Includes index.
     ISBN 0-87842-376-1 (alk. paper)
     1. Wild flowers—North America—Identification.   2. Desert plants—
North America—Identification.   3. Wild flowers—North America—
Pictorial works.   4. Desert plants—North America—Pictorial works.
I. Title.
QK110.T39   1998
582.13'754'097—dc21   98-12109
                                                                        CIP

PRINTED IN HONG KONG BY MANTEC PRODUCTION COMPANY

Mountain Press Publishing Company
P.O. Box 2399 • Missoula, MT 59806
406-728-1900 • 1-800-234-5308

To all those people who have labored toward
the protection and preservation of North American
desert ecosystems and their unique inhabitants.

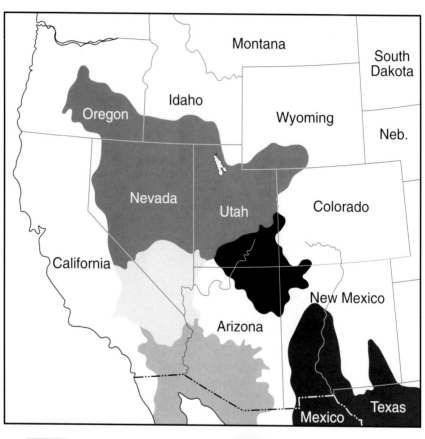

Great Basin Desert

Mojave Desert

Sonoran Desert

Painted Desert

Chihuahuan Desert

Contents

Preface

Disappointment.
Creosote bush, treeless plain.
Dust and tumbleweed twirling
in spiraling heat.
Look closer . . .
Closer.

Wonderment!
Fragrant creosote, wildflower-strewn plain.
Dust devils and tumbleweed dancing
a spiraling jig.
Look closer . . .
Closer.

—Rhonda Taylor

My interest in desert plants and fascination with deserts in general were triggered during a plant taxonomy field trip into the Great Basin and Mojave Deserts. I was an undergraduate student majoring in wildlife conservation, and I shall not age myself by giving the date of the field trip. I will admit, though, to having taken a picture of a fellow student sitting on a rock facing the Flamingo Hotel of Las Vegas—with nothing but desert at his back. A few years later while in the Air Force and stationed at Williams Air Force Base, near Phoenix, I made frequent forays into the desert with my young bride, a lady who is still my "bride" despite the intervening years. My limited exposure to the desert environment in those early years—camping under the stars, smelling creosote bush, marveling at the diversity of wildflowers, dodging the ubiquitous spiny shrubs and cacti—made an everlasting impression on me.

When I got out of the Air Force I went back to school, receiving a degree in botany and subsequently a professorship at a university. My favorite subjects as a college teacher were plant ecology and evolution, in which I emphasized adaptations to arid climates, plant taxonomy, and plant geography. These courses provided the opportunity and excuse to visit the deserts repeatedly, to study the ecology and collect photographs for classes and seminars. This book on wildflowers and the ecology of North American deserts is the natural result of my cultured interest in and fascination with our deserts. It does not, however, adequately reflect the depth of my feelings.

My daughter, Rhonda Taylor, shares my love of desert habitats and joins me in describing our wish that more people would take time to appreciate and preserve desert habitat:

> Most Americans' mental image of "the desert" derives from books, movies, and television. The media tend either to romanticize the desert or to portray it as a veritable wasteland. These seemingly inhospitable lands teem with a vast variety of plants, animals, reptiles, insects, and birds, all uniquely adapted to harsh desert conditions. North American deserts are as varied as the flora and fauna that live there, from the salt flats of Nevada and the sand dunes of California's Death Valley to the rugged canyons of Arizona and the strikingly colorful rock formations of Utah.
>
> Today we live in an era of supermobility, and every year thousands of people visit or pass through desert lands. While a person may gain a certain measure of appreciation for the singular beauty, grandeur, and mystique of the North American deserts by peering through the windows of a speeding automobile, deeper appreciation comes only to those willing to stop and look closer . . . willing to allow the senses to be filled with the ageless balm of silence . . . willing to brave intense heat to witness firsthand the delicate balance of desert life . . . willing to wait motionless at a water hole at sunset for the advent of wild creatures in search of life-sustaining moisture . . . willing to inhale deeply of aromatic, desert air . . . willing to stand silently, looking out at an endless expanse of sky through the distortion of quivering heat . . . willing, for a moment in time, to become more than just an observer or intruder into the untamed desert.
>
> We should not allow first impressions to become irreversibly fixed. Desert habitats provide incomparable opportunities for the visitor to enjoy a distinctly complex and valuable part of our natural heritage. With familiarity comes appreciation, and with appreciation comes the desire to protect and preserve these hardy but delicate domains for generations to come. The North American deserts are not mere unimportant backdrops to our busy lives; they are vibrant, thriving regions of ageless beauty and grandeur. They are worth a second look.

Introduction

I planned and wrote this book for the amateur botanist and anyone who appreciates the desert environment and its varied wildflowers. The ecological background and emphasis, unusual in popular wildflower guides, should answer questions of what deserts are and why they exist. Readers seeking a more detailed discussion of desert topics may consult the Selected References at the back of the book. A section on adaptations explains the multitude of fascinating strategies employed by the desert denizens to deal with their hostile environment. In keeping with the ecological emphasis, the major dominant plants of the varied desert communities have been given special consideration, including distribution maps.

The plants described in this book are arranged by family. Treatment by family has several advantages: it is convenient; it gives the reader a sense of relationships among plants; and a family description reduces repetitive descriptions for species in the same family. The families are arranged alphabetically by common name. In each family, the plants are again treated alphabetically but by their scientific name, since there is seldom any correlation between common names and the relationship of species. Organization by scientific name allows related plants to be grouped together. A strict alphabetization is violated on occasion to facilitate the matching of descriptions with photographs. The coverage of plants within families is by no means complete. In the larger genera only a small sample of the total species has been included—the most common or showiest. Some groups, such as the grasses, are poorly represented, either because working with them requires a high level of expertise or because they are too small or too inconspicuous to be noticed. Although terminology has been kept as simple as practical, we cannot accurately describe plants without reference to their parts. A glossary and labeled plant drawings have been provided at the back of the book. A key for identifying families, noting their location in the text, also is included.

Scientists sometimes change plants' Latin names as additional information becomes available. The result is that many earlier published names become unacceptable or controversial in the scientific community. Eventually, the multiple-volume *Flora of North America* (in preparation) will be the ultimate authority on plant nomenclature. In this book, I have referred to *Higher Plants of California: The Jepson Manual* and *A Utah Flora* as the primary authorities for Latin names. The common names reflect my own bias, since they vary so much from region to region. A good resource for common names is *Desert Wild Flowers,* by E. C. Jaeger, cited in the bibliography.

Many or most plants grow in more than one desert region, so I have opted against treating the plants on a desert-by-desert basis. Also, I have intentionally avoided giving specific flowering times, since the unpredictable environment plays an important role in triggering flowering. Besides, flowering times vary according to elevation and geography. In general, annuals and herbaceous perennials bloom in the spring in their respective ranges, but only if there is sufficient moisture. In droughty years, the deserts are essentially devoid of annuals. In deserts with biseasonal precipitation, some plants bloom in late summer or may even flower twice. Succulents and woody plants generally bloom later in the season, but many flower only sporadically, again based on environmental conditions. So, if you are planning a single trip to the deserts to observe the wildflowers, you should wait for a spring when precipitation has been abundant, and visit sites at various elevations to maximize seasonal progression.

The regional map shows that this book does not systematically treat the Mexican component of the Sonoran and Chihuahuan Deserts, even though their names are derived from Mexican states. The exclusive treatment is a matter of practicality, but there is much overlap in the desert flora of the United States and Mexico. The geographical limits of the deserts, as seen on the map (adapted from Jaeger's *North American Deserts*), are defined primarily on the basis of the vegetation. The same is true of the elevation limits. Species that grow along waterways are included only if they are limited to desert regions.

What Are Deserts and Why Do They Exist?

"Desert" is difficult to define, because environmental and biotic factors vary. Deserts share several features, though, and thus can be readily characterized. These commonalities relate to climate, weather, soils, vegetation, and animal life. Most important, deserts combine low precipitation, high daytime temperatures, and nearly constant wind. The result is that evaporation from the soil and from plants (transpiration) exceeds precipitation, with drought the inevitable consequence. The situation is exacerbated by the irregularity of rainfall and the general impenetrability of the desert pavement.

Why do deserts exist? The aridity of North American deserts is the result of mountain rain shadows and the global factor, which relates to the circulation of the atmosphere in response to the spinning of the earth. Deserts typically form between 20 and 30 degrees north (and south) latitudes as a result of the subtropical anticyclonic phenomenon along the western edge of major continents. Subtropical anticyclones block humid air masses from entering this region. As the wind moves northward in the equatorial zone it is swept aloft, cools, and dumps its moisture. At about 30 degrees latitude it descends toward the south, warms, and picks up surface moisture—creating desert conditions.

Desert Ecosystems

PRECIPITATION

Annual precipitation in deserts is usually less than 10 inches. Equally as important as the amount of rainfall is its seasonality and periodicity. Precipitation is much more effective if it comes during periods of low evaporation. Winter rains tend to last longer and have lower intensity than the cyclonic summer rains, so there is much less surface runoff from winter rain. Deserts with precipitation predominantly in the winter are less arid than those with a summer rainfall season, assuming equal annual precipitation. The Great Basin and Mojave Deserts predominantly receive winter and spring rain, from storms originating in the Pacific Ocean. By contrast, most of the rainfall in the Chihuahuan Desert comes in late summer, from storm cells originating in the Gulf of Mexico. The bulk of the rainfall in the Sonoran Desert and the Painted Desert is biseasonal because of their intermediate geological location.

Relating to periodicity, rainfall comes in pulses or irregular showers, which may be heavy. A biologically effective pulse is one that wets the soil enough for seed germination and seedling establishment. The gap between such pulses varies from a few days to many months or even years. Some years the deserts are in full bloom. These spectacular displays of wildflowers result from two to several shortly spaced biologically effective pulses.

TEMPERATURE

Precipitation is unpredictable, but mean annual temperatures vary little from year to year. Also, monthly means are highly consistent from one year to the next: moderate to low in winter and high in summer. The average high during July and August in North American deserts is generally about 90 degrees Fahrenheit, but in some areas, such as Las Vegas, highs regularly exceed 100 degrees. The mean daily temperatures are much lower. With so little plant cover, heat loss in the desert is considerable during the night, and nighttime temperatures are typically 30 to 50 degrees cooler then daytime temperatures. The average low in December and January varies from below freezing in the Great Basin Desert to the mid-40s in the Chihuahuan Desert, which is nearly frost free.

SOILS

Desert soils have been classified into several technical types based primarily on chemical composition, yet they have much in common. The profiles or layers are poorly developed, largely because of the near absence of organic material. They are deficient in nitrogen but rich in essential inorganic elements. In many areas, the soil surface is covered by small rocks of more or less uniform size cemented together by clay and iron oxides. This surface crust is termed *desert pavement*. It resists weathering and tends to seal the surface, preventing water penetration and promoting runoff and flooding. Calcium carbonate typically accumulates below or occasionally at the soil surface, forming a water-impervious caliche layer.

Despite the dry climate and a scarcity of organic material, the desert soils are alive with microorganisms, chiefly bacteria, algae, and fungi. These organisms are particularly abundant at the base of dominant shrubs and are active following rain showers. The microorganisms carry out such beneficial functions as decomposition and nitrogen fixation. Together with lichens, they form surface crusts that store liquid water, slowing runoff but also reducing infiltration.

Desert soils are often alkaline because of accumulated salts from "run-on" of water rich in salts leached from above. Also, evaporation of water from the soil pulls salts to the surface, particularly in basins with high water tables. Each of these processes can lead to alkali flats or playas.

Soil texture is as important as soil chemistry because it influences water infiltration as opposed to runoff. Water penetrates fast and deep in sandy soils, thus reducing evaporation and more readily supplying the roots of woody plants and deep-rooted herbs. Sandy soils store less water than clayey soils, though, and thus are more quickly depleted. Regardless of soil texture, water infiltration rarely exceeds root depth, and all water is either absorbed by roots or evaporated. Evaporation takes place mainly in the upper 4 inches of the soil, which dries completely in five to twenty-five days, depending on temperature, wind, and soil texture. Evaporation of water between the 4- to 12-inch soil layer requires several weeks. Water loss from depths greater than 12 inches results primarily from absorption by roots and subsequent evaporation (transpiration) from leaves.

WIND

Wind velocity in deserts seldom exceeds that in the surrounding areas, but the wind has a more pronounced impact because it is less impeded by vegetation. In deserts near mountain ranges, winds tend to alternate directions between night and day. At higher elevations, the air cools more rapidly in the evening, becomes heavier, and descends. During the day, the air at lower elevations warms first, becomes lighter, and sweeps upward. Desert winds are often erratic and occasionally violent. Sandstorms scour the surface of rock structures, create drifts around shrubs, bury vegetation, and form unstable dunes. Dust storms frequently blacken the sky for miles, and cyclonic dust devils dance across the desert landscape, tearing at the vegetation in their path. The greatest impact of wind in the desert ecosystem is that it increases water evaporation from the soil and transpiration from leaf surfaces. But more obvious is its effect on vegetation by shaping plants and by the movement of silt and sand. The desert is indeed a place of shifting, whispering sand.

VEGETATION

Interaction Among Plants

It seems logical that with so little available soil moisture, competition among plants for this limited resource would be strong. The density of desert annuals, however, normally much greater under the canopy of large shrubs, suggests a lack of competition. The explanation is simple: the various plant species use water stored at different levels in the soil. Fast-growing ephemerals, annuals, and herbaceous perennials use water stores between 4 and 12 inches. On the other hand, shrubs draw their water mainly from stores below 12 inches. These deeper stores are only slightly affected by evaporation and are thus more stable. Two or more inches of rainfall in a short period of time is required to replenish water stores deeper than 12 inches. Therefore, the drier the climate and the more unpredictable the precipitation, the greater the proportion of annuals.

So competition does exist between plants rooted at similar levels and is responsible for the even-spacing of dominant shrubs over the desert landscape. The small amount of competition between the dominant shrubs and the shallow-rooted ephemerals is insignificant compared to the benefits the latter group of plants gains from the association. The shrub canopy moderates temperature and reduces evaporation and transpiration under it. This extends the time period of accessible moisture. Also, shrubs enhance microbial activity and increase soil fertility. Thus desert annuals ride on the coattails of plants like creosote bush.

Species Diversity

As in any biome, the diversity of species in deserts depends on the diversity of available resources. As environmental variability increases, so do the number of available niches. And the greater the number of niches, the greater will be the number of species whose resource requirements will be met. Also, as noted above, competition is primarily among species that share the same habitat and have the same resource requirements. In a heterogeneous environment, therefore, competition will not be a major factor in limiting number of species. By and large, the desert environment is heterogeneous as a result of variation over space, the variation expressed in terms of soil chemistry and texture, topographic features, precipitation patterns, temperature, groundwater, and various disturbances. So deserts have a rich assortment of life forms with alternative ways of coping with drought, including annuals, herbaceous perennials, shrubs, small trees, succulents, and so on. Coupled with the variability of life forms is a high degree of species diversity. The Sonoran Desert is especially rich in life forms and species because of the biseasonal precipitation pattern. But whether it's the Sonoran or any other North American desert, most visitors will be impressed by the diversity, abundance, and sheer beauty of wildflowers when the deserts are in bloom.

Desert Dominants
The dominant plants of any community are those that have the greatest impact on other plants and animals in the community and the most profound effect on the ecosystem as a whole. They achieve dominance through size, distribution, and abundance. The major dominants have been noted in the discussion of the respective deserts and have been identified by a symbol (✸) and given special consideration, including distribution maps, in their respective families.

ADAPTATIONS
Desert plants must be adapted to survive drought, and the adaptations take a multitude of forms, both physiological and morphological. Routinely, plants are categorized according to their strategy of dealing with drought. Plants can be grouped simplistically as drought escapers, drought avoiders, and drought endurers.

Drought Escapers
Drought escapers are annual plants that grow rapidly, completing their entire life cycle during or following a rainy period. The cells of the leaves are of a type and orientation that maximize photosynthesis, and the first priority of photosynthetic energy is the development of reproductive structures. For these plants it is essential that the seeds can remain dormant for many years and will not germinate unless there is sufficient moisture to ensure reproductive success. It is critical that the plants are in tune with the environment. In many species, the seed coats contain inhibitors, which must be leached out before the seeds will germinate. The amount of rain required to leach the inhibitors should be sufficient to jump-start the plant's life cycle. Other seeds run on poorly understood "internal water clocks," limiting germination to conditions favorable to seedling survival.

Still, on occasion the drought escapers will be tricked by environmental vagaries, so it is important that the seeds of a species are sufficiently heterogeneous that they don't all germinate at the same environmental signal. An entire species' population could be wiped out if conditions fall short of adequate for completion of the life cycle. Once these annuals embark on life's journey, there is no turning back; the next generation depends on the success of their brief and frenetic existence.

Drought Avoiders
Most desert perennials fall into the general category of drought avoiders. These plants don't avoid the drought as such but survive it by avoiding the deleterious effects of drought. Most of the water lost by plants is by transpiration—evaporation from the

surface of plant organs. In most plants, transpiration is primarily from leaves, eloquently designed photosynthetic factories. The expanded leaf surface with its thousands of pores (stomates) optimizes the absorption of carbon dioxide, the carbon source of sugars produced through photosynthesis. In desert plants, the expanded, perforated, sievelike surface area also results in an excessive loss of water, which is usually in short supply. The dilemma for plants, then, is to maximize water preservation without overcompromising photosynthesis. Adaptations must be cost effective. Sugars produced must be sufficient to meet the energy requirements associated with growth and reproduction and to build up reserves necessary to survive periods of dormancy. Since the leaves are involved both in photosynthesis and in transpiration, they have been subjected to intense selective pressures, the result being a large variety of compromising adaptations. Some of the more common types of adaptations are discussed below:

Thick cuticle. The cuticle is a waxy, impervious layer covering the surface cells (epidermis). The thicker the cuticle, the lower the water loss, except through stomatal pores, which cannot be covered without blocking carbon dioxide uptake. The disadvantage of a thick cuticle is that its construction requires diversion of limited photosynthetic resources, and most water lost through transpiration is through stomates.

Hairs. Many leaves are covered by hair (pubescence), which reduces transpiration by providing a moist buffer zone between the leaf surface and the surrounding dry air. This greatly restricts the drying effect of breezes. Also, white or gray pubescence reflects the sun's rays, cooling the plant and further reducing transpiration. There is a construction cost of hairs, though, and carbon dioxide absorption is somewhat reduced.

Leaf curling. Many desert plants, especially grasses, have enlarged cells with thin cuticles regularly spaced on either the upper or lower leaf surface. These specialized (bulliform) cells fill with water during moist periods, fully expanding the leaves. As drought develops, they quickly lose their water, collapse, and the leaf surface shrinks, causing the leaf to curl or fold. This reduces the leaf surface exposed to the atmosphere by approximately half and greatly lessens transpiration. At the same time, it also reduces photosynthetic efficiency by restricting light and carbon dioxide absorption.

Sunken stomates. In many desert plants, the stomates are in crypts or depressions along the lower leaf surface. The relative humidity inside the crypts is much higher than that of the atmosphere, so the difference between relative humidity (the vapor pressure gradient) inside and outside stomatal pores is reduced, and absorption from the leaf (transpiration) is lessened. Protecting the stomates from drying breezes further reduces transpiration.

Cellular compaction. Leaves normally have a great deal of air space associated with photosynthetic cells. This facilitates diffusion of carbon dioxide throughout the leaf but allows water to be lost more readily from these cells. So the reduction of internal air space, cellular compaction, restricts transpiration but reduces photosynthetic efficiency—the price for survival.

Multiple epidermal layer. Some desert plants have one to several layers of tightly compacted, nonphotosynthetic cells below the epidermis on one (the upper) or both leaf surfaces. The adaptiveness of this "hypodermis," which lies between the epidermis and the photosynthetic cells, is that it acts as a water storage area, results in less internal air space, and has a cooling effect by reducing the amount of radiation striking the photosynthetic cells. At the same time, though, it also decreases photosynthetic efficiency.

Reduced surface-to-volume ratio. The greater the surface area of a leaf, the higher the rate of transpiration. It follows, therefore, that natural selection has favored smaller, more compact leaves characteristic of many desert plants, especially shrubs. The cost of this adaptation is significant in terms of reduced carbon dioxide uptake and photosynthetic efficiency.

Sclerophylly. A sclerophyllous leaf is one with a great deal of nonliving, hard, strengthening tissue (*sclero,* hard; *phyll,* leaf). These leaves are adaptive in a desert ecosystem in that less water is lost from nonliving cells, and the strengthening tissue helps prevent severe wilting. The physical stresses associated with wilting from dehydration can cause disruption and tearing of cell membranes, leading to cell death. So the strengthening tissue protects the leaves, but the cost of replacing photosynthetic cells by sclerophyll tissue is considerable.

Leaf orientation. The leaves of many desert plants orient themselves so only the thin edges are exposed to direct sunlight. This reduces the heat load and lessens transpiration without greatly affecting carbon dioxide absorption.

Drought-deciduous leaves. Most desert shrubs are drought deciduous, that is, they drop their leaves as drought progresses. This reduces transpirational loss by up to 95 percent but shuts down photosynthesis, except in plants with green stems. This adaptive strategy is energetically expensive.

Not all adaptations of drought avoiders are expressed in the leaves. Woodiness is adaptive because woody tissue is nonliving and water is conserved through a reduction in metabolically active cells in relation to the total dry weight of a plant. The ratio of nonliving to living tissue must not drop so low that the plants are unable to carry out their vital functions, including reproduction.

Adaptations are also expressed in root systems, which are flexible within species—they respond to water conditions in their habitat. Some species have extensive shallow root systems that effectively mine the upper soil layers for minerals and water and can benefit from light rain showers. Other plants have deeper root systems that depend on periodic heavy rains to replenish water reserves. Some species, termed *phreatophytes,* have very long, deep roots that tap underground water sources. Mesquite, a common phreatophyte, has been reported to have roots that penetrate more than 200 feet deep in the soil! Phreatophytes must overcome two problems: (1) establishing seedlings, in that roots must pass through dry soil to reach a residual water supply and (2) lifting water from great depths. the plants solve the first problem mainly by growing in desert washes, where water penetrates more deeply. The plants overcome the second problem by having a high internal salt concentration (low osmotic potential) that strongly draws water up from the roots. Phreatophytes also combine water-conserving adaptations, such as those described above.

Another drought-avoiding strategy is succulence. Many people associate deserts with cacti and other succulents. These plants have the ability to store enough water to survive extensive periods of drought. The water-storage capacity, coupled with several other adaptations, places the succulents among our most successful desert plants. Many have no leaves but have green, roundish stems covered by a thick cuticle. This minimizes the surface-to-volume ratio and reduces transpiration. The plants have extensive, shallow root systems that take advantage even of light showers by extracting water from the upper few inches of soil before it evaporates. Finally, cacti and other succulents have an unusual but highly adaptive photosynthetic strategy that involves the absorption of carbon dioxide at night. In most plants, stomates are closed at night and open during the day, when carbon dioxide is needed for photosynthesis. In these succulents, the stomates are open at night, when the air is cool and transpiration is low, and closed during the day. Carbon dioxide is thus absorbed at night and stored until daylight, when it can be converted into sugar. The problem with this system is that carbon dioxide is always in short supply, and in concert with the cost of its storage and the reduced surface area, the result is very low photosynthetic efficiency. The plants have paid a great price for the ability to effectively manage their water supply and avoid the consequences of drought. Because of their limited photosynthetic resources, succulents must have a low rate of metabolism not to burn more energy than they can assimilate. They "grow slow and live low"—they are the laid back members of desert communities.

Drought Endurers

Drought endurers are evergreen shrubs that remain active throughout the year. They are the masters of water economy. The characteristics of the living tissue allow them to carry out photosynthesis and maintain some growth even under extreme water stresses. The plants can also extract water that is limited and strongly bound to soil particles. This ability to draw water from "dry" soils, combined with extreme water economy, yields a high resistance to water loss, making drought endurers ideal xerophytes (literally, "dry plants"). The resistance to water loss is based on a combination of adaptations described above for drought avoiders, including, in particular, small, sclerophyllous leaves. As might be expected, these admirably adapted xerophytes, including the ubiquitous creosote bush, are usually dominant members of desert communities.

Another important category of desert plants that includes both the drought avoiders and the drought endurers is halophytes, literally, "salt plants." These are plants that live in salt flats or playas or in other areas rich is soil salts. These plants must deal with drought arising from low precipitation and the physiological drought associated with saline soils. Few plants can survive in salty soils because the salt draws water from the plants, and they die from dehydration. If plants are to survive, the concentration of salts and other soluble materials inside the cells must exceed that in the soil. Thus, halophytes survive by storing salt. Greasewood is our most conspicuous desert halophyte. It is a medium-sized shrub with small, succulent leaves that are salty to the taste.

Herbivory Defense

Not all adaptations are designed to protect plants from drought; some are responses to herbivores, large and small. The fact that deserts have more than their share of spiny plants is not a coincidence. The "profit margin" of desert plants is lower than that of other plants; the difference between energy assimilated via photosynthesis and the energy expended to stay alive and reproduce is small because of all the photosynthetic compromises plants must make to conserve water. They cannot afford to be generous with freeloaders, and defense mechanisms have taken many

step; to save the deserts we must understand and respect them, we must abandon our pioneer mentality directed toward taming the deserts. The North American desert ecosystems can withstand drought but not the disruptive forces to which they are being so indiscriminately subjected.

Geologic History of North American Deserts

BASIN AND RANGE PROVINCE

The Basin and Range Province includes Nevada, southeastern California, southern Arizona, and southwestern New Mexico. The Great Basin, Mojave, and Sonoran Deserts occupy this province, along with the northern part of the Chihuahuan Desert. This province is a collapsed portion of a massive regional uplift that resulted from interactions of the North American and Pacific tectonic plates giving rise to the Rocky Mountains, the adjacent Colorado Plateau, and the Great Plains. Associated with this gravitational collapse, or perhaps because of it, has been extensive folding and faulting. These fragmenting forces, in the past 20 million years, have given rise to a series of north-south trending mountains separated by broad desert basins. Except for some of the higher mountains, the elevation of the Basin and Range Province is less than that of surrounding provinces, ranging from below sea level in Death Valley to several thousand feet. Because of the low elevation of the desert basins, water drains in but not out, resulting in salt flats and saline seas.

COLORADO PLATEAU

The Colorado Plateau includes northeastern Arizona, southeastern Utah, the western edge of Colorado, and northwestern New Mexico. About 90 percent of the plateau drains into the Colorado River. Many parks and monuments attest to the beauty of the plateau. During the Cretaceous period, centered about 100 million years ago, an inland sea extended from the Gulf of Mexico north through the center of North America. By the end of Cretaceous time, about 65 million years ago, what is now the Colorado Plateau was mainly a coastal, sandy plain marked by a series of basins. Colorful sand dunes rich in iron and magnesium swept across the plain. A major uplift that began about 60 million years ago and continues today has raised the plateau as much as 3 miles in places to an average elevation of more than 5,000 feet. Today, the plateau includes the Painted Desert, with its spectacular canyons and red and buff sandstone desert. Red shales and white to bluish gray limestones further paint the desert landscape. Volcanic plugs frequently protrude through the sandstone, adding to the overall beauty of this desert area. At higher elevations, the desert gives way to grassy plains and piñon-juniper woodlands.

North American Deserts

GREAT BASIN DESERT

The boundaries of the Great Basin Desert are arbitrary, largely because scientists disagree about where desert communities end and other, less arid, communities begin. In this book, I have followed the boundaries suggested by Edmond Jaeger and shown in the regional map. The desert lies in the rain shadow of the southern Cascade–Sierra range, which forms the western boundary. To the east it is bounded by the Rocky Mountains, which block weather fronts from the plains. The northern edge of the desert comes in contact with the sagebrush steppe (sagebrush country), which differs subtly in vegetative structure. The southern boundary coincides more or less with the northern limit of creosote bush distribution and the Mojave Desert.

Throughout its geologic history, the Great Basin Desert has been subjected to extensive faulting and folding, with formation of several north-south oriented mountain ranges. The mountains separate the broad basins, which are pockets of aridity. These basins have no drainage outlets; water accumulates at the lowest elevations and simply evaporates, resulting in barren salt flats—playas—some of them several miles across.

The climate of the Great Basin "cold desert" is semiarid and temperate, as opposed to the arid and subtropical climates of the "hot deserts" to the south. Precipitation ranges mainly from 6 to 12 inches, most of it falling in the winter as snow and in the early spring. Temperature ranges are extreme, both seasonally and diurnally. Mean winter lows are below freezing, with extremes as much as 30 degrees below zero Fahrenheit. Summer highs often exceed 100 degrees. Windstorms are common and often severe. The topograghy of the desert area is variable, with elevation ranging from 2,000 to 5,000 feet and averaging about 4,000 feet. The higher mountains in the Great Basin exceed 12,000 feet.

The landscape of the Great Basin Desert looks monotonous most of the year, with dominant gray, low, rounded shrubs, which give the impression that if you've seen one, you've seen 'em all. Most of these shrubs are wind pollinated and lack colorful flowers, adding to their drab appearance. In the drier sites, especially in alkaline soil, species of the goosefoot family (Chenopodiaceae) dominate. These include shadscale *(Atriplex confertifolia)*, hopsage *(Grayia spinosa)*, winterfat *(Ceratoides lanata)*, and greasewood *(Sarcobatus vermiculatus)*. Where the soil is less alkaline, as on the gravelly foothills of the mountain ranges, tall sagebrush *(Artemisia tridentata)* is the major dominant, often associated with one of two species of desert-tea *(Ephedra nevadensis* and *E. viridis)* and other species of *Artemisia,* such as spiny sagebrush *(A. spinescens)*. In sandy flat areas, rabbitbrushes *(Chrysothamnus* species) typically dominate. These low shrubs bloom in the fall and differ from the other shrubs mentioned above in having dense clusters of bright yellow flowers. The horsebrushes *(Tetradymia* species), which are locally abundant, also have bright yellow flowers but bloom in the spring. In contrast with the hot deserts to the south, cacti here are unimportant except in areas where overgrazing has perpetuated the spread of the prickly-pear cactus *(Opuntia polyacantha)*.

The wildflowers here are less abundant and less spectacular than in other North American deserts, but they are represented in most communities. Among the most common and conspicuous species are desert mallow *(Sphaeralcea ambigua)*, lupines *(Lupinus* species), prince's plume *(Stanleya pinnata)*, desert primroses *(Oenothera* species), desert paintbrush *(Castilleja chromosa)*, locoweeds *(Astragalus* species), penstemons *(Penstemon* species), phacelias *(Phacelia* species), and a variety of difficult-to-identify "DYCs" (damned yellow composites), members of the sunflower or aster family.

Progressing up the mountain slopes, the desert communities gradually become more steppelike, dominated by tall sagebrush and bluebunch wheatgrass *(Agropyron spicatum)*. At still higher elevations, and on rocky outcrops, piñons and junipers appear, sparse at first then forming dense woodlands.

Chenopod desert near Tonopah, Nevada

Chenopod-sagebrush community, Great Basin Desert, with Timber Mountain in the background

PAINTED DESERT

Many, or perhaps most, desert ecologists include the Painted Desert as a southeastern extension of the Great Basin Desert. This argument is based primarily on floristic similarities. However, there are important distinctions, especially in the nature of plant communities. The climatic pattern also differs, with a significant portion of the precipitation falling in the summer in the Painted Desert. Finally, the origin of the two deserts involved different geologic processes; the Great Basin was formed from the collapse of the Basin and Range Province, and the Painted Desert is part of the Colorado Plateau, mainly an uplifted inland sea.

The Painted Desert lies above and north of the Sonoran Desert and lacks conspicuous hot desert dominants, such as creosote bush and saguaro cactus. It covers northeastern Arizona, southeastern Utah, southwestern Colorado, and southwestern

*Painted
Desert with
piñon-juniper*

*Painted
Desert
scene*

*Mixed desert
scrub of
blackbrush,
ephedra, and
rabbitbrush in
the Painted
Desert*

New Mexico, and includes the Navajo and Hopi Indian Reservations. Because a large part of it is in the Navajo Reservation, it has been called the Navahoan Desert. It is a high-elevation desert (3,500 to 5,500 feet), and the landscape drains into the Little Colorado, Upper Colorado, Green, and San Juan Rivers. Because of the high elevation the winters are cold, with frequent snow. But the summers are hot, with temperatures occasionally exceeding 100 degrees. Precipitation is biseasonal, with about half of it falling in the summer, often associated with severe thunderstorms. Annual precipitation is usually less than 10 inches; effective rainfall is even less because of high evaporation and runoff following summer storms. In many areas, the desert is made more arid by erosion of the sandstone substrate, forming arroyos that drain the landscape and lower the water table.

Plant communities are largely determined by the soil type. In sandy soils, where the water penetrates readily, species diversity is highest. In some areas, the blowing sand is piled around and over dominant desert-tea species, forming conspicuous hummocks. The dominant teas include *Ephedra viridis,* especially var. *viscida,* and *E. torreyana.* Rabbitbrushes (*Chrysothamnus* species) and dwarf yuccas (*Yucca navajoa* and *Y. harrimaniae*) are also common in sandy soils, along with the attractive and conspicuous Indian ricegrass *(Oryzopsis hymenoides).* Among the most abundant wildflowers in these sandy habitats are dwarf lupine *(Lupinus pusillus),* crescent locoweed *(Astragalus amphioxys),* desert primroses (*Oenothera* species), long-beaked twist-flower *(Streptanthella longisrostris),* and golden cryptanth *(Cryptantha confertiflora).* Over much of the desert landscape the soil is thin, rocky, and typically red. The major dominant in these soils is blackbrush *(Coleogyne ramosissima).* The showy Cisco woody aster *(Xylorhiza venusta)* is often associated with blackbrush but grows in other communities as well. In low, usually alkaline areas with silty or clayey soils, *Atriplex* species typically dominate. The most prevalent of these small, rounded shrubs are mat saltbush *(A. corrugata),* Gardner saltbush *(A. gardneri),* and shadscale *(A. confertifolia).* Along the upper reaches of the desert, especially in deeper soil, tall sagebrush *(Artemisia tridentata)* becomes the primary dominant, and the landscape takes on the appearance of the sagebrush steppe. Above the blackbrush and sagebrush communities, the deserts give way to piñon–juniper woodlands. Some of the high plateaus support grassland communities, where one of the dominants is galleta grass *(Hilaria jamesii).*

Perhaps more than other North American deserts, the Painted Desert has suffered from overgrazing by sheep and cattle. Range scientists have estimated that the desert will support only about five cows per square mile. When this number is exceeded, as it often is, the palatable plants are replaced by less palatable and weedy species. Prickly-pear cactus and introduced annual grasses and mustards are frequent indicators of a history of overgrazing. Perhaps less damaging to the desert ecosystem but more obvious disturbances are those associated with recreational activities. Off-road vehicles have left conspicuous scars across the desert landscape and on the slopes of prominent pinnacles.

The Painted Desert does not have the rich and colorful assortment of wildflowers for which the hot deserts to the south are famous. But it makes up for this deficiency with its spectacular scenery, carved from the unstable, mainly red, sandstone substrate. Erosion has cut deep canyons and arroyos, leaving walls and pinnacles with multicolored layers of sand, shale, and calcium carbonate. The badlands, dissected by canyons and sculpted with colorful pinnacles, alcoves, arches, and natural bridges, are popular tourist attractions.

MOJAVE DESERT

The Mojave is the smallest North American desert. It lies between the Great Basin Desert to the north and the Sonoran Desert to the south, including the northern half of southeastern California, southern Nevada, and a bit of eastern Arizona and Utah. It is bounded on the west by the southern tip of the Sierra Nevada range and to the east by the Colorado River. It is an upland desert, ranging between 2,000 and 4,000 feet. Death Valley, however, which formed with the gravitational collapse of the Basin and Range Province, lies below sea level. At the end of the Ice Age, the Mojave River, arising in the San Bernardino Mountains; the Amargosa River, flowing from the uplands of southwestern Nevada; and the Owens River, flowing from the southeastern slopes of the Sierra Nevada, emptied into Death Valley and formed Lake Manly, which was about 100 miles long and 600 feet deep. Today these riverbeds for the most part are dry, with water flowing in only a few portions of the Mojave and Amargosa Rivers and reaching Death Valley only after heavy rains. Thus, with the exception of some drainage into the Colorado River, the desert is composed of undrained basins, many of which, like Lake Manly, are dry lake beds.

The Mojave lies in the rain shadow of the Sierra Nevada, San Bernardino, and San Gabriel Mountains and is the driest of North American deserts. Precipitation ranges from about 5 inches in the western part to less than 2 inches to the east, falling mainly in winter and early spring. Winters are cold and snow often covers the ground. The occasional isolated summer cloudburst sometimes results in excessive runoff, with water crashing down the canyons carrying sand and debris and causing local flash floods.

The variable terrain reflects the geologic history of the Mojave Desert. North-south oriented mountain ranges scarred with eroded canyons traverse the desert, separating the dry, alkaline lake beds. Volcanic cones and extensive lava flows mark the landscape and reveal the tumultuous past. Beds of clay deposited in ancient lakes have been carved into colorful pinnacles and eroded into multilayered embankments. Extensive limestone deposits have been eroded away to form grotesque sculptures and subterranean caverns. Ancient sand deposits have been activated to form the most extensive sand dunes found in American deserts.

The Mojave Desert landscape is often subdivided, arbitrarily, into the upper and lower bajadas (Spanish for "slopes"). Upper bajadas tend to have coarse-textured soils and are dominated by Joshua tree *(Yucca brevifolia),* an attractive and unusual small tree that more than any other plant characterizes the Mojave Desert. Some of the more common associates of Joshua-tree–dominated communities are other yuccas; various cacti; Nevada tea *(Ephedra nevadensis);* wolfberries (*Lycium* species); *Atriplex* species; desert grasses, especially big galleta *(Hilaria rigida);* the ubiquitous creosote bush *(Larrea tridentata);* and a wide assortment of herbaceous wildflowers. At higher elevations, the Joshua tree communities intergrade with the piñon-juniper woodlands.

The lower bajadas generally have finer soils and are dominated by creosote bush, usually in conjunction with bur sage *(Ambrosia dumosa).* Common associates include Mojave yucca *(Yucca schidigera);* banana yucca *(Y. baccata);* various cacti, principally beavertail cactus *(Opuntia basilaris)* and chollas; goldenhead *(Acamptopappus schockleyi);* cheese bush *(Hymenoclea salsola),* mainly in sandy washes; ratany (*Krameria* species); desert holly *(Atriplex hymenelytra)* and other *Atriplex* species; and numerous showy annuals. In basins, playas, the soil is fine and typically alkaline. Here the dominants are usually members of the goosefoot family—chenopods—similar to those that grow in alkaline sites of the Great Basin Desert.

Creosote bush, brittlebush, bur sage, and cholla of the lower bajada Mojave Desert

Ephedra, Joshua tree, saltbushes, and cholla of the upper bajada Mojave Desert

Lower bajada community of creosote bush and bur sage, Mojave Desert near Las Vegas

High Mojave Desert with Mojave goldenbush, blackbrush, and juniper near Kingman

Along the northern limit of the Mojave Desert the vegetation intergrades with that of the Great Basin Desert. In both deserts such low shrubs as shadscale *(Atriplex confertifolia),* saltbushes (other *Atriplex* species), hopsage *(Grayia spinosa),* greasewood *(Sarcobatus vermiculatus),* wolfberries *(Lycium* species), thorny horsebrush *(Tetradymia spinosa),* and desert-teas *(Ephedra* species) are abundant and often dominant. Creosote bush drops out, however, and tall sagebrush *(Artemisia tridentata)* appears.

SONORAN DESERT

The Sonoran Desert has the greatest species diversity of all North American deserts and is typically divided by desert ecologists into six or more subdivisions, primarily on the basis of vegetation. The large number of plant (and animal) species relates to the variation in the desert landscape and climate—the greater the number of habitats, the richer the plant and animal life. Precipitation varies from less than 2 inches in the western part of the Colorado Desert subdivision to more than 12 inches in the eastern part of the Arizona Upland subdivision, where much of it falls in the summer. A large part of the desert lies in Mexico, and it derives its name from the Mexican state of Sonora. The Sonoran is also the hottest North American desert; much of the vegetation shows tropical affinities, especially in Mexico. Of the six or more subdivisions, only the Arizona Upland subdivision and the Lower Colorado River subdivision are in the United States; this book examines only these two subdivisions.

Arizona Upland Desert

This mountainous region of south and central Arizona is the "typical" Sonoran Desert of the United States. It lies at higher elevations than other subdivisions and is therefore generally cooler. It also receives more precipitation, including summer and winter rainy periods. For these reasons, it is also the most floristically diverse. The bajadas are largely granitic, with rugged volcanic outcrops. Of the several rivers that drain the bajadas, the Gila is the largest, flowing across nearly all of Arizona, from the northeast to the southwest.

The upper bajadas are dominated by saguaro cactus *(Carnegiea gigantea)* and littleleaf palo verde *(Cercidium microphyllum).* Because saguaro is so abundant and distinctive, this upland area has been called the Saguaro Desert. Also, more than any other plant, saguaro cactus has come to symbolize the American deserts. When most Americans think "desert," they visualize saguaro. However, the palo verde is no less conspicuous, especially when its bright yellow blooms blanket the desert landscape.

Several additional plants are locally abundant and often dominant in the upper bajadas. Ocotillo *(Fouquieria splendens)* is particularly conspicuous when in bloom, with its brilliant red or orange-red, tubular flowers pollinated by hummingbirds. It is an unusual plant, with several unbranched, spiny, green stems that drop their leaves when water stresses develop. Ironwood *(Olneya tesota),* a large shrub or small tree with attractive blue and white, sweetpealike flowers, is common, especially in washes. Mesquite *(Prosopis* species) often forms thorny, impenetrable thickets where the water table is high, again, primarily along washes. Brilliant-flowered cacti are abundant, especially the teddy-bear or jumping cholla *(Opuntia bigelovii).* Regal yuccas are conspicuous with their large white flowers. Finally, annual wildflowers make a major contribution to the beauty of the upper bajadas, one group flowering in response to winter and spring rains, another group initiated by summer rains.

The lower bajadas are dominated by the ubiquitous drought-resistant creosote bush, which sometimes forms pure stands but is usually associated with bur sage

Palo verde, saguaro, ocotillo, creosote bush, and teddy-bear cholla, upper bajada Sonoran Desert near Tucson

Creosote bush with desert dandelion, lower bajada Sonoran Desert near Palm Springs

Palo verde–saguaro upper bajada community, Sonoran Desert near Phoenix

Sonoran Desert grassland with acacia and palo verde near Ajo, Arizona

(Ambrosia dumosa) or triangular-leaved bur sage *(Ambrosia deltoidea).* Here also there are many colorful cacti, chollas, prickly-pears, and barrel cacti. Brittlebush *(Encelia farinosa)* is a common and showy plant of rocky slopes, with its numerous stems bearing attractive gray leaves and large, yellow, sunflower-like heads. Other members of the sunflower family are also often conspicuous, and the display of annual wildflowers can be spectacular following rainy periods.

Colorado Desert

As treated here, this, the Lower Colorado Valley, is the largest subdivision of the Sonoran Desert, often further divided by desert ecologists into the Yuman and Colorado Deserts. With this division, the Yuman Desert would include the southwest quarter of Arizona, and the Colorado Desert would be restricted to southeastern California and adjacent Mexico, west of the Colorado River. The lumping of the entire region into the "Colorado Desert" is justified by vegetative similarities even though floristic differences are noted, as would be expected over such a broad geographical area.

The Colorado Desert is low lying, much of it below sea level. The scattered hills are drained mainly by the Colorado River, from which the desert gets its name. The lower basins have no outlet and become increasingly alkaline as the inflowing water evaporates, leaving a salty residue. The lowest basin is the Salton Sink, 273 feet below sea level. This sink has become the Salton Sea, formed from flooding of the Colorado River and a change in direction of flow from the Gulf of California into the Salton Sink. The landscape consists primarily of sandy plains and low, highly eroded mountains of granitic and volcanic rock. Desert pavement covers much of the lowlands, restricting plant growth, especially shrubs.

The annual precipitation of the Colorado Desert is less than 5 inches; and the severity of water stresses is magnified by the low frequency and irregular pattern of rainfall, coupled with high summer and winter temperatures. Still, species diversity is impressive. Creosote bush dominates more or less throughout the desert, often in association with bur sage. Brittlebush is abundant and conspicuous, particularly when in bloom. Buckhorn *(Opuntia acanthocarpa)* and teddy-bear *(O. bigelovii)* chollas abound along gravelly foothills and plains. Beavertail, barrel, and hedgehog cacti *(Opuntia basilaris, Ferocactus acanthodes,* and *Echinocereus engelmannii,* respectively) grace the rocky hillsides with their brilliant flowers. Desert marigold *(Baileya multiradiata)* often lines the roads, forming golden yellow transects across the desert. In sandy areas, sand verbena *(Abronia villosa),* desert primrose *(Oenothera deltoides),* desert sunflower *(Geraea canescens),* and the bluebonnet *(Lupinus sparsiflorus)* singly or in combination put on spectacular displays of color. Other particularly common and colorful wildflowers distributed across the desert landscape include apricot globemallow *(Sphaeralcea ambigua),* Arizona lupine *(Lupinus arizonicus),* desert carnation *(Chaenactis fremontii),* phacelias *(Phacelia* species), suncups *(Camissonia brevipes),* and desert dandelion *(Malacothrix glabrata).* Large shrubs and small trees dominate the washes. These include mesquite, acacias, palo verdes, and the less widespread and singularly beautiful desert willow *(Chilopsis linearis)* and smoke tree *(Psorothamnus spinosa).*

CHIHUAHUAN DESERT

Although the Chihuahuan is a huge desert, only a small part of it lies in the United States, in western Texas and southern New Mexico. The desert, named for the Mexican state in which much of it lies, is separated from the Sonoran Desert by the southern extension of the Rocky Mountains, which is covered mainly with grasslands. The Chihuahuan Desert is cooler than the other North American hot deserts because of its high elevation, ranging from about 1,200 feet along the Rio Grande to over 6,000 feet in Mexico. It also receives the most rainfall, averaging nearly 10 inches, almost all in the summer months. The soil is diverse over this huge desert, largely volcanic with many limestone deposits. In some areas "sand" dunes of nearly pure gypsum (calcium sulfate) cover many square miles—for example, at White Sands National Monument near Alamogordo, New Mexico.

The Rio Grande drains much of the northern Chihuahuan Desert. As in other deserts, however, large portions have no outlet to the sea, and runoff collects in alkaline basins, some of which are dry lake beds. These alkaline flats are dominated by

Agave and lechuguilla in Chihuahuan Desert near El Paso

Creosote bush–grass community in Chihuahuan Desert, northern Mexico

salt-tolerant halophytes, including saltbush *(Atriplex canescens),* a plant that thrives in similar habitats in all North American deserts.

Creosote bush is the most widespread and dominant species in the Chihuahuan Desert, as in other hot deserts of North America. It covers about half of this desert, extending its range into grasslands in areas of overgrazing. Ocotillo is also a widespread and conspicuous inhabitant, as it is in the Sonoran Desert. But the Chihuahuan Desert has its own mascot. While the Mojave is best known for the Joshua tree and the Sonoran for the saguaro cactus, the Chihuahuan has its lechuguilla *(Agave lechuguilla).* This attractive, yellow-flowered agave is the major dominant in what has been called lechuguilla scrub, a community found primarily in limestone soils. Lechuguilla and other leaf succulents, agaves, yuccas, and sotols *(Dasylirion* species) characterize the landscape of the Chihuahuan and distinguish it from the Sonoran Desert, which lies just over the grassy slopes of the southern Rockies.

Other indicator species of the northern Chihuahuan Desert include tarbush *(Flourensia cernua),* a yellow-flowered composite; crucifixion thorn *(Koeberlinia spinosa),* a viciously spiny shrub as the common name suggests; narrow-leaved sotol *(Dasylirion wheeleri),* an attractive "lily" resembling yucca but having smaller flowers borne in a plumelike inflorescence; and bisnaga *(Echinocactus wislizenii),* a barrel cactus. A few other important plants of the northern Chihuahuan Desert are various *Opuntia* species, *O. phaeacantha* and *O. engelmannii* in particular, two closely related prickly-pears with yellow to peach-colored flowers; yuccas, especially the stately soaptree *(Yucca elata),* which frequently grows in gypsum dunes; the thorny mesquites *(Prosopsis* species) and acacias *(Acacia* species), found primarily in washes; and three-leafed sumac *(Rhus trilobata),* perhaps the most common species of gypsum dune habitats. As is true of other hot deserts, annuals constitute an important and colorful component of Chihuahuan Desert communities, especially soon after the summer rains commence. Most of these annuals also grow in other North American deserts.

In Mexico, the Chihuahuan Desert occupies a vast plateau lying between the Sierra Madre Occidental and the Sierra Madre Oriental. The vegetation of this southern and major portion of the Chihuahuan has received less study than the northern portion and is less well known. The area is immense, and what is known is that the vegetation is diverse. Three of the characteristic plants of this southern portion are lechuguilla, candelilla *(Euphorbia antisyphilitica),* and guayule *(Parthenium argentatum).*

Desert Wildflowers

D denotes desert dominant species

ACANTHUS FAMILY   Acanthaceae

Although Acanthaceae is a large family, it is mainly tropical; only a few species range as far north as the deserts of North America. The family is characterized primarily by bilaterally symmetrical, tubular flowers, adapted in shape and color for pollination by hummingbirds. The flowers have only two stamens, which are fused to the corolla tube and positioned at the top of the tube, facilitating pollination. The ovary is superior, developing into a capsule that explodes at maturity in some species, scattering the seeds. Although our desert species are not thorny, Acanthaceae is often called the "thorn family" (*acanth*, "thorn").

Desert Honeysuckle   *Anisacanthus thurberi*

Shrub, up to 6 feet tall. **Leaves** opposite, not lobed or toothed (entire), elliptical, and pointed at the tip, about 2 inches long and less than half as wide. **Flowers** red to yellowish orange, an inch or more long, borne in groups of 2 to several in upper leaf axils; corolla tube with 3 lower and 1 upper lobe; sepals 5, very narrow, fused only at the base. **Fruit** a 2-chambered capsule, each chamber bearing 2 large seeds.

When in bloom, desert honeysuckle and the related **chuparosa (*Justicia californica*)** put on brilliant displays along the banks of desert washes and on rocky canyon walls. Both grow in the Sonoran Desert of Arizona, with chuparosa, which has smaller leaves and brighter red flowers, ranging westward into California.

ALLTHORN FAMILY   Koeberliniaceae

Sometimes the allthorn family is included in Capparaceae, the caper family. When treated as a separate family, as it usually is, it has only one genus, named after the German botanist Koeberlin. North American deserts are home to only a single species, allthorn.

Allthorn   *Koeberlinia spinosa*

Roundish **shrub,** usually less than 5 feet tall; **stems** pale to dark green, hairy, extensively branched; the numerous branches are rigid and mainly reduced to blackish spines 1 to 2 inches long. **Leaves** minute, only a fraction of an inch long, soon deciduous, photosynthesis thus being carried out by the green stem. **Flowers** whitish to pale green, ½ inch across, parts in fours (4 sepals, 4 petals, and 8 stamens), borne in clusters along the spinelike branches. **Fruit** a shiny, black berry.

Allthorn is appropriately named; it looks like a mound of vicious green thorns. Even the flowers pale in comparison to the thorns. It ranges from the Sonoran Desert of California, where it is rare, across southern Arizona into the Chihuahuan Desert, where it is locally abundant and often dominant. It prefers sandy or gravelly soils of desert plains and foothills.

Desert Honeysuckle *Anisacanthus thurberi*   **Chuparosa** *Justicia californica*

Allthorn *Koeberlinia spinosa*

AMARANTH FAMILY   Amaranthaceae

All kinds of species—from small annual herbs to trees—are in the amaranth family. Some species are cultivated for food, others as ornamentals; many are bothersome weeds. Only a few species are native in North American deserts, and only one genus, *Tidestromia,* is described in this book. The family is characterized by inconspicuous flowers that lack petals and are associated with small, often spiny bracts.

Honeysweet   *Tidestromia* species

Low, extensively branched and more or less matlike **herbs,** densely covered with short, branched, feltlike hair, giving the plants an overall white or grayish appearance. **Leaves** alternate at the base of the stems, opposite or 3 per node above, egg-shaped, about ½ inch long but variable in size. **Flowers** minute, only a fraction of an inch across, yellowish, borne in leafy clusters at the nodes and the tips of branches. **Fruit** a 1-seeded achene.

Two species are widely distributed in our deserts, *Tidestromia lanuginosa,* an annual, and *T. oblongifolia,* a perennial. Both prefer sandy or gravelly soils and are often conspicuous along roadsides. The common name derives from the sweet flower aroma.

BARBERRY FAMILY   Berberidaceae

The barberry family is diverse and includes herbs, but only shrubs occur in the deserts of North America. Because it is diverse, it is held together only by the characteristics of the flowers. The sepals and petals are usually similar in color and shape and appear in a few to several whorls of three. Stamens, too, come in two to several sets of three. The ovary is superior.

Desert Barberry   *Berberis fremontii*

Large (up to 14 feet), extensively branched **shrub. Leaves** evergreen, alternate, pinnately compound; the 3 to 7 leaflets are leathery, wavy, lance-shaped to triangular, up to 1 inch long, and bear vicious spines along the margins and at the tip. **Flowers** yellow, about ⅓ inch long and wide, borne in racemes from leaf axils and at the tips of branches; sepals 9 in three whorls of 3; petals 6 in two whorls of 3; stamens 6. **Fruit** a yellow-orange to purplish berry.

Although this species is widely distributed in the Southwest, it grows primarily in the Mojave Desert of Nevada and the Painted Desert of Utah, New Mexico, and Arizona. It prefers gravelly soil and ranges upward into piñon-juniper woodlands.

The berries are eaten by animals, particularly birds. Some people gather them to make into jellies. In the past, Indians used the purple juice of the berries to paint their skin and dye pottery, and they extracted a yellow dye from the wood.

Red barberry (*B. haematocarpa*) is closely related and similar to desert barberry, and distribution of the two species overlaps in the Mojave Desert. Red barberry, which is more common in the Sonoran and Chihuahuan Deserts, can be distinguished by its relatively narrow terminal leaflet, 3 to 10 times as long as broad, compared with 1½ to 2½ times as long as broad in desert barberry, and smaller berries, less than ⅓ inch in diameter but more than ⅓ inch in desert barberry. The name *haematocarpa,* literally "blood fruit," relates to the color of the berries.

Honeysweet *Tidestromia lanuginosa*

Fruit of Desert Barberry *Berberis fremontii*

Red Barberry *Berberis haematocarpa*

BIGNONIA FAMILY
Bignoniaceae

Bignoniaceae comprises many of the most conspicuous trees, shrubs, and vines of tropical forests, adorned with a profusion of large, bilaterally symmetrical flowers that are adapted for pollination by birds, bats, and large bees. The family is closely related to the figwort family, which has similarly shaped flowers, but in the bignonia family the podlike fruits are long and typically hang downward. Only two species, described below, reach into the deserts of North America.

Desert Willow
Chilopsis linearis

Large, willowlike **shrub** or small tree, up to 20 feet tall, with dark brown to black bark. **Leaves** deciduous, mainly alternate but sometimes opposite or even whorled, very narrow (linear), 4 to 10 inches long, not toothed or lobed, typically arched downward. **Flowers** more than an inch long, bilaterally symmetrical, showy and fragrant, borne in racemes at the tips of branches; sepals about ½ inch long, fused with two "lips"; petals (corolla) fused into a somewhat flattened tube with 2 upper and 3 lower, wavy lobes, white to pinkish with yellow markings and conspicuous purple lines (nectar guides) on the lower lobes and throat of the tube; stamens 4, fused to the corolla tube. **Fruit** a hanging, pencil-like capsule, 5 to 8 inches long, with many small, hairy seeds.

Several varieties of *Chilopsis linearis* have been recognized, one or more in each of our hot deserts—the Mojave, Sonoran, and Chihuahuan. It grows in sandy washes.

The desert willow is often grown ornamentally in appreciation of its graceful habit and beautiful, fragrant flowers. It has strong, decay-resistant wood, leading to its use as fence posts.

Yellow Trumpet Flower
Tecoma stans

Medium-size **shrub,** up to 7 feet tall. **Leaves** deciduous, opposite, pinnately compound with 5 to 11 lance-shaped, toothed leaflets, each 2 to 3 inches long. **Flowers** about 2 inches long, trumpet-shaped, borne in racemes at the tips of branches; sepals (calyx) fused into a tube with 5 lobes; petals (corolla) bright yellow, fused into a tube with an upper, 2-lobed lip and a lower, 3-lobed lip; stamens 4, fused to the top of the corolla tube. **Fruit** a linear, somewhat flattened, podlike capsule 4 to 8 inches long and ¼ inch wide; seeds winged.

Yellow trumpet flower has a wide range, from southeastern Arizona into Texas, but is seldom abundant. It grows on the rocky slopes of desert mountains, where it is not easily overlooked, because of its profusion of brilliant yellow flowers. It is a beautiful shrub, often grown as an ornamental.

Desert Willow *Chilopsis linearis*

Yellow Trumpet Flower *Tecoma stans*

BORAGE FAMILY   Boraginaceae

A combination of characteristics makes Boraginaceae one of the easiest families to recognize. The radially symmetrical flowers typically are in a coiled cluster (scorpioid cyme or raceme) along the tips of stems and branches; sepals (calyx) fused at the base, generally densely hairy; the petals (corolla) are fused into a narrow tube with five spreading, perpendicular lobes; in the "mouth" of the corolla tube, at the base of each lobe, a small, usually hairy appendage is borne; the five stamens are also fused to the corolla tube, alternating with the appendages; the ovary matures into four 1-seeded nutlets; and the plants are usually completely covered with stiff, sometimes bristlelike, hairs. The leaves are alternate and generally neither lobed nor toothed. The family is large and includes everything from small annuals to fairly large trees. In the deserts of North America the family is best represented by drought-escaping annuals. The white hair clothing the plants reflects the sun's radiation, cooling the plants and reducing water loss, and limiting insect predation.

Fiddlenecks   *Amsinckia* species

Annual **herbs,** completely covered with stiff, sharp hairs that may penetrate human skin; **stems** generally erect, usually branched, 8 to 24 inches tall. **Leaves** basal and alternate, linear or narrowly lance-shaped. **Flowers** yellow to orange, sometimes with reddish marks, ½ inch long or less, borne in a coiled spike at the tip of the stem and branches; **Fruit** 4 nutlets.

Several fiddleneck species grow in all North American deserts, similar in appearance and separable by technical characteristics. They are abundant in disturbed areas and benefit from heavy grazing by cattle and sheep. Fiddlenecks contain bitter and toxic alkaloids that render them inedible. The two most common and widespread species are **devil's lettuce *(Amsinckia tessellata),*** which has warty (tessellate) nutlets, and **rancher's fireweed *(A. menziesii).***

White Cryptanth (White Forget-Me-Nots)   *Cryptantha* species

Annual or perennial, erect to prostrate **herbs,** densely covered with stiff, white hairs, **stems** up to 18 inches tall, usually branched. **Leaves** basal and alternate or sometimes opposite near the stem base, narrowly elliptical to lance-shaped. **Flowers** white in scorpioid inflorescences; appendages at the mouth of the corolla tube usually yellow and conspicuous, a bull's-eye nectar guide. **Fruit** 4 smooth or roughened, pyrimidal or lance-shaped nutlets.

Numerous white cryptanths grow in North American deserts, separable only by technical characteristics. Many are dinky plants with small flowers and go unnoticed, but a few are showy.

Rancher's Fireweed *Amsinckia menziesii*

Slender Cryptanth *Crypthantha tenuis*

Narrow-Leaf Cryptanth
Crypthantha angustifolia

Cockscomb Cryptanth
Crypthantha celosoides

Golden Cryptanth
Cryptantha confertiflora

Perennial **herb,** usually with several clustered stems up to 12 inches tall. **Leaves** linear, 1 to 5 inches long. **Flowers** showy, golden yellow, about ½ inch long, densely clustered at the tip of the stem and branches. **Fruit** 4 smooth, glossy, triangular nutlets.

This, the showiest of several *Cryptantha* species, grows in rocky soils of the Mojave Desert and, particularly, the Painted Desert, where it is abundant and conspicuous.

Salt Heliotrope
Heliotropium curvassavicum

Succulent, hairless (glabrous), perennial **herb,** with freely branched, more or less prostrate stems. **Leaves** varying in position from alternate to opposite or even whorled, narrowly oblong (wider above the middle), ½ to 2 inches long. **Flowers** about ¼ inch long and across, borne in coiled, 2 to 5 inch spikes, which are usually in pairs, sometimes in groups of 3 to 5, at the stem tip; corolla trumpet-shaped with 5 shallow teeth, white with a yellow to purplish star (a bull's-eye nectar guide) in the throat of the trumpet. **Fruit** 4 nutlets, each covered with long, barbed prickles that aid in their dispersal.

As the common name suggests, this plant grows in saline areas, with greasewood or other salt-tolerant shrubs. It is widespread, with one variety or another in all our deserts. Other *Heliotropium* species grow in North American deserts; some are very attractive, resembling morning glory. One is **Gregg's heliotrope** *(Heliotropium greggii),* a common plant in the Chihuahuan Desert, growing in low, clayey sites where water accumulates after heavy rains. It is a rhizomatous, perennial herb with trumpet-shaped, inch-wide white flowers with a yellow star in the throat.

Gregg's Coldenia
Tiquilia (Coldenia) greggii

Low, extensively branched and compact, roundish **shrub,** 1 to 2 feet tall; the twigs stiff and almost spiny. **Leaves** deciduous, so numerous on the branches that their arrangement is obscured; elliptical, ¼ to ½ inch long and about half as wide, covered with white-woolly hair (felty). **Flowers** pink to lavender, about ⅓ inch long, borne in ball-like clusters at the branch tips; calyx obscured by long, smoky-colored, feathery hairs; corolla funnel-shaped, with 5 rounded lobes. **Fruit** usually a single, 1-seeded nutlet (3 of the 4 nutlets typical of borages abort). The calyx tightly embraces the nutlet, and with its long feathery hairs, facilitates wind dispersal of the nutlet.

When in full bloom this is a strikingly attractive shrub, even though the individual flowers are small. It prefers limestone soils in the Chihuahuan Desert and often forms dense populations.

Golden Cryptanth *Cryptantha confertiflora*

Salt Heliotrope *Heliotropium curvassavicum*

Gregg's Coldenia *Tiquilia (Coldenia) greggii*

BUCKTHORN FAMILY
Rhamnaceae

The buckthorn family is a large, primarily tropical family, including shrubs, trees, and vines. The leaves are simple, usually alternate, sometimes conspicuously veined, and often clustered together. The flower parts are usually in fives—five sepals, five petals (petals absent in some genera), and five stamens. All flower parts except the ovary are borne on a floral cup (hypanthium). The ovary is superior or made partly inferior by the fusion of the hypanthium to the base of the ovary. North American deserts support only a few species of the buckthorn family.

Mountain Lilac
Ceanothus species

Small to medium-size **shrubs,** branches numerous and sometimes spiny at the tip. **Leaves** simple, sometimes toothed, alternate in some species, opposite in others, usually with 3 prominent veins. **Flowers** small but showy, white or blue, borne in umbel-like clusters in leaf axils and/or stem tips. **Fruit** a 3-chambered capsule, each chamber bearing a single, large seed.

Many species of *Ceanothus* grow in the southwestern United States, most of them in chaparral biomes of California, where they are notably adapted to periodic fires. A few species extend downward into the desert mountains. **Desert mountain lilac *(Ceanothus greggii),*** a low shrub with woolly, unarmed stems, is the most widespread of these drought-adapted species. The leaves are only about ½ inch long and half as wide, opposite and evergreen. The flowers are white to purplish in open clusters, making up in number what they lack in size. It ranges from California northward into Nevada and eastward into Arizona, New Mexico, Texas, and Utah and is best represented in the Painted Desert.

Mexican Crucillo (Abrojo)
Condalia warnockii

Compact, densely branched **shrub,** 3 to 6 feet tall, the branches velvety and spine-tipped. **Leaves** alternate but generally clustered, deciduous, narrow, only ¼ inch long. **Flowers** tiny and inconspicuous with no petals, borne along the branches; sepals white. **Fruit** a purplish, edible drupe (cherrylike with a pit).

This is a variable species, ranging from the Sonoran Desert of southeastern Arizona into the Chihuahuan Desert. It prefers rocky soils and usually grows along canyon walls and in washes.

Graythorn *(Ziziphus obtusifolia)* is a closely related, thorny shrub, often placed in the same genus *(Condalia)*. It, too, is a variable species, differing from Mexican crucillo by having egg-shaped, somewhat larger leaves and flowers with petals. The flowers are tiny and inconspicuous. It grows on rocky slopes and ridgetops in the Sonoran, Mojave, and Chihuahuan Deserts.

Desert Mountain Lilac *Ceanothus greggii*

Mexican Crucillo *Condalia warnockii*

Graythorn *Ziziphus obtusifolia* —Donald Pinkava photo

BUCKWHEAT FAMILY   Polygonaceae

The buckwheat family is extremely diverse, varying in habit from small annuals to trees. It is generally held together by the nature of the flowers and fruit. The perianth segments (sepals and petals) are similar or the petals are absent, and the fruit is a one-seeded achene. Several genera, including *Polygonum* and *Rumex,* have papery stipules that wrap around the stem above the nodes. Some genera, including *Eriogonum* and *Chorizanthe,* have umbellate inflorescences surrounded by bracts (involucral bracts). Many species in these latter two genera grow in North American deserts.

Brittle Spineflower   *Chorizanthe brevicornu*

Annual, erect **herb,** up to 1 foot tall; **stems** yellowish green and photosynthetic, branches in pairs (dichotomously branched), brittle (readily breaking at the nodes), clothed with short, stiff hairs. **Leaves** basal (stem leaves reduced to bracts), narrowly elliptical, ½ to 2 inches long and only ⅛ as wide. **Flowers** with 6 whitish but small and inconspicuous perianth segments and 3 stamens, borne in the axils of branches and surrounded by a whorl of spine-tipped bracts, thus the common name. **Fruit** a 3-angled, 1-seeded achene.

This is the most widespread of many desert species of *Chorizanthe.* All are low, unattractive annuals, sometimes growing in dense populations. Brittle spineflower inhabits all North American deserts except the Chihuahuan Desert, and is frequently associated with creosote bush.

Bicolored Buckwheat   *Eriogonum bicolor*

Low, mat-forming **shrub,** 1 to 4 inches tall; **stems** up to 8 inches long but spreading horizontally from a woody root crown. **Leaves** alternate, ¼ to ½ inch long, narrowly elliptical, the lower surface covered by white, woolly hair but largely hidden by the leaf margins, which are rolled downward. **Flowers** borne in compact umbels surrounded by an involucre of 5 partially fused bracts; perianth segments 6, in 2 sets of 3, white to pink, usually with darker, reddish stripes along their midvein; stamens 9. **Fruit** a brown, 1-seeded, triangular achene.

Bicolored buckwheat is an attractive shrub, complimenting the colorful rocky landscape of the Painted Desert where it grows. Another attractive, mat-forming species is **cushion buckwheat (*Eriogonum ovalifolium*).** It has ball-shaped, white or yellow to reddish flower clusters borne on leafless stems arising from the leafy cushion. The leaves are up to 2 inches long, elliptical, and densely covered with white wool. This variable species grows in rocky soils from deserts to alpine ridges, most notably in the Great Basin.

Brittle Spineflower *Chorizanthe brevicornu*

Bicolored Buckwheat *Eriogonum bicolor*

Cushion Buckwheat *Eriogonum ovalifolium*

Mojave Buckwheat
Eriogonum fasciculatum

Low **shrub,** up to 3 feet tall; **stems** several from a branched root crown, clump-forming. Some branches often lie on the ground, rooting and increasing the width of the clump. **Leaves** alternate, leathery, narrowly elliptical, up to ½ inch long and ¼ as wide, the lower surface white-woolly; leaf margins rolled under. Clusters (fascicles) of secondary leaves are typically borne in the axils of the lower primary leaves. **Flowers** white to pinkish in congested, ball-like umbels at the tip of the stems; involucral bracts and perianth segments woolly-pubescent. **Fruit** a triangular achene.

    Eriogonum fasciculatum is an extremely complex species, and several varieties have been recognized. The habitat is equally diverse, ranging from piñon-juniper woodlands and chaparral to Mojave and Sonoran Desert scrub. Some of the varieties are invasive and thrive in disturbed areas. Wherever it grows, it is an important nectar source for bees. The species is particularly common in California and has been called "California buckwheat." Another ecologically important, wide-ranging desert buckwheat is **Wright buckwheat *(Eriogonum wrightii),*** an extensively branched subshrub with numerous small umbels of white or pinkish flowers.

Desert Trumpet
Eriogonum inflatum

Annual or biennial **herb,** varying from a few inches tall in particularly dry sites to 3 feet tall where moisture is readily available; **stems** inflated immediately below the first whorl of branches, the characteristic responsible for the Latin and common names. **Leaves** all basal, usually hairy; leaf blades oblong to round or heart-shaped, up to an inch long, typically with wavy margins; leaf stalks (petioles) longer than the blades. **Flowers** pale yellow to reddish, tiny, borne in small, compact umbels at the tip of threadlike branches. **Fruit** a triangular achene.

    Although desert trumpet lacks showy flowers, it is the best known of the many *Eriogonum* species, easily recognized by its inflated stem. It grows in sandy and gravelly soils in all North American deserts except the Chihuahuan Desert, where it is replaced by **annual buckwheat *(E. annuum),*** the showiest of many additional annual species of *Eriogonum.*

Canaigre
Rumex hymenosepalus

This large, succulent **herb** is easily recognized. It grows in sandy soils of all North American deserts, but is most abundant in the Painted Desert. The common name is probably derived from Indians who ate the stems and leaves and used a root extract to treat colds. The fleshy, acidic leaf petioles have been used by Mexicans as a rhubarb substitute; the species is often called **"wild rhubarb."**

Mojave Buckwheat
Eriogonum fasciculatum ssp. *polifolium*

Desert Trumpet
Eriogonum inflatum

Annual Buckwheat *Eriogonum annuum*

Canaigre *Rumex hymenosepalus*

BUTTERCUP FAMILY Ranunculaceae

Ranunculaceae is among our most primitive families and probably shared the earth with dinosaurs a hundred million years ago. The primitive qualities are evident in the lack of reduction in and fusion of flower parts. The family is thus characterized by having many stamens, multiple pistils, and unfused sepals and petals. With a few notable exceptions, the flowers are radially symmetrical and pollinated by nonspecialized insects.

Although the family is large, only a few species have adapted to the harsh desert environment, most of them in the genus *Delphinium*. *Delphinium* is one of the most advanced genera in the family, unusual in having bilaterally symmetrical flowers.

Larkspurs *Delphinium* species

Perennial, erect **herbs** with shallow, thickened, fibrous roots; **stems** solitary, usually branched above, 1 to 2 feet tall. **Leaves** basal and alternate, the former with long stalks (petioles), the alternate ones reduced upward on the stem, eventually becoming bractlike; leaf blades roundish in outline, 1 to 2 inches wide, palmately divided into narrow segments. **Flowers** borne in open racemes; sepals blue, about ½ inch long, showier than the petals, the upper of 5 modified into a blade and a ½- to 1-inch posterior spur; petals 4 in two distinct pairs, the upper pair paler than the lower; pistils 3 to 5, which mature into many-seeded pods (follicles).

The most common desert larkspur is, appropriately, **desert larkspur (Delphinium parishii).** This species has strikingly attractive flowers with vivid, sky-blue to lavender-blue sepals. The two upper petals are white and the two lower are blue, with a conspicuous tuft of hair on the inside. Desert larkspur grows on gravelly soils in the Mojave and Sonoran Deserts, primarily in the upper bajadas.

Another common species is **Anderson larkspur (D. andersonii),** which has dark blue flowers. Two varieties are recognized: *andersonii,* primarily a Great Basin plant, growing in gravelly soils with sagebrush, shadscale, and saltbush species, and *scaposum* of the Mojave, Sonoran, and Painted Deserts. The latter variety is essentially scapose—it has no well-developed stem leaves.

Larkspurs' flowers are specialized for pollination by bumblebees. These strong and clever insects push the petals aside and struggle through the tangle of stamens and styles to reach the mouth of the spur, where they probe for nectar. Larkspurs are also equipped to deal with herbivores, producing alkaloids that place them among the most poisonous of desert plants.

CACTUS FAMILY Cactaceae

The cactus family more than any other symbolizes the North American desert. It is here that the family achieves its greatest success, both in species diversity and in ecological importance. Several adaptations combine to make the cacti successful: the ability to store and conserve water; extensive, shallow root systems that enable the plants to absorb water after even minor rainstorms; the lack of leaves, so the surface area where water can be lost is greatly reduced; and a photosynthetic system that allows them to open stomates at night when it is cool and relative humidity is high, thus greatly restricting water loss through transpiration. All these adaptations have their cost, though, in photosynthetic efficiency. Cacti are survivors, even though they have compromised metabolic activities and growth rate through their preoccupation with staying wet.

Desert Larkspur
Delphinium parishii ssp. *parishii*

Anderson Larkspur
Delphinium andersonii var. *scaposum*

Anderson Larkspur
Delphinium andersonii

Jumping Cholla
(*Opuntia bigelovii*)
and Saguaro
(*Carnegiea gigantea*)

Another problem with the adaptive strategy of cacti is that they have become water reservoirs that can be tapped by animals. In response to this vulnerability, the cacti have shown strong selection for some mechanism of defense, and the spiny armament has been the response of selective pressure. The spines are borne in clusters from an area called an "areole."

Their beautiful flowers, as well as the unusual sculpturing of the plants, place cacti among the most attractive members of desert communities. Cactus flowers are usually large, in shades of red and yellow, and resemble a brightly colored cup or bowl. Each has a single style, topped by several fingerlike stigmas arising from the center to be surrounded by a profusion of stamens. The sepals and petals (perianth segments) are mostly undifferentiated. The flower is a playground or feeding place for a variety of insects.

☼ Saguaro Cactus   *Carnegiea gigantea*

Slow-growing, succulent **tree,** the trunk (stem) as much as 40 feet tall and 2 feet in diameter, typically with 1 to several strictly erect branches nearly equaling the trunk in size. An extensive, shallow root system extends outward in all directions from the trunk, efficiently absorbing water that penetrates only the upper few inches of soil. Several vertical ridges (ribs) traverse the full length of the trunk and branches, bearing numerous clusters of spreading spines. **Leaves** none. **Flowers** greenish white, waxy, 3 to 5 inches in diameter, opening primarily at night; sepals and petals several, indistinct; stamens numerous; ovary large, maturing into a fleshy, edible red **fruit** 1 to 2 inches in diameter.

Although the saguaro cactus has come to symbolize the deserts of North America, its distribution is almost restricted to the Arizona component of the Sonoran Desert, where it is a conspicuous figure in the upper bajadas. On these rocky desert slopes it typically shares dominance with littleleaf palo verde, which provides important shade where saguaro seedlings can become established.

The saguaro cactus, the state flower of Arizona, is a habitat in itself. The flowers produce an abundance of nectar, providing food for bees and various other insects during the day and moths and bats at night. Even doves visit the flowers for a drink of the energy-rich nectar. A variety of animals, including humans, feed on the fleshy fruits. Woodpeckers punch holes in the stems for nest sites, which other birds use, too.

Other columnar cacti species grow in North American deserts. Saguaro is distinct from these by having a single, typically branched stem. **Organpipe *(Lemaireocereus thurberi)*** has several stems up to 20 feet tall and 10 inches in diameter, with 12 to 20 vertical spiny ribs. Its flowers are white, 2 to 3 inches across, and open at night. The fruit is round, about 3 inches in diameter, and densely spiny but sweet and sought after by native peoples. This large cactus replaces saguaro in most of Mexico and southern Arizona, where a national monument has been established for its preservation. It overlaps in range with **senita *(Lophocereus shottii),*** which is equally large and also has multiple stems. Senita is distinct in having only 5 to 8 prominent ribs and pink flowers.

Saguaro *Carnegiea gigantea* **and Littleleaf Palo Verde** *Cercidium microphyllum*
Inset: Saguaro *Carnegiea gigantea*

Organpipe *Lemaireocereus thurberi*   **Senita** *Lophocereus shottii*

Eagle's Claw
Echinocactus horizonthalonius

Stems flattened to round, becoming cylindrical with age, gray blue, usually solitary, 6 to 12 inches tall; ribs rounded and very prominent, usually 8; areoles aligned along the ridges, filled with white wool; **spines** 5 to 10 per cluster, gray to yellow or reddish, an inch or more in length, spreading in all directions but often arched inward like the claws of an eagle. **Flowers** solitary at the top of the stem, pale pink to red, 2 to 3 inches in diameter, the perianth segments spreading wide, horizontal to the stem top. **Fruit** fleshy, cylindrical, 1 to 1½ inches long and half as wide, densely covered with white wool.

Like many cacti, eagle's claw has suffered from collection and marketing by unscrupulous people who are too greedy and impatient to start the slow-growing plants from seed. The species ranges widely in the Chihuahuan Desert but is rarely abundant.

Clustered Barrel Cactus
Echinocactus polycephalus

Stems round to cylindrical, usually in clusters of 3 to several, 1 to 2 feet tall; ribs 13 to 21 prominent but obscured by the spination; **spines** 10 to 14 per cluster, red or yellowish, up to 3 inches long, spreading in all directions and usually slightly curved. **Flowers** solitary at the top of the stem, about 2 inches in diameter, yellow, or the petals sometimes with a pink central stripe. **Fruit** dry when mature, roundish, about 1 inch thick, densely covered with white wool.

The common and Latin names (*poly,* "many"; *cephalus,* "head") relate to the distinctive multistemmed habit of this cactus. The clustered stems along with the red spines make it one of our most attractive cacti, even when not in flower. It grows along rocky slopes in the Mojave and Sonoran Deserts.

Horse Crippler
Echinocactus texensis

Stems round to somewhat flattened, up to 1 foot tall; ribs 13 to 25, prominent but obscured by the spination; **spines** 6 to 8 per cluster, usually red with a white base, up to 3 inches long, typically curved but stout and rigid. **Flowers** solitary at the top of the stem, about 2 inches across; petals red to orange at the base and pink to white at the tip, usually with a purplish central stripe. **Fruit** fleshy, roundish, about 1 inch thick, not covered by white wool.

This cactus is also known as devil's head and devil's pincushion, which, with "horse crippler," suggest how vicious the spines are. The species grows in gravelly soils, primarily in the Chihuahuan Desert and plains of Texas.

Strawberry Cactus
Echinocereus enneacanthus (stramineus)

Stems numerous, forming large mounds, cylindrical, up to 12 inches long and 3 inches in diameter; ribs 10 to 12, obscured by the spination; **spines** 8 to 14 per cluster, straw-colored the first year (*stram,* "straw-colored"), generally becoming white with age; the central spine(s) may be more than 3 inches long. **Flowers** solitary on the top of the stem, up to 5 inches across; perianth segments magenta; stamens yellow; stigma lobes green. **Fruit** fleshy and spiny, round, about 1 inch in diameter, red.

Several varieties of this species are recognized, apparently all restricted to the Chihuahuan Desert. The common name is derived from the strawberry-like fragrance and flavor of the fruit.

Eagle's Claw
Echinocactus
horizonthalonius

Clustered Barrel
Cactus *Echinocactus*
polycephalus

Horse Crippler *Echinocactus texensis*
—Richard Worthington photo

Strawberry Cactus
Echinocereus enneacanthus **var.** *stramineus*

Engelmann Hedgehog Cactus   *Echinocereus engelmannii*

Stems cylindrical, up to 18 inches tall and 4 inches in diameter, usually several forming mound-shaped clumps; ribs 10 to 13, obscured by the spination; **spines** variable in color (the species thus sometimes called "calico cactus"), 10 to 18 per cluster, including 2 or more well-developed central spines, although one is generally much longer than the others (up to 3 inches long), and several spreading lateral spines, ¼ to ½ inch long. **Flowers** more or less funnel-shaped, up to 3 inches across, borne on the side of the stem near the top; outer perianth segments magenta to lavender, inner segments purplish, especially at their base; stamens yellow; stigma lobes green. **Fruit** round, about 1 inch in diameter, red, fleshy and edible but spiny, the spines eventually falling away.

This is probably the most widespread and common of several hedgehog cacti (*Echinocereus* species). It grows in all North American deserts except the Chihuahuan Desert, where it is replaced by strawberry cactus. In much of its range it overlaps with claret-cup cactus, and the two species are difficult to distinguish when the plants are not in bloom. The perianth segments of claret-cup are more distinctly red, and the anthers are pink to red rather than yellow. In the Sonoran Desert of Arizona, Fendler hedgehog cactus is locally abundant and is easily confused with Engelmann hedgehog cactus. Fendler hedgehog cactus has a single, well-developed central spine, the flowers are typically darker, and the stems are usually fewer in number. Like other cacti, Engelmann hedgehog cactus prefers well-drained, gravelly soils.

Fendler Hedgehog Cactus   *Echinocereus fendleri* **var. rectispinus**

Stems cylindrical, 4 to 18 inches long and 3 inches in diameter, solitary or 2 to 6 in a clump; ribs 8 to 12, prominent; **spines** gray to brown, the single central spine stiff, straight, and up to 4 inches long; marginal spines about 8, spreading and much shorter than the central spine. **Flowers** more or less funnel-shaped, 2 to 3 inches across, borne on the side of the stem near the top, strikingly attractive, with dark magenta perianth segments; stamens pale yellow; stigmas green. **Fruit** round, about 1 inch in diameter, purplish red, fleshy and edible but spiny.

Echinocereus fendleri is sometimes split into several varieties, and the description above applies to var. *rectispinus,* which means "straight spine." This variety appears to be restricted to the Sonoran Desert of Arizona and adjacent Mexico. It grows in rocky and sandy areas, usually in less dry sites than the similar Engelmann hedgehog cactus, with which it overlaps in range. The distinguishing characteristics of the two cacti are noted in the above description of Engelmann hedgehog cactus.

Claret-Cup Cactus   *Echinocereus triglochidiatus*

Stems numerous, generally forming large mounds, cylindrical, up to 10 inches tall and 4 inches in diameter; ribs 7 to 12 though somewhat obscured by the spination; **spines** 3 to 12 per cluster, gray to white or in some forms black, variable in length, the central one(s) often more than 3 inches long. **Flowers** borne near the stem tip, cup-shaped, 2 to 3 inches across; perianth segments scarlet to claret red; stamens red; stigma lobes green. **Fruit** fleshy and spiny, cylindrical, about 1 inch long and ⅔ as wide, purplish red.

Claret-cup is a variable and widely distributed species, found in all North American deserts in one form or another. It grows on rocky slopes in desert mountains, where it is strikingly conspicuous when in bloom. The Latin name *(triglochi)* describes some forms that have only 3 spines per cluster.

Engelmann Hedgehog Cactus *Echinocereus engelmannii*
Inset: Flower of Engelmann Hedgehog Cactus *Echinocereus engelmannii*

Fendler Hedgehog Cactus
Echinocereus fendleri **var.** *rectispinus*

Claret-Cup Cactus
Echinocereus triglochidiatus **var.** *melancanthus*

Rainbow Cactus
Echinocereus dasyacanthus

Stems solitary or in small clusters, cylindrical, up to 12 inches tall and 4 inches in diameter; ribs 15 to 20, obscured by the spination; **spines** numerous in each cluster, wide spreading, up to ½ inch long, pale gray or straw-colored to pink or reddish brown. An outstanding characteristic of the species is the horizontal bands of colored spines, each band a different color, producing a rainbow effect. **Flowers** solitary on the top of the stem, up to 5 inches across; inner perianth segments yellow with a green base, outer segments green; stamens yellow; stigma lobes green. **Fruit** fleshy and spiny, green to purplish.

The nomenclature of rainbow cactus is confusing. By whatever name, though, the exceptionally large flower and bands of different colored spines make it distinctive. It grows in the Chihuahuan Desert and southern Arizona.

California Barrel Cactus
Ferocactus acanthodes (cylindraceus)

Stems usually solitary, at first round, becoming cylindrical (columnar) with age, up to 6 feet tall and 18 inches in diameter; ribs 20 to 30; **spines** 10 to 18 per cluster, spreading and interwoven, variable in size and color (gray, yellow, or red), the central one(s) flattened, curved, conspicuously cross-ribbed, and up to 5 inches long. **Flowers** several, embedded among the spines on the top of the stem, about 2 inches across; perianth segments greenish yellow; stamens and stigma lobes yellow. **Fruit** egg-shaped, up to 1½ inches long and 1 inch wide, yellowish, dry at maturity.

This interesting cactus is widely scattered over the deserts of California and Arizona but is only locally abundant. It ranges northward into southern Nevada and the southwest corner of Utah. It grows on gravelly hillsides and sandy plains and appears to prefer limestone soils. Like many of our native cacti, California barrel cactus has suffered greatly from collection and is becoming rare in areas of former abundance.

Along with other barrel cacti, California barrel cactus is said to be an emergency thirst quencher, and large animals occasionally feed on the fleshy tissue. In my experience, however, the juice is slimy and bitter, hardly the cool, refreshing drink one would enjoy on a hot afternoon in the desert.

A related and even larger barrel cactus is **southwestern barrel cactus (*Ferocactus wislizenii*),** growing up to 10 feet tall and 2 feet in diameter. It ranges across the Sonoran Desert of Arizona into the Chihuahuan Desert, where it is most abundant. It has yellow-orange or red-orange flowers, the only obvious difference between this species and the California barrel cactus.

Peyote
Lophophora williamsii

Stems solitary or clustered, gray green or bluish green, flattened, only 1 to 3 inches tall and 2 to 4 inches in diameter; ribs typically 8, very pronounced; **Spines** none, except on seedlings. **Flowers** funnel-shaped, up to an inch across; perianth segments pale pink, darker in the middle. **Fruit** cylindrical, about ½ inch long, pink to red, fleshy and spineless.

This dwarf cactus grows in limestone soils in the Chihuahuan Desert of Texas and Mexico. It is known to be narcotic and has been used in ceremonies by Indians to produce hallucinations. Peyote is also called "mescal button."

Rainbow Cactus
*Echinocereus
dasyacanthus* —Richard
Worthington photo

**Southwestern
Barrel Cactus**
Ferocactus wislizenii

Left: California Barrel Cactus trolls *Ferocactus acanthodes*
Left Inset: California Barrel Cactus *Ferocactus acanthodes*

Right: Peyote *Lophophora williamsii* —Donald Pinkava photo

Buckhorn Cholla   *Opuntia acanthocarpa*

Medium-size **shrub** with a single, freely branched stem, seldom more than 6 feet tall; branches cylindrical, jointed, covered by short ridges (tubercles) 1 to 2 inches long and ¼ inch high; **spines** 12 to 20 per cluster, 1 to 2 inches long, pale yellow to brownish. **Leaves** small, cone-shaped, and succulent, present only on seedlings. **Flowers** borne on terminal branch segments, bowl-shaped, 1 to 2 inches across; perianth segments yellow to bronze-colored or reddish brown; stamens yellow; stigma lobes pale yellow to greenish. **Fruit** dry at maturity, about 1 inch long, brownish, tubercled and spiny (*acanthocarpa,* "spiny fruit").

Buckhorn may be the most widely distributed cholla, ranging more or less throughout the Mojave and Sonoran Deserts, often forming dense populations but not as impenetrable as stands of teddy-bear cholla.

✸ Teddy-Bear Cholla   *Opuntia bigelovii*

Succulent and spiny, treelike **shrub,** up to 8 feet tall, with a solitary stem and short, jointed (segmented) branches, the segments cylindrical, not flattened; **spines** about 1 inch long, silvery yellow to golden brown, round, sharp, and barbed, borne in clusters of 4 to 10 on ridged, congested tubercles. The spines become dark brown with age, giving the stem and older branches a blackish appearance. **Flowers** pale yellowish green, 1 to 2 inches in diameter; perianth segments (sepals and petals) several, undifferentiated; stamens numerous, with conspicuously green filaments and yellow anthers; stigmas green. **Fruit** ½ to 1 inch long and nearly as wide, yellowish green, leathery, bearing tubercles but no spines.

Of the many cholla species, this is the most abundant if not the most widespread. In gravelly desert plains, particularly in outwash fans, it often grows in dense populations, usually in association with creosote bush.

Although teddy-bear cholla is a handsome plant, beware—it is not cuddly. The barbed spines reach out, latch on, and refuse to let go. The terminal segment of a branch readily detaches, and the impaled animal walks away carrying the spiny armament. The species is also called jumping cholla, perhaps because these spiny segments seem to jump out at you as you walk by. More likely, the name relates to the plant's jumping hither and yon through transport of these detachable segments; each will develop into a new plant.

Cane Cholla   *Opuntia imbricata*

Treelike **shrub,** up to 8 feet tall, extensively branched; branches cylindrical, canelike, only about 1 inch in diameter; tubercles prominent, 1 to 2 inches long; **spines** 10 to 25 per cluster, ½ to 1 inch long, tan to reddish, strongly barbed. **Leaves** small, roundish, present only on seedlings. **Flowers** borne at the tips of branches, 2 to 3 inches across; perianth segments reddish purple. **Fruit** fleshy, oblong, 1 to 2 inches long, tuberculate and spiny.

This is probably the most common cholla of the Chihuahuan Desert, ranging westward into the Sonoran Desert of Arizona. It grows in gravelly and sandy soils, where it is often a major dominant.

Buckhorn Cholla *Opuntia acanthocarpa*
Inset: Flowers of Buckhorn Cholla *Opuntia acanthocarpa*

Teddy-Bear Cholla community *Opuntia bigelovii*
Inset: Flowers of Teddy-Bear Cholla *Opuntia bigelovii*

Cane Cholla *Opuntia imbricata*

Silver Cholla   *Opuntia echinocarpa*

Medium-size **shrub** seldom more than 5 feet tall, with a single, freely branched stem; branches cylindrical, segmented, covered by tubercles ¼ to ½ inch long and half as high; **spines** borne in clusters of 8 to 20, about 1 inch long, silvery white to straw-colored. **Leaves** small and cone-shaped, succulent, present only on seedlings. **Flowers** borne on terminal branch segments, bowl-shaped, 1 to 2 inches across; perianth segments greenish on the inside, often bronze on the outside; stamens yellow; stigma lobes greenish yellow. **Fruit** dry at maturity, pale green to yellowish, tubercled, densely spiny (*echinocarpa,* "hedgehog fruit," relating to the spination).

This cholla closely resembles buckhorn cholla, and large portions of their ranges overlap. The two species, which probably hybridize, are separated by the size and shape of stem tubercles, length of the terminal branch segments, and flower color. Silver cholla tends to be more scattered and rarely forms dense populations.

Desert Christmas Cactus   *Opuntia leptocaulus*

Small **shrub,** 1 to 3 feet tall, sparingly branched except at the base; branches cylindrical, only ½ inch in diameter (*leptocaulus,* "slender stemmed"); tubercles not prominent; **spines** usually solitary, gray to straw-colored, 1 to 2 inches long, not barbed. **Leaves** small, roundish, succulent, present only on seedlings. **Flowers** borne along the branches, only 1 inch across; perianth segments greenish yellow to bronze. **Fruits** fleshy, egg-shaped, about ½ inch long, not tuberculate, bright red, with scattered, minute spines.

Unusual for cacti, this species prefers heavy, fine soils and is most common in silty drainages. It ranges through the Sonoran Desert of Arizona into the Chihuahuan Desert. It is rarely abundant.

Pencil cholla *(Opuntia arbuscula)* also grows in southern Arizona and resembles desert Christmas cactus. It is somewhat larger in all respects, is much more extensively branched, and has yellow-green rather than red fruits.

Staghorn Cholla   *Opuntia versicolor*

Treelike **shrub,** 3 to 10 feet tall, freely branched above a short trunk; branches cylindrical, ¾ inch in diameter, with prominent, 1-inch tubercles; **spines** 6 to 12 per cluster, up to 1 inch long. **Leaves** small, roundish, succulent, present only on seedlings. **Flowers** borne at the tip of short branches, 1 to 2 inches across, cup-shaped; perianth segments usually red to reddish purple, occasionally yellowish. **Fruit** egg-shaped, about 1 inch long, fleshy, not tuberculate, with small, scattered spines.

This is a scattered but locally abundant cholla in the Sonoran Desert of Arizona. It grows in gravelly and sandy soils.

Silver Cholla *Opuntia echinocarpa*

Desert Christmas Cactus *Opuntia leptocaulus*

Staghorn Cholla *Opuntia versicolor*

✖ Texas Prickly-Pear   *Opuntia engelmannii*

Shrub, 1 to 5 feet tall with segmented branches that spread horizontally over the ground; segments (pads) flat, disk-shaped or egg-shaped, bluish green, up to 10 inches long and ½ inch thick. **Spines** 1 to 2 inches long, straight, borne in clumps of 3 to 10 on areoles separated by 1 to 2 inches. **Flowers** usually bright yellow but sometimes orange or even reddish, 3 to 4 inches across; sepals and petals many, similar in appearance; stamens numerous with white filaments and pale yellow anthers; stigmas green with whitish (pollen-receptive) ridges. **Fruit** fleshy, reddish purple, 2 to 3 inches long, pear-shaped, bearing several areoles with miniature spines.

Texas (or Engelmann) prickly-pear is widely distributed and dominant over large areas, particularly in the Chihuahuan Desert. It prefers gravelly soils and grows in all habitats, from the driest, hottest part of the desert to the cool desert grasslands above. Over much of its range it overlaps and hybridizes with the highly variable **dusky prickly-pear *(Opuntia phaeacantha),*** which is distinctly smaller and more prostrate, with pads that are more pear-shaped and petals typically reddish at the base.

Besides having beautiful flowers, prickly-pears are valuable members of desert communities. Rodents and some larger animals, notably peccaries or javelinas, derive water and nutrition from chewing on the pads. The fleshy fruits and their seeds are eaten by many animals, including humans, who must first singe off the spines. Many species of prickly-pears become a serious nuisance in overgrazed areas.

Hybridization Among *Opuntia* Species

Opuntia species, chollas and prickly-pears alike, are notoriously difficult taxonomically because of their propensity to hybridize. Several previously proposed species are now thought to be hybrids. Even within "good" species, gene flow resulting from past hybridization has increased the genetic variation and added to the difficulty of drawing the line between one species and another. Hybridization results from the close relationship among the various species and their pollination strategy. The principal pollinators of cacti are mostly flies and beetles, which do not discriminate between flowers of different species, freely mixing pollen as they randomly visit flowers within their forage range. The showy **Vasey prickly-pear (*Opuntia vaseyi*)** is an example of a formerly described species now thought to be a hybrid. It resembles dusky prickly-pear, which is probably one of the parental species.

Texas Prickly-Pear *Opuntia engelmannii*
Inset: Texas Prickly-Pear with fruit *Opuntia engelmannii*

Dusky Prickly-Pear with flowers
Opuntia phaeacantha

Vasey Prickly-Pear (note salmon-colored flower) *Opuntia vaseyi*

Beavertail Cactus
Opuntia basilaris

Low growing **herb, stems** blue gray, clumped, erect and/or spreading, padlike, up to 14 inches long, 12 inches wide, and ½ inch thick; **spines** usually none, but numerous small bristles (glochids) arise from each of several equally spaced areoles. **Flowers** borne along the upper edge of the pads, 2 to 3 inches across; perianth segments pinkish magenta; stamens (filaments) red; stigma lobes white. **Fruit** dry when mature, egg-shaped, 1 to 2 inches long, tan to greenish purple, covered with areoles bearing bristles.

Beavertail cactus is widespread, growing in all North American deserts except the Chihuahuan Desert. It is conspicuous in spring, since it is one of the first perennial plants to bloom and has strikingly attractive flowers. It grows in rocky habitats.

Mojave Prickly-Pear
Opuntia erinacea

Low-growing **subshrub, stems** gray green, clustered, segmented, the segments flat, roundish to pear-shaped, up to 10 inches long and nearly as wide, ½ inch thick; **spines** whitish, 1 to several per cluster (areole) but sometimes present only on the upper areoles, up to 4 inches long; small bristles (glochids) straw-colored, many per areole. **Flowers** borne along the top of the terminal stem segments, about 2 inches across; perianth segments variable in color from pinkish magenta to yellow; filaments white; stigma lobes green. **Fruit** dry at maturity, tan to brownish red, generally spiny, 1 to 2 inches long.

This is a variable and taxonomically confusing species, and several varieties have been proposed. It overlaps in range and probably hybridizes with other prickly-pears, adding to the confusion. In one form or another it grows in all North American deserts except the Chihuahuan Desert. Like most cacti, Mojave prickly-pear prefers gravelly soils.

Plains Prickly-Pear
Opuntia polyacantha

Low **subshrub; stems** clustered, usually gray green, segmented, the segments flat and pear-shaped, up to 8 inches long and 6 inches wide, ½ inch thick; **spines** 5 to 12 per cluster (areole), up to 3 inches long, gray to straw-colored; bristles (glochids) numerous per areole, straw-colored. **Flowers** borne singly or in clusters at the tip of terminal stem segments, 2 to 3 inches across; perianth variable in color from bright yellow to red; stamens pale yellow; stigma lobes green. **Fruit** dry at maturity, oblong, 1 to 2 inches long, tan to reddish, covered with bristles and usually spiny.

This is primarily a Great Basin and Painted Desert species, but it ranges southward into the hot deserts. Several varieties have been proposed, and the variation is increased through hybridization. It grows in sandy soils in dry, gravelly plains.

Beavertail Cactus *Opuntia basilaris*

Mojave Prickly-Pear *Opuntia erinacea*

Plains Prickly-Pear *Opuntia polyacantha*

Purple Prickly-Pear
Opuntia violacea

Subshrub to treelike, up to 5 feet tall but usually much smaller; **stems** segmented, the segments flattened, roundish, 5 to 8 inches in diameter, ¼ to ½ inch thick; conspicuously reddish purple pigmented; **spines** usually restricted to the upper margin of the pad, where they are solitary or in pairs, 3 to 4 inches long, dark purple to black; the areoles are filled with numerous reddish brown bristles (glochids). **Flowers** borne on the upper margin of the pads, 3 inches across; perianth segments pale yellow with a reddish base. **Fruit** cylindrical, 1 inch long, reddish purple and fleshy.

Two varieties of this species (*macrocentra* and *santa-rita*) are recognized in the Chihuahuan Desert, distinguishable mainly on the basis of pad shape and spination. Both varieties are abundant and often form dense populations. The purplish pads make the species conspicuous over the gravelly Chihuahuan landscape.

Johnson Devil-Claw
Sclerocactus johnsonii

Stems usually solitary, cylindrical, up to 10 inches tall and 6 inches in diameter; ribs 15 to 20, prominent; **spines** yellowish to red, 10 to 15 per cluster, the central ones up to 3 inches long, straight or somewhat curved. **Flowers** 1 to 3, borne on top of the stem, cup-shaped, 2 to 3 inches across; perianth usually greenish yellow, sometimes pink or magenta; stamens and stigma lobes yellow. **Fruit** dry, yellowish, scaly, about ½ inch long and half as wide.

This attractive but devilish barrel cactus is an occasional plant on rocky slopes and ridgetops in the Mojave Desert. The related and taxonomically difficult **Whipple fishhook cactus (*Sclerocactus whipplei*)** grows in similar habitats, primarily in the Painted Desert, ranging upward into open forests. It is a larger cactus with pinkish violet to magenta flowers. Its larger spines are ribbonlike and hooked at the tip.

CALTROP FAMILY
Zygophyllaceae

Although the caltrops comprise a small family, it is variable, and the genera are not easily seen to be related. Unifying characteristics mainly relate to the flowers, which are radially symmetrical with parts in fives—five sepals, five petals, ten stamens, and a superior ovary with five compartments. The leaves are opposite and compound. Most species grow in warm, dry areas. Only creosote bush and fagonia, described below, are native to and common in North American deserts.

Fagonia
Fagonia laevis

Subshrub, up to 2 feet tall; **stems** dichotomously and extensively branched, yellow green and appearing varnished; angled; sandpapery from minute, stiff hairs. **Leaves** opposite, compound, with 3 spine-tipped leaflets less than ⅓ inch long. Four spine-tipped bracts are at the base of each pair of leaves. **Flowers** lavender, solitary in leaf axils, ⅓ to ½ inch across; petals narrowed at the base, often twisted like a propeller. **Fruit** a 5-lobed, 5-seeded capsule.

Fagonia is locally abundant, covering the rocky desert hillsides where it grows. It ranges more or less throughout the Mojave and Sonoran Deserts.

Purple Prickly-Pear
Opuntia violacea

**Whipple
Fishhook Cactus**
Sclerocactus whipplei

Johnson Devil-Claw
Sclerocactus johnsonii

Fagonia
Fagonia laevis

Creosote Bush

Larrea tridentata

Large, erect to nearly prostrate, unarmed **shrub. Stems** several, dark gray to blackish, limber, about 1 inch thick at the base and up to 12 feet tall, freely branched, the branches spreading and often drooping. **Leaves** opposite, compound with 2 nonstalked, nontoothed, asymmetrical leaflets that are joined at the base, up to ⅓ inch long, and varnished with resin. **Flowers** solitary on short branches from leaf axils; petals 5, bright yellow and showy, about ¼ inch long, very narrow at the base (clawed), appearing stalked, typically twisted like the blades of a fan; sepals 5, smaller than the petals, uneven in size; stamens 10; ovary superior, densely covered with stiff, silvery white hairs. **Fruit** densely hairy, 5-lobed, each lobe splitting off into a 1-seeded nutlet.

Creosote bush grows in the driest and hottest regions of North America. It is so successful and widespread that the hot deserts have collectively been called the *Larrea tridentata* province or biome by many leading ecologists. In desert plains and on lower slopes, it often forms pure stands or shares dominance with bur sage. In the upper bajadas, it is a frequent associate of such dominants as saguaro cactus in the Sonoran Desert, Joshua tree in the Mojave Desert, or lechuguilla in the Chihuahuan Desert. It is not particularly salt tolerant and does not grow in alkali flats or playas.

Creosote bush is an evergreen, drought-enduring plant. When soil water is readily available, the leaves are dark green, becoming olive brown as drought becomes severe. Since the leaves are persistent, they must be adapted to conserve water. The highly varnished surface reflects sunlight, thus having a cooling effect; the epidermis is impregnated with resins, sealing the leaves against water loss; the photosynthetic cells are adaptively arranged and very compact, thus reducing transpiration. The leaves also produce chemicals, water-soluble phenolics as well as the resins, that protect against herbivores.

The name *creosote bush* derives from the sweet and arguably pleasant, resinous scent of the plant. The perfume is particularly strong in the rainy season. Resinous extractions from the leaves have been used medicinally by Native Americans and Mexicans to treat such disorders as tuberculosis, gastric problems, and rheumatism, and as an antiseptic for wounds and burns. Resin extractions were also used by Native Americans to waterproof baskets.

Creosote Bush community *Larrea tridentata*

Creosote Bush with flowers *Larrea tridentata*

Creosote Bush with fruit *Larrea tridentata*

CAPER FAMILY Capparaceae

Capparaceae is a widespread family of mainly tropical plants, with some species extending into the temperate zone in arid habitats. The family includes everything from small annuals to trees, characterized by the flowers and fruits. The flowers resemble those of the mustard family, with four sepals, four petals, and six stamens, and presumably the two families are related. The ovary is superior and matures into a capsule, usually with a long stalk. The many seeds are produced in two rows along the capsule wall, another characteristic shared with mustards. The leaves are generally alternate and palmately compound.

Yellow Bee Plant *Cleome lutea*

Robust annual **herb,** the **stems** erect, up to or exceeding 3 feet high, usually, but sparingly, branched. **Leaves** alternate, palmately compound with 3 to 7 (generally 5) leaflets, these narrowly elliptical and up to 2 inches long, borne on a long stalk (petiole). **Flowers** about ½ inch across, borne in an elongate, leafy raceme along the top of the stem and branches; petals bright yellow; stamens extend well beyond the petals. **Fruit** a narrowly elliptical, many-seeded, 1- to 3-inch pod, borne on a long stalk.

Yellow bee plant grows in all North American deserts except the Chihuahuan Desert. It prefers sandy flats, particularly if the soil is a bit alkaline, often forming dense populations—a sea of yellow when in bloom. It also tends to be weedy, growing in disturbed areas and along roadsides. The common name relates to the fragrant flowers, which attract bees and other insect foragers.

Rocky Mountain Bee Plant *Cleome serrulata*

Robust annual **herb,** the **stems** erect, up to 5 feet tall but usually much less, often branched above. **Leaves** alternate, 3 foliate, the three leaflets elliptical, up to 3 inches long, and ½ inch wide, borne on a long stalk (petiole). **Flowers** about ½ inch across, borne in a dense, leafy raceme along the top of the stem and branches; petals pale lavender to purple; stamens extend well beyond the petals, filaments lavender, anthers green. **Fruit** a narrowly cylindrical, stalked pod, 1 to 3 inches long.

Like yellow bee plant, this species is weedy and grows primarily in disturbed areas and along roadsides. It prefers sandy soils and is most common in the Great Basin and Painted Deserts.

Clammy-Weed *Polanisia uniglandulosa*

Robust annual, glandular-clammy **herb,** the **stems** erect, 1 to 3 feet tall, sometimes branched. **Leaves** alternate, trifoliate, the three leaflets elliptical, 1 to 2 inches long and half as wide, the petiole equally long. **Flowers** densely congested in a leafy raceme along the top of the stem and branches; petals white, about an inch long, narrowed into a threadlike base; stamens lavender purple, extending well beyond the petals. **Fruit** an elliptical, somewhat inflated, more or less erect pod, 3 to 4 inches long.

This strikingly attractive plant grows in sandy washes and along arroyos of the Chihuahuan Desert. In other American deserts, it is replaced by the more widespread *Polanisia dodecandra,* which is similar but has smaller flowers and is less showy.

Yellow Bee Plant *Cleome lutea*   Clammy-Weed *Polanisia uniglandulosa*

Rocky Mountain Bee Plant *Cleome serrulata*

Stinkweed
Cleomella **species**

Annual **herbs; stems** erect, 6 to 30 inches tall, often branched from the base. **Leaves** alternate, trifoliate, the three leaflets narrowly elliptical, up to ½ to 2 inches long, borne on a long stalk (petiole). **Flowers** borne in a dense raceme along the upper half of the stem; petals yellow; stamens extending well beyond the petals. **Fruit** a more or less diamond-shaped, somewhat inflated, leathery pod, borne on an elongate stalk.

Several species of *Cleomella* grow in our deserts, mainly in alkaline flats. The most common is **blunt-leaf stinkweed *(C. obtusifolia),*** found in the Mojave and Sonoran Deserts. In the Great Basin Desert, it is replaced by **Hillman stinkweed (*C. hillmanii).***

Cleomella is closely related to *Cleome* (treated on page 62) and means "little *Cleome*." The major distinction is that the fruits of *Cleome* are elongate, much longer than wide.

Bladderpod
Isomeris arborea

Profusely branched, medium-size, spherical **shrub,** up to 5 feet tall. **Leaves** alternate, trifoliate, the three leaflets elliptical, ½ to 2½ inches long, borne on an inch-long stalk (petiole). **Flowers** borne in racemes at the tips of branches, about ¾ of an inch across; sepals partly fused at the base, green; petals bright yellow; stamens yellow, extending beyond the petals. **Fruit** a leathery pod (capsule), becoming inflated and bladderlike at maturity, borne on a long stalk, thus hanging down and out from the flower.

Bladderpod is widely distributed in California in the Mojave and Sonoran Deserts. It grows in dry washes and sandy flats, often as the major dominant. It is also known as "burro-fat," suggesting that it is a valuable browse plant—this despite the foul-smelling, skunky leaves.

CYPRESS FAMILY
Cupressaceae

The cypress family is a large conifer family of evergreen trees and shrubs. The leaves are scalelike and twice opposite, in four rows, completely covering the twigs. The seed cones are small and woody or berrylike. The pollen cones are smaller yet and look like a continuation of the twig tips.

Junipers
Juniperus **species**

Most members of the cypress family grow in environments where moisture is not limiting, and only the junipers are sufficiently drought tolerant to withstand desert conditions. Even these rugged denizens of arid habitats can grow only on the upper fringes of true deserts, in desert mountains. On the other hand, desert species are often associated with junipers or grow in the understory of juniper woodlands. A few of the frequent associates are saguaro cactus, Joshua tree, various chollas, sagebrush, blackbrush, and ephedras.

Several juniper species grow in the American West. They can be large **trees** under ideal conditions, becoming smaller in stature and **shrublike** as the environment becomes more hostile. The **bark** is thin and peels off in strips, giving the trunk a ragged appearance. The twigs are narrow and hidden by the scalelike **leaves,** which individually measure only a small fraction of an inch. With few exceptions, the plants are unisexual, with male and female "cones" on separate plants. The **pollen cone** measures only about ⅙ of an inch and is made up of several minute scales, each with

Hillman Stinkweed *Cleomella hillmanii*

Bladderpod *Isomeris arborea*
Inset: Bladderpod flowers *Isomeris arborea*

Juniper with berries *Juniperus osteosperma*

Caper Family/Cypress Family ❖ **65**

2 or more pollen sacs. The **seed cone** is ¼ to ½ inch in diameter and is fleshy and berrylike, with the cone scales fused together and in some species not apparent.

Junipers are ecologically important. They are the dominant members of most communities where they grow. They provide shelter for a wide variety of animals and the berries are eaten by birds and mammals. Indians, too, gathered the berries, which they ate fresh or ground into cakes. Juniper wood is highly resistant to decay, and the plants have been used extensively as fence posts and for construction of shelters. Junipers are often regarded as a nuisance, and large tracts of woodlands have been decimated by clearing and burning to promote grass growth and to enhance grazing.

As soil moisture increases, piñon pines become important associates of juniper, forming the piñon-juniper biome. At higher elevations and farther north, but still under droughty conditions, the less-cold-tolerant piñons again drop out, leaving pure stands of juniper.

DOGBANE FAMILY   Apocynaceae

Dogbane, a large family with worldwide distribution, is best represented in the tropics. It includes herbs, shrubs, trees, and vines, many ornamentals, and some poisonous and medicinal plants. An outstanding characteristic of the family is the milky juice in leaves, stems, and all other plant parts. The flowers are radially symmetrical with parts in fives—five sepals, five petals, and five stamens. The corolla (petals) typically is fused into a narrow tube with five spreading lobes. The stamens are borne on the corolla tube, sometimes near the base, sometimes at the mouth. Each flower has two pistils, with their styles and stigmas fused, the latter much enlarged and often disk-shaped. Only a few species of this large family grow in North American deserts.

Blue-Star   *Amsonia tomentosa*

Perennial **herb,** typically covered with grayish, felty wool; **stems** numerous, up to 2 feet long, spreading and sprawling from a woody base. **Leaves** alternate but crowded, broadly lance-shaped below, narrower above, 1 to 2 inches long. **Flowers** borne in dense, umbel-like clusters at the tips of stems and branches; sepals fused only at the base, with 5 pointed, threadlike lobes; corolla dusky blue, the tube ⅓ to ½ inch long, narrowest just below the pointed lobes that form a star. **Fruit** a pair of narrowly elliptical pods (follicles) that are constricted between the seeds.

This is the showiest and most widespread of three species of *Amsonia* that grow in North American deserts—in the Sonoran, Mojave, and Painted Deserts. It prefers sandy soils and often grows with saltbush, blackbrush, or ephedras.

Rock-Trumpet   *Macrosiphonia macrosiphon*

Perennial **herb,** up to a foot tall; **stems** usually several, erect to spreading from a woody base. **Leaves** opposite, broadly elliptical, 2 to 3 inches long, woolly. **Flowers** usually solitary at the tip of stems; corolla white to pinkish, fused into a narrow, 2- to 4-inch tube with 5 to 6 lobes that are typically oriented like propeller blades; stamens borne on the corolla tube and wrapped around the style and enlarged stigma. **Fruit** a pair of many-seeded pods; each seed bears a tuft of hair that aids in wind dispersal.

Rock-trumpet is aptly named. The flowers resemble a trumpet, and the plant grows among rocks in the Chihuahuan Desert. The redundant Latin name means large *(macro)* tube or pipe *(siphon)* and relates to the corolla tube.

Juniper woodland in the Painted Desert

Blue-Star *Amsonia tomentosa*

Rock-Trumpet *Macrosiphonia macrosiphon*

EPHEDRA FAMILY
Ephedraceae

Ephedraceae is one of those families that has been around a long time, but its place in the evolutionary history of other seed plants is obscure. By definition, ephedras are gymnosperms (*gymno*, "naked"; *sperm*, "seeds"); that is, the seeds are not enclosed within an ovary. The plants have conelike reproductive structures, male and female, but they appear to be more closely related to flowering plants (angiosperms) than to conifers. Arguments have been made that they either are ancestors to angiosperms or are a sister group derived from a common ancestor. Whatever their position in the evolutionary scheme of things, they are an important fixture in the desert landscape.

Ephedraceae is a small family with a single genus, *Ephedra,* and several species, all adapted to grow in arid Old and New World habitats. All species are small to medium shrubs with jointed, greenish stems and conspicuous nodes. The branches are ridged or grooved, stiffly erect or spreading, and opposite or whorled. The leaves are reduced to nongreen scales, two to three per node. Individual plants are unisexual, bearing either male or female cones singly or in whorls of two to several at the stem nodes. Male cones, about ¼ inch long, consist of a central stalk with several small scales; two to several stamens are borne inside and at the base of each scale. As the stamens mature they extend outward beyond the scales, the anthers open, and the pollen is carried on the wind. Seed (female) cones, one to three per node, are up to ½ inch long and produce 1 to 3 seeds each. The ephedras, or desert-teas, are important members of many desert communities. In general they prefer sandy soils, where they are often major dominants. Separation of the species is difficult and is based on technical characteristics.

✖ Nevada Ephedra (Nevada Tea)　　*Ephedra nevadensis*

Erect, unisexual **shrub,** up to 6 feet tall, with straight but spreading, nonspiny, pale green, jointed branches. **Leaves** opposite, reduced to deciduous scales less than ¼ inch long. **Flowers** technically not produced, replaced by small cones opposite or clustered at the branch nodes; male (pollen) cones elliptical, ¼ inch long or longer; female (ovulate) cones roundish, about ⅓ inch long, with 3 to 5 pairs of bracts. **Seeds** 1 to 2 per female cone. Of several *Ephedra* species that grow in North American deserts this is the most widely distributed and the most variable. It can be found in all North American deserts in one form or another.

Green ephedra *(Ephedra viridis)* overlaps in distribution with Nevada ephedra, especially in the Great Basin and Painted Deserts. It resembles Nevada ephedra, but the branches are yellowish green rather than pale green, smaller, and more or less parallel, giving the plant a broomlike appearance. Another common species is **Mormon tea *(E. torreyana),*** which differs from the above species by having 3 leaves and 3 cones per node. **Mojave ephedra *(E. fasciculata),*** of the Mojave and Sonoran Deserts, resembles Mormon tea, but the leaves and cones are paired, 2 per node.

Many medicinal uses have been ascribed to ephedras, including a cure for venereal diseases. The drug ephedrine, now produced synthetically, was derived from an Asian species of *Ephedra*. In North America the various species have been used extensively as a medicinal tea, a tonic.

**Green Ephedra
community**
Ephedra viridis

Mojave Ephedra
Ephedra fasciculata

Nevada Ephedra male plant
Ephedra nevadensis

Mormon Tea male *Ephedra torreyana*
Inset: Mormon Tea female *Ephedra torreyana*

EVENING PRIMROSE FAMILY   Onagraceae

The evening primrose family contains woody plants, even trees, but all North American desert species are herbs, though sometimes with a woody base. Typically the flower parts are in fours—four sepals, four petals, eight stamens, and four compartments in the ovary. A narrow floral tube (hypanthium) extends from the top of the inferior ovary, and the sepals, petals, and stamens are borne at the mouth of the tube. In most species the flowers are radially symmetrical and showy.

In many species the flowers open at night. These species have extremely long floral tubes, and the abundant nectar produced at the base of the tube can be accessed only by hawkmoths, which are active at night and have exceptionally long proboscises.

Calylophus   *Calylophus hartwegii*

Mound-forming perennial **herb,** up to 15 inches tall, with numerous stems arising from a branched woody base. **Leaves** alternate, linear to narrowly lance-shaped, 1 to 2 inches long, sometimes toothed. **Flowers** solitary in leaf axils, usually opening in the afternoon or early evening; floral tube 1 to 3 inches long; sepals reflexed backward; petals bright yellow, 1 to 2 inches long; filaments attached to the center of the anthers; stigma disk-shaped. **Fruit** a cylindrical, ½-inch, many-seeded capsule.

This extremely variable species is divided into several subspecies or varieties. It is best represented in the Chihuahuan Desert, particularly in Texas, where it often grows in gypsum or limestone soils. It ranges north into the Painted Desert of Utah and west into Arizona.

Suncup   *Camissonia brevipes*

Annual, erect, occasionally branched **herb,** up to 2 feet tall but usually much shorter. **Leaves** basal and low on the stem, the blades toothed or not, 1 to 4 inches long, simple and broadly lance-shaped to pinnately compound with irregularly shaped and sized leaflets, the terminal leaflet much the largest; leaf stalks nearly as long as the blades. **Flowers** few to numerous in a raceme, opening in the evening and remaining open through the next day; sepals reflexed backward; petals bright yellow, sometimes with red spots near their bases, ¼ to ¾ inch long; stamens 8, the filaments attached to the center of the anthers; stigma ball-shaped. **Fruit** a narrowly cylindrical, many-seeded capsule.

This is the best known of many evening primroses, often forming expansive, colorful populations across the rocky desert landscape, particularly in the Mojave and Sonoran Deserts.

Booth Evening Primrose   *Camissonia boothii*

Annual, usually hairy or glandular-sticky erect **herb,** up to 2 feet tall but usually much less; bark of the stem whitish and tending to peal as the stem ages. **Leaves** variable in size (1 to 5 inches long), in shape (narrowly elliptical to egg-shaped and from nontoothed to pinnately lobed), and in position (sometimes primarily in a basal rosette, sometimes alternate or nearly opposite on the stem, sometimes a combination). The leaves are often reddish and/or marked with purplish spots. **Flowers** borne in a nodding, often dense raceme, opening at dusk and remaining open through the next day; floral tube about ¼ inch long; sepals reflexed backward; petals white to reddish orange, often with small, red spots near the base, about ⅓ inch long; filaments

Calylophus *Calylophus hartwegii*

Suncup *Camissonia brevipes* var. *brevipes* community
Inset: Suncup *Camissonia brevipes* var. *brevipes*

Booth Evening Primrose *Camissonia boothii* ssp. *condensata*

attached to the center of the anthers; stigma ball-shaped. **Fruit** a narrow, nonstalked, many-seeded capsule, ½ to 1½ inches long, widest at the base.

Many *Camissonia* species are complex and taxonomically difficult, and this is one of those species. The problem is that much variation exists among individual plants, but the variation is more or less continuous. Also, species separation is often complicated by hybridization. The result is that many previously accepted species have now been lumped together to form one large species with several varieties or subspecies. Two of the most common of these are **ssp. *decorticans,*** often called **bottle-washer** because of the dense, cylindrical inflorescence, and **ssp. *condensata.*** In some form or another, Booth evening primrose grows in the Mojave, Sonoran, Painted, and Great Basin Deserts, often in abundance. It prefers sandy or gravelly soils.

Another equally or even more difficult species is **club-fruited evening primrose *(Camissonia claviformis),*** with many varieties and subspecies, some with yellow flowers, some with white flowers, usually with red spots at the base of the petals. In this species, the fruits are stalked and club-shaped *(claviformis,* "club shaped"), separating it from Booth evening primrose. It, too, prefers sandy or gravelly soils and grows in all but the Chihuahuan Desert.

A third closely related species with a similar range and habitat requirement is **narrow-leaved evening primrose *(Camissonia refracta).*** The key distinction between this species and forms of Booth and club-fruited evening primroses is the shape of the capsule, cylindrical in *refracta,* rather than broader near the base (Booth evening primrose) or at the top (club-fruited evening primrose). In general, but not always, *refracta* has narrower leaves, as the common name suggests. Also, the basal, rosette leaves usually wither and die before the plant blooms. Narrow-leaved evening primrose is most abundant in the northern part of the Mojave Desert, in southern Nevada.

Painted Desert Evening Primrose   *Camissonia eastwoodiae*

Annual **herb;** stems erect and unbranched or branched from the base, 5 to 14 inches tall. **Leaves** basal and alternate near the stem base, simple, sometimes toothed; leaf blades egg-shaped or broadly lance-shaped, ½ to 3 inches long, stalk (petiole) nearly as long. **Flowers** borne in nodding racemes; floral tube (hypanthium) ⅓ to ¼ inch long; sepals 4, spreading or reflexed backward; petals bright yellow with numerous red spots, ¼ to ½ inch long; stamens 8, the filaments attached to the bottom of the anthers; stigma ball-shaped. **Fruit** a cylindrical but curved, many-seeded capsule up to 1½ inches long.

This attractive species is endemic to the Colorado Plateau in the Four Corners region of the Painted Desert. It seems to prefer slightly alkaline soils and often grows with mat saltbush.

Booth Evening Primrose
Camissonia boothii ssp. *decorticans*

Club-Fruited Evening Primrose
Camissonia claviformis ssp. *integrior*

Narrow-Leaved Evening Primrose
Camissonia refracta

Painted Desert Evening Primrose
Camissonia eastwoodiae

Hill Suncup
Camissonia graciliflora

Hairy annual **herb,** only a few inches tall, stems usually branched. **Leaves** linear to narrowly lance-shaped, up to 4 inches long, neither toothed nor lobed. **Flowers** solitary or few; sepals 8, spreading; petals 8, bright yellow, about ⅓ of an inch long; stamens 8, filaments attached to the base of the anthers; stigma ball-shaped. **Fruit** conspicuously 4-angled, ⅓ to ¼ inch long.

This distinctive evening primrose grows in clayey soils along the upper slopes (hills) of the Mojave and Great Basin Deserts, often in Joshua tree communities.

Tooth-Leaved Evening Primrose
Camissonia strigulosa (dentata)

Low, annual, roundish **herb,** 4 to 12 inches tall; **stems** white, extensively branched and spreading, more or less zig-zag. **Leaves** alternate, linear to narrowly elliptical, up to 1½ inches long, minutely toothed. **Flowers** borne in loose, nodding, leafy racemes along the branches, opening at dusk and closing the next morning; floral tube (hypanthium) a small fraction of an inch long; sepals 4, fused together into 2 pairs; petals 4, bright yellow, sometimes with 2 red dots at the base, about ½ inch long and wide; stigma ball-shaped. **Fruit** a cylindrical, curved, many-seeded capsule, 1 to 3 inches long.

This is a distinctive, handsome plant with its many brilliant yellow flowers and white, wiry stems. It prefers sandy soils and often grows in dunes. It is distributed in the Sonoran and, particularly, Mojave Deserts.

Scarlet Gaura
Gaura coccinea

Perennial **herb,** up to 3 feet tall; **stems** usually several, erect, unbranched above the ground. **Leaves** alternate, narrowly elliptical to linear, 1 to 3 inches long, becoming progressively smaller upward on the stem. **Flowers** slightly bilaterally symmetrical, borne in a narrow raceme; floral tube ¼ to ½ inch long; sepals reflexed backward; petals ⅓ to ½ inch long, narrowed at the base into a stalk (claw), at first white but soon turning red (scarlet); stamens 8, the filaments attached to the center of the anthers; stigmas 4, spreading, starlike. **Fruit** a four-angled "nut" bearing 3 to 4 seeds.

Scarlet gaura's mix of white and red flowers is unusual and attractive. It is widespread in the American West, often growing in such profusion that it becomes a pest. In the desert regions, it grows primarily in limestone soils along mountain slopes, the upper bajadas. Although scattered, it can be found in all our deserts.

A less common, equally attractive species is **prairie gaura** *(Gaura lindheimeri),* a hairy, perennial herb that resembles scarlet gaura but has white to pale lavender petals that are oriented to one side of the flower. As the common name suggests, it is more at home in the prairies than the deserts but does grow along the border between the desert grasslands and the Chihuahuan Desert. It is often cultivated because of its beauty.

Hill Suncup
Camissonia graciliflora

**Tooth-Leaved
Evening Primrose**
*Camissonia strigulosa
(dentata)*

Scarlet Gaura *Gaura coccinea*   **Prairie Gaura** *Gaura lindheimeri*

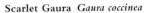

Fragrant Evening Primrose   *Oenothera caespitosa*

Perennial **herb** from a thick, woody taproot; **stems** lacking or no more than a few inches tall. **Leaves** basal in a rosette, variable in size (1 to 12 inches long), shape (usually narrowly elliptical in outline), and degree of lobing varying from nontoothed to pinnately divided, usually hairy, particularly along the leaf margin. **Flowers** borne singly or in small clusters from the center of the leaf rosette; floral tube up to 6 inches long; sepals reflexed backward; petals white but fading pink, heart-shaped, about 2 inches long and wide; stamens 8, filaments attached to the center of the anthers; stigma lobes 4. **Fruit** a many-seeded, cylindrical capsule, 1 to 2 inches long.

This species is as variable as beautiful, growing in one form or another in all the North American deserts, usually in rocky sites. **California evening primrose (Oenothera californica)** is similar in having a basal rosette of leaves and large, showy flowers with white, heart-shaped petals. It is an annual, though, and usually has better-developed stems. Preferring sandy soils, it is locally abundant in the Mojave Desert, ranging southward into the Sonoran Desert of California.

Another stemless species is **early evening primrose (Oenothera primiveris),** an annual herb with equally large, yellow, heart-shaped petals that become purplish with age. Both its common and Latin names (*primiveris,* "first spring") reflect the blooming time of this beautiful desert plant. It is an important early spring nectar source for hungry hawkmoths, as well as a welcome sight for late winter or early spring travelers across the desolate desert landscape. It prefers sandy soils, usually in desert washes and arroyos. It ranges from the Great Basin south through the Mojave and Sonoran Deserts and east into Texas.

Of all the beautiful evening primroses, none can match the panoramic display of **dune evening primrose (Oenothera deltoides).** This is a bushy herb, up to 2 feet tall, with numerous branched, erect to spreading leafy stems. As the common name suggests, it prefers sand dune areas (stabilized), where it typically grows in association with sand verbena and/or phacelias, resulting in a beautiful display of white mixed with shades of purple. It ranges across the Mojave and Sonoran Deserts. It is also called **basket evening primrose,** a name that describes the shape of old plants; the outer stems curve inward to form the "basket."

The flowers of most *Oenothera* species are fragrant and open in late afternoon, remaining open through the night. Nocturnal hawkmoths are attracted by the sweet fragrance and white color and hover over the flowers while probing for the abundant nectar concealed at the base of the long floral tube. Only a hawkmoth has a proboscis sufficiently long to reach the nectar.

Fragrant Evening Primrose *Oenothera caespitosa*

Dune Evening Primrose *Oenothera deltoides*

Early Evening Primrose *Oenothera primiveris* ssp. *bufonis*

White-Stemmed Evening Primrose   *Oenothera albicaulis*

Taprooted annual **herb,** 4 to 10 inches tall; **stems** white (*albicaulis,* "white stem"), erect, simple or branched from the base. **Leaves** basal in a rosette and alternate on the stem, elliptical, up to 4 inches long, usually toothed or pinnately lobed, the stem leaves more deeply divided than the basal leaves. **Flowers** borne in leaf axils near the stem tip, nodding in bud; floral tube about 1 inch long; sepals reflexed backward; petals white but fading pink, heart-shaped, 1 to 1½ inches long and wide; stamens 8, filaments attached to the center of the anther; style elongate; stigma lobes 4. **Fruit** a many-seeded, linear capsule, 1 to 2 inches long.

In some sandy areas, populations of this striking evening primrose are dense and expansive, turning the desert landscape snow-white with a tint of pink from fading flowers. It is particularly common in the Painted and Chihuahuan Deserts. A similar species, **pale evening primrose (Oenothera pallida),** overlaps in distribution with the white-stemmed evening primrose but is more common in the Great Basin. It is a perennial herb and lacks the basal rosette of leaves.

FERN FAMILY   Polypodiaceae

Ferns usually bring to mind images of moist tropical or temperate forests. Most ferns live where they don't have to worry about where their next drink of water is coming from, but a few species have adapted to the desert environment. These few hardy specimens have tough, leathery, compound leaves (fronds) that function with very little water. The fronds are derived directly from scaly rhizomes—there is no aboveground stem. Ferns reproduce by spores produced in spore sacs on the lower surface or along the margin of leaf segments (pinnae).

In recent taxonomic treatments the classical Polypodiaceae has been split into several families. Among these only the **brake-fern family (Pteridaceae)** is well represented in American deserts. In this family the rhizomes are scaly, an adaptation that reduces water loss; the lower surface of leaf segments is covered with hair, scales, or powdery material, another water-saving adaptation; and the spore sacs are borne along the veins or margins of leaf segments. Three common representatives of this diverse family are treated here: **Jones cliff break (Argyrochosma [Pellaea] jonesii),** **scaly cloak fern (Astrolepis [Notholaena] integerrima),** and **fairy swords (Cheilanthes lindheimeri).** In their respective ranges, all grow in rocky areas, such as rock outcrops, rock crevices, and canyon walls.

Jones cliff break has fronds that are clustered, twice pinnately compound, narrowly triangular in outline, and up to 6 inches long. The leaf segments, only ¼ inch long, are curved upward and the margins are rolled under, partially covering the spore sacs that are produced along the leaf margins. The frond stalk is dark-colored and less than an inch long. This fern is common in the Mojave and Sonoran Desert mountains.

In scaly cloak fern the fronds are clustered, pinnately compound, narrowly elliptical, up to 24 inches long, and no more than 2 inches wide. The leaf segments are about ⅓ inch long, sometimes lobed, and covered by minute, star-shaped scales. The spore sacs are borne at the tip of prominent veins, protected and hidden by the leaf scales. The frond stalk is somewhat shorter than the blade, dark-colored, and wiry.

White-Stemmed Evening Primrose
Oenothera albicaulis

Pale Evening Primrose
Oenothera pallida

Jones Cliff Break
Argyrochosma
(Pellaea) jonesii

Scaly Cloak Fern
Astrolepis (Notholaena)
integerrima

Scaly cloak fern grows primarily in the Chihuahuan Desert, ranging west into the Sonoran Desert of Arizona.

In fairy swords, the fronds are loosely clustered or scattered along a creeping rhizome. The frond blade is lance-shaped in outline, thrice pinnately compound, and about 8 inches long and 2 inches wide. The leaf segments are tiny and are covered by woolly pubescence. The margins of the leaf segments are rolled under, covering and protecting the spore sacs. The frond stalk is dark-colored and wiry but shorter than the blade. This is a common fern of the Chihuahuan Desert and the Sonoran Desert of Arizona.

FIG MARIGOLD FAMILY   Aizoaceae

Fig marigold is a large family of mainly tropical plants, with the center of distribution in Africa. In North America, the family is best represented along the sandy shores of oceans and salty lakes, with only a few species growing in deserts. Many species are cultivated for their beauty and their ability to tolerate neglect.

The most outstanding characteristic of the family is succulence—an adaptation to aridity and saline soils. In most species, the flowers are radially symmetrical, large, and showy. They have a short floral tube (hypanthium), from which many stamens are derived. The flowers usually have five sepals and anywhere from no petals at all to numerous petals.

Western Sea Purslane   *Sesuvium verrucosum*

Succulent, nonhairy, perennial **herb, stems** many, freely branched, weak and sprawling over the ground, up to 2 feet long. **Leaves** opposite, up to 2 inches long, linear to more or less spoon-shaped. **Flowers** solitary in leaf axils; sepals 5, reddish purple and showy, about ⅓ inch long, with a greenish appendage coming from the underside near the tip; petals none; stamens numerous, the filaments fused at the base, reddish; ovary half inferior, the floral tube arising from midway on the ovary. **Fruit** a cone-shaped capsule the top of which separates, like the lid of a sugar bowl, releasing the numerous seeds.

This species is scattered over the hot deserts of North America, in seasonally wet saline flats and along the margins of salty lakes.

A surprisingly similar plant, **chisme *(Portulaca mundula),*** in the related **purslane family (Portulacaceae),** is common in the Chihuahuan Desert. This, too, is a succulent herb with weak, sprawling stems and reddish purple, similarly sized flowers that have numerous stamens. Also, the fruit is a capsule with a separating lid. The leaves of chisme are alternate, linear, very numerous and ¼ to ½ inch long. A tuft of woolly hair grows in the axils of the leaves. The flowers are borne singly or in small clusters at the stem tips. They have 2 sepals, 5 reddish purple petals, about ⅓ inch long, and numerous stamens, as noted above. Chisme grows in sandy and gravelly soils in desert washes and arroyos and along roadsides.

Fairy Swords *Cheilanthes lindheimeri*

Western Sea Purslane *Sesuvium verrucosum*

Chisme *Portulaca mundula*

FIGWORT FAMILY Scrophulariaceae

The figwort family is large and variable and is held together mainly on the basis of floral characteristics. Although there are many exceptions, in general the family has evolved to exploit the skills and nutritional needs of bumblebees. The typical figwort flower is bilaterally symmetrical, giving it a unique shape and making the floral rewards difficult to access, often requiring manipulation that only the clever and strong bumblebee can perform. The petals (corolla) are fused into a tube, narrow at the base and flaring at the top to form the "gullet." The underside of the gullet is expanded and together with the lower corolla lobes forms a landing platform for the bumblebee. The platform has color markings (nectar guides) that specifically direct the bee's movement into the gullet, where it probes the narrow tubular base for nectar. The stamens are fused to the top of the corolla tube, making contact with the bee as it enters the flower and depositing pollen in a precise, strategic location so it can be transferred to the stigma of the next flower the bee visits. The flower has a unique, pleasing perfume, which the bee relates to, along with shape and color. Finally, the floral reward must be great enough to make the bumblebee concentrate its efforts (major) on that species but low enough that the bee sequentially visits many flowers to meet its immediate nutritional needs or to fill its "larder" to carry back to the hive.

Twining Snapdragon *Antirrhinum filipes*

Annual or short-lived perennial **herb; stems** thin, viny, usually branched, clambering over other vegetation. **Leaves** opposite, low on the stem, ½ to 1 inch long, lance-shaped; upper leaves alternate, reduced in size, linear. **Flowers** borne singly from upper leaf axils on long, threadlike, prehensile pedicels; calyx fused at the base with 5 lobes; corolla bright yellow, ½ inch long, tubular at the base, 2-lipped, the lower lip with an enlarged, hairy, red-dotted "palate"; stamens 4, positioned under the upper lip. **Fruit** a round, many-seeded capsule.

Although twining snapdragon is common in sandy soils of the Mojave and Sonoran Deserts, it goes unnoticed when not in bloom because the stems and leaves are small and normally are obscured by the foliage of supporting shrubs, such as creosote bush. The flowers are beautiful and conspicuous, and not easily missed.

Desert Paintbrush *Castilleja chromosa*

Perennial, pubescent **herb** with clustered stems up to 18 inches tall. **Leaves** alternate, lower ones linear to lance-shaped, usually nonlobed, upper ones with 1 to 3 pairs of lateral lobes. **Flowers** borne in a dense, brilliantly pigmented spike varying from yellow to red; individual flowers derived from the axils of lobed, pigmented bracts; calyx fused with 4 narrow lobes, colored the same as the bracts; corolla green, fused into a narrow tube at the base and 2-lipped above, the upper lip (the galea) ½ inch long and beaklike, the lower lip consisting of 3 small lobes; stamens 4, fused to the corolla tube. **Fruit** a many-seeded, ½-inch capsule.

This plant is the most strikingly attractive figwort. It has a broad range, growing in gravelly soils of all North American deserts except the Chihuahuan. **Narrow-leaf paintbrush (*Castilleja angustifolia*)** is closely related and equally attractive if not as brilliant. Sometimes the two paintbrushes are combined in the same species *(C. angustifolia)*. Narrow-leaf paintbrush is primarily a Great Basin species. It has a distinctive coloration with a hint of purple.

Twining Snapdragon *Antirrhinum filipes*

Desert Paintbrush *Castilleja chromosa*

Narrow-Leaf Paintbrush *Castilleja angustifolia*

Purple Owl's Clover   *Castilleja (Orthocarpus) exserta*

Annual, hairy and glandular-sticky **herb,** 4 to 15 inches tall. **Leaves** alternate, ½ to 2 inches long, pinnately divided with 5 to 9 linear lobes. **Flowers** borne in a dense, bracteate spike; bracts divided into 5 to 9 narrow, lavender to purple lobes; calyx fused into a tube with 4 lavender purple lobes; corolla ½ to 1 inch long, tubular at the base and 2-lipped above the middle, upper lip lavender purple, beaklike with a hooked tip, lower lip saclike, tricolored, lavender below, reddish in the middle, and white to orange toward the tip; stamens 4, fused within the upper lip. **Fruit** a many-seeded capsule, about ½ inch long.

This species has traditionally been placed in the genus *Orthocarpus (O. purpurascens)* and is still treated that way by many taxonomists. The common name is more uniformly accepted than the Latin name. But by whatever name it is known, it is a beautiful plant and often grows in dense, expansive populations, coloring the landscape lavender to reddish purple. It grows in gravelly plains of deserts and grasslands, ranging from the Great Basin through the Mojave and Sonoran Deserts.

White-Felted Paintbrush   *Castilleja lanata*

Perennial **herb,** covered with white, feltlike pubescence; **stems** clustered, often branched, up to 2 feet tall, derived from a woody root crown. **Leaves** alternate, nondivided, narrowly lance-shaped, 2 to 4 inches long. **Flowers** borne in a bracteate spike; bracts red, entire or with a pair of lateral lobes; calyx fused into a tube with 4 red lobes; corolla tubular at the base and 2-lipped above, the upper lip 1 to 2 inches long and beaklike, green with a red margin, the lower lip small and 3-lobed; stamens 4, fused within the upper lip. **Fruit** a many-seeded capsule, about ½ inch long.

This paintbrush grows in gravelly plains and along rocky slopes of the Chihuahuan Desert, extending westward into the Sonoran Desert of Arizona.

It is an unusual sight seeing this and other paintbrushes, particularly desert paintbrush, growing and blooming alongside such desert shrubs as creosote bush and ephedras in a dry period. With the exception of hairiness, they have no obvious adaptations to protect against drought. So, how can they survive? They are root parasites! They tap the roots of associated, deep-rooted shrubs, deriving various nutrients from them, including precious water. Thus, they have an ingenious way of avoiding the drought.

Bird's-Beak   *Cordylanthus* **species**

Annual **herb** with a single, erect, branched stem. **Leaves** alternate, usually divided into narrow segments. **Flowers** bilaterally symmetrical, borne in spikes, racemes, or sometimes solitary; calyx fused with a slit down one side; corolla more or less club-shaped, 2 lipped, the upper lip resembling a bird's beak, enclosing the stamens and style, lower lip nearly as long, somewhat inflated, pouchlike. **Fruit** a many-seeded capsule.

Several species grow in North American deserts. All are root parasites, resembling paintbrushes in this respect. Although the plants are generally ungainly, the flowers are unusually shaped, often combining purple and yellow in an attractive combination. A common representative is **Wright bird's-beak** *(Cordylanthus wrightii),* a sand-loving species of the Painted Desert.

Purple Owl's Clover *Castilleja (Orthocarpus) exserta* ssp. *venusta*
Inset: Purple Owl's Clover *Castilleja (Orthocarpus) exserta* ssp. *venusta*

White-Felted Paintbrush *Castilleja lanata*   Bird's-Beak *Cordylanthus* species

Bush Beardtongue   *Keckiella antirrhinoides*

Medium-size, roundish **shrub,** up to 6 feet tall; **stems** freely branched, hairy when young. **Leaves** opposite, drought-deciduous, appearing varnished, narrowly elliptical, up to 1 inch long. **Flowers** bilaterally symmetrical, borne in leafy racemes at branch tips; calyx fused at the base with 5 lobes; corolla bright yellow, ½ to 1 inch long, tubular at the base, 2-lipped with an enlarged throat; stamens 4, positioned under the upper lip; a fifth sterile, yellow bearded stamen (a bearded tongue) extends outward in the throat. **Fruit** a many-seeded, cone-shaped capsule.

This is an occasional but very attractive shrub of the Sonoran Desert. It prefers rocky slopes of desert mountains and often grows in association with Joshua tree.

Texas Silver-Leaf   *Leucophyllum frutescens*

Low to medium-size, roundish **shrub,** up to 7 feet tall; **stems** freely branched, woolly white when young. **Leaves** alternate, congested toward the branch tips, broadly elliptical to spoon-shaped, about 1 inch long and nearly as wide, densely covered with branched, felty, silvery white hairs (*leucophyllum,* "white leaf"). **Flowers** slightly bilaterally symmetrical, borne in dense, leafy spikes at the tips of branches; calyx fused at the base with 5 lobes; corolla rosy purple, about an inch long, bell-shaped, with a narrow tubular base, an inflated throat, and 2 upper and 3 lower lobes; the palate in the throat of the corolla tube is bearded and often marked with white spots; stamens 4, positioned under the 2 upper corolla lobes. **Fruit** a tough, leathery, many-seeded capsule.

Texas silver-leaf is strikingly attractive when in bloom, its profusion of showy flowers highlighted against the background of silvery white leaves. In some regions of the Chihuahuan Desert of Texas, particularly on limestone soils, Texas silver-leaf is a major community dominant. Here, the desert landscape assumes a gardenlike aspect when the plants burst into bloom.

Big Bend Silver-Leaf   *Leucophyllum minus*

Low, round **shrub,** 2 to 3 feet tall; **stems** freely branched. **Leaves** alternate, about ½ inch long, spoon-shaped, densely covered with branched, silvery white hair. **Flowers** slightly bilaterally symmetrical, borne in leaf axils along the branches; calyx fused at the base with 5 linear lobes; corolla lavender, ½ to 1 inch long, fused into a narrow, tubular base and an expanded, whitish throat, with 2 upper and 3 lower lobes, each hairy at the base; stamens 4, positioned under the 2 upper corolla lobes. **Fruit** a tough, leathery, many-seeded capsule.

Like Texas silver-leaf, this species is a very attractive and frequently dominant shrub. It differs in being smaller and having a bluer flower with a narrower throat. It grows along rocky slopes and gravelly flats in the Chihuahuan Desert and is most abundant in the Big Bend country of Texas.

Bush Beardtongue *Keckiella antirrhinoides*

Texas Silver-Leaf *Leucophyllum frutescens*

Big Bend Silver-Leaf *Leucophyllum minus*
Inset: Big Bend Silver-Leaf flowers *Leucophyllum minus*

Violet Snapdragon Vine · *Maurandya antirrhiniflora*

Perennial **herb, stems** freely branched, long and viny, twining over and through associated vegetation. **Leaves** alternate or irregularly scattered on the stem; blades arrowhead-shaped, about 1 inch long and an equal distance from lateral point to lateral point; leaf stalk (petiole) ½ to 1 inch long, flexuous and prehensile. **Flowers** bilaterally symmetrical, borne singly on long, flexuous, threadlike stalks (pedicels) from leaf axils; sepals 5, narrowly lance-shaped; corolla fused into a pale lavender tube with 2 upper and 3 lower violet-colored lobes; stamens 4, positioned under the upper corolla lobes. **Fruit** a round, many-seeded capsule.

The yellowish white palate at the bottom of the lower corolla lobes is enlarged, closing the throat and blocking access to the nectar at the base of the tube. In this respect the flowers resemble snapdragons (*antirrhini,* "snapdragon"; *flora,* "flower"). Only bumblebees are strong enough to push past the blocked throat and access the nectar.

This attractive vine grows in sandy or rocky areas, climbing over shrubs or boulders or sprawling over the ground. Preferring limestone or even salty soils, it is common in the plains of the Chihuahuan Desert, ranging westward across southern Arizona into California. In southern Arizona a form with brilliant scarlet flowers can occasionally be found. It is frequently cultivated and is well adapted for growth on garden trellises.

Dune Snapdragon Vine · *Maurandya wislizenii*

Perennial **herb; stems** freely branched, long and viny, clambering over other vegetation. **Leaves** alternate; blades arrowhead-shaped, up to 2 inches long and an equal distance between lateral points; leaf stalks (petioles) 1 to 3 inches long. **Flowers** bilaterally symmetrical, borne singly on short stalks from leaf axils; sepals 5, narrowly lance-shaped; corolla pale lavender, about 1 inch long, fused into a somewhat squashed tube with 5 short lobes, 2 upper and 3 lower; the corolla lobes are marked by purplish lines (nectar guides) that lead into the throat; the palate is ridged and hairy but is not enlarged to the extent of closing the throat; stamens 4, positioned beneath the 2 upper corolla lobes. **Fruit** a roundish, leathery, many-seeded capsule.

As the common name suggests, this vine generally grows in sand dune areas, climbing on desert shrubs and sprawling over the dunes. It is most common in the Chihuahuan Desert, ranging westward into Arizona.

Violet Snapdragon Vine *Maurandya antirrhiniflora*

Violet Snapdragon Vine *Maurandya antirrhiniflora*

Dune Snapdragon Vine *Maurandya wislizenii*

Bigelow Monkey Flower

Mimulus bigelovii

Low, erect, annual **herb,** 2 to 10 inches high; **stems** reddish, sometimes branched at the base. **Leaves** opposite, sometimes reddish, ⅓ to 1½ inches long, narrowly triangular with a pointed tip, often having long, white hair. **Flowers** only slightly bilaterally symmetrical, borne singly in leaf axil; calyx fused into an angled tube with 5 teeth, generally covered with short, often glandular hair; corolla rose to dark magenta, fused into a narrow tube with 5 spreading lobes; the throat of the corolla is darker in color and has two golden ridges on the bottom (palate); stamens 4, positioned along the top of the corolla tube. **Fruit** an egg-shaped, many-seeded capsule, ½ inch long.

This is the most widespread of many annual *Mimulus* species, many of them having reddish flowers. It is also one of the most attractive, sometimes growing in extensive populations, particularly along sandy washes of the Mojave and Sonoran Deserts.

One of the showiest of several yellow-flowered desert species is **Parry monkey flower *(Mimulus parryi),*** which is about the same size as Bigelow monkey flower, and the flowers are similarly shaped. The yellow corolla is marked with magenta dots in the throat of the tube and by 2 elliptical spots at the base of each of the 3 lower corolla lobes. It grows in gravelly soils of the Great Basin and northern Mojave Deserts.

Short-Flowered Mohavea

Mohavea breviflora

Annual **herb, stems** erect, sometimes branched at the base, 2 to 8 inches tall. **Leaves** alternate, broadly lance-shaped, ½ to 1½ inches long, covered with short, glandular-sticky hairs. **Flowers** bilaterally symmetrical, borne singly in leaf axils; sepals 5, glandular-hairy; corolla bright lemon yellow, ⅔ inch long, fused into a tube with 2 upper and 3 lower lobes; the lower part of the throat (palate) is enlarged and marked with maroon dots and splotches; stamens (fertile stamens) 2, positioned under the upper lip (2 corolla lobes). **Fruit** a many-seeded, egg-shaped capsule, ⅓ inch long.

This is an occasional Mojave Desert wildflower, growing in gravelly soils, typically in washes. Another species of *Mohavea,* differing primarily in flower shape and color, is **ghostflower *(M. confertiflora).*** The corolla of this species appears somewhat transparent, ghostly. The lobes are yellowish white with maroon dots, and the throat is marked with gold and maroon, particularly the enlarged palate. Ghostflower, too, prefers sandy to gravelly desert washes and grows in the Mojave and Colorado Deserts.

**Bigelow
Monkey Flower**
Mimulus bigelovii

**Parry
Monkey Flower**
Mimulus parryi

Short-Flowered Mohavea
Mohavea breviflora

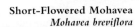

Ghostflower
Mohavea confertiflora

PENSTEMONS
Penstemon species

The genus *Penstemon* is large and complex, with many species, some poorly defined. Hybridization has contributed to the problem of formulating a clear-cut classification system. In general, the species are genetically similar and depend on the fidelity of pollinators to retain species integrity. When pollinators are promiscuous, visiting flowers of different species, hybridization is likely. The principal pollinators are hummingbirds and bees, especially bumblebees.

The bee flowers typically come in shades of blue or lavender and are usually strongly bilaterally symmetrical and 2-lipped, the lower lip functioning as a landing platform. The flowers have an enlarged throat, into which the bee crawls to reach into the narrow tubular base for nectar. The 4 functional stamens are strategically positioned under the upper lip. A sterile, fifth *(pen-)* stamen, which is usually hairy near the tip, lies tonguelike in the corolla throat and is responsible for the alternate genus name, "beardtongue." Hummingbird flowers are more nearly radially symmetrical, have long, narrow corolla tubes, and are bright red.

Sand-Dune Penstemon
Penstemon accuminatus

Perennial, hairless, bluish green (glaucous) **herb,** 6 to 20 inches tall; **stems** thick and succulent, solitary to several, spreading. **Leaves** thick and leathery, basal and opposite, basal ones elongate and stalked, stem leaves broadly lance-shaped and stalkless (sessile), 1 to 3 inches long. **Flowers** clustered in the axils of reduced upper leaves; corolla bright blue to lavender or purple, about ⅔ inch long, 2-lipped with 2 upper and 3 lower lobes; sterile stamen not much enlarged, yellow-bearded near the tip. **Fruit** an elliptical, many-seeded capsule.

This is a Great Basin species that grows in sandy flats and dune areas, as the common name suggests, often in abundance.

Cleveland Penstemon
Penstemon clevelandii

Perennial **herb,** 1 to 2 feet tall; **stems** usually several from a woody, branched root crown. **Leaves** opposite, fused together in the variety *connatus* ("grown together"), thick and leathery, 1 to 2 inches long, toothed or not. **Flowers** borne in paired open clusters from leaf axils; corolla magenta to red, nearly an inch long, the basal tube gradually expanding into the throat, 2-lipped, with 2 upper and 3 lower lobes; sterile stamen not much enlarged and usually not bearded. **Fruit** an elliptical, many-seeded capsule.

This strikingly handsome species grows along rocky hillsides in the Sonoran Desert of California. It is named in honor of Daniel Cleveland, a California attorney, not after the city in Ohio.

Mistaken Penstemon
Penstemon confusus

Perennial **herb,** 8 to 24 inches tall; **stems** 1 to several from a woody root crown. **Leaves** opposite, rather thick and leathery, nontoothed, narrowly elliptical, basal ones up to 3 inches long, upper ones progressively smaller. **Flowers** bilaterally symmetrical, borne in clusters in upper leaf axils; corolla pinkish lavender to bluish violet, ⅔ inch long, the throat somewhat expanded, paler in color than the 5 corolla lobes and often marked with red guidelines; sterile stamen not much enlarged and usually not hairy.

This confusing species grows in sandy and gravelly soils of the Great Basin.

Sand-Dune Penstemon
Penstemon accuminatus

Mistaken Penstemon
Penstemon confusus

Cleveland Penstemon *Penstemon clevelandii*
Inset: Cleveland Penstemon *Penstemon clevelandii*

Firecracker Penstemon
Penstemon eatonii

Perennial **herb,** 10 to 30 inches tall; **stems** erect to spreading, 1 to several from a woody root crown. **Leaves** opposite, thick and leathery, lance-shaped, the margin wavy but not toothed, 1 to 6 inches long, upper ones reduced in size. **Flowers** only slightly bilaterally symmetrical, borne singly or in clusters of 2 to 5 from leaf axils; corolla brilliant scarlet, about 1 inch long, fused into a narrow tube without an inflated throat; corolla lobes 5, small, projected forward; sterile stamen small, not bearded, and hidden in the corolla tube. **Fruit** an egg-shaped, many-seeded capsule.

The strikingly attractive flowers of this penstemon are adapted for pollination by hummingbirds. The long, narrow corolla tube restricts access to the nectar, and few insects can see red colors. The species is wide-ranging as well as beautiful, occupying all North American deserts except the Chihuahuan. It prefers rocky sites, often growing along canyon walls.

Scented Penstemon
Penstemon palmeri

Robust, perennial **herb,** up to 5 feet tall; **stems** erect, clustered from a branched, woody root crown. **Leaves** opposite, toothed, thick and leathery, broadly lance-shaped, 1 to 5 inches long, upper ones reduced in size, becoming bractlike. **Flowers** strongly bilaterally symmetrical and adapted for bumblebee pollination; corolla pale lavender, 1 to 1½ inches long, with a short, narrow tube and broadly inflated throat, conspicuously 2-lipped, the upper lip with 2 erect lobes, the lower lip consisting of 3 forward-projected, red-striped lobes; sterile stamen bearded with golden hair and projected outward from the throat.

This beautiful, fragrant penstemon prefers sandy and rocky soils and ranges from the eastern Mojave and adjacent Sonoran Deserts into the Great Basin.

Parry Penstemon
Penstemon parryi

Robust, perennial **herb,** up to 4 feet tall. **Leaves** narrowly lance-shaped, 1 to 4 inches long. **Flowers** borne in clusters of a few to many along the upper stem; corolla rosy magenta, ⅔ inch long, funnel-shaped, the throat not much inflated; sterile stamen only slightly bearded, not extending beyond the corolla tube.

Parry penstemon is rarely abundant and is restricted in range to the Sonoran Desert of Arizona, but it deserves mention here because of its unusually showy flowers.

Showy Penstemon
Penstemon speciosus

Perennial **herb,** up to 2 feet tall; **stems** erect, usually clustered from a woody root crown. **Leaves** opposite and nontoothed; the lower ones are elliptical and stalked, the upper ones are lance-shaped, often folded, and clasp the stem. **Flowers** showy (*speciosus,* "showy"), more than an inch long, borne in panicles from leaf axils; corolla sky blue to purplish, strongly 2-lipped, with 2 upper and 3 lower lobes; sterile stamen not bearded and not extending beyond the throat of the corolla. **Fruit** an egg-shaped, many-seeded capsule.

This is one of our most beautiful penstemons, even though the flowers are not as striking as the red-flowered species. It also has a broad ecological tolerance, ranging from the subalpine zone to desert mountains. It prefers sandy or gravelly soils and grows mainly in the Great Basin Desert and sagebrush steppe.

Firecracker Penstemon
Penstemon eatonii

Scented Penstemon *Penstemon palmeri*
Inset: Scented Penstemon *Penstemon palmeri*

Parry Penstemon *Penstemon parryi*

Showy Penstemon *Penstemon speciosus*

High-Desert Penstemon   *Penstemon pseudospectabilis*

Robust **subshrub**, 2 to 4 feet tall. **Stems** woody at the base, clustered from a branched root crown, erect and spreading. **Leaves** opposite but fused around the stem, triangular to egg-shaped, 1 to 4 inches long and nearly as wide, sharply toothed along the margin, thick and leathery. **Flowers** slightly bilaterally symmetrical, borne on 2 or more branched stalks from leaf axils; corolla dark pink, about 1 inch long, more or less funnel-shaped, the narrow tubular base gradually expanding into the throat, the lower surface of which is marked with red lines; the 5 corolla lobes are nearly equal in size and spread perpendicularly to the tube; sterile stamen not bearded, contained within the throat. **Fruit** an egg-shaped, many-seeded capsule.

This species grows primarily in rocky washes of the Mojave and Sonoran Desert mountains. The specific epithet *(pseudospectabilis)* might suggest that the plant is not conspicuous or visible, but the opposite is true. The name relates not to the similarity but to the distinction from *Penstemon spectabilis,* a chapparal species.

Another species with sharply toothed leaves that are fused at the base is **bicolor penstemon *(P. bicolor),*** a plant that grows in gravelly and rocky soils in the Mojave Desert. Its flowers are about ⅔ inch long and strongly bilaterally symmetrical. The corolla is dark pink to magenta, with the lower lobes and throat lined with dark reddish stripes. In addition, a narrow white band is usually at the base of the three lower corolla lobes. The sterile stamen has a thick, golden yellow beard. The upper stem, inflorescence, and even the flowers are glandular-sticky.

Utah Penstemon   *Penstemon utahensis*

Perennial **herb**, 6 to 30 inches tall; **stems** erect, usually clustered from a branched, woody root crown. **Leaves** opposite, thick and leathery, narrowly elliptical, 1 to 4 inches long, reduced and bractlike upward on the stem. **Flowers** slightly bilaterally symmetrical, borne in long, often branched stalks from leaf axils; corolla crimson to scarlet, ⅔ to 1 inch long, narrowly tubular without a well-defined throat; corolla lobes spreading perpendicular to the tube; sterile stamen contained within the corolla tube, not bearded. **Fruit** an egg-shaped, many-seeded capsule.

This beautiful penstemon grows in gravelly washes and on rocky slopes of the Painted Desert, ranging east into the Mojave Desert of California and southern Nevada.

Farther south in Arizona, the Utah penstemon is replaced by the similar **Arizona scarlet-bugler *(P. subulatus).*** The stems of this species are solitary or few and the leaves are very narrow, linear, folded or keeled, and 2 to 5 inches long. The corolla is radially symmetrical or nearly so and the tube is narrow its full length. The 5 corolla lobes are short and spread perpendicular to the tube. The corolla thus resembles a bugle—a brilliant scarlet bugle. Like the Utah penstemon, this species is adapted for pollination by hummingbirds. It prefers rocky soils of desert hillsides and canyon walls and grows only in the Sonoran Desert of central and southern Arizona.

**High-Desert
Penstemon**
*Penstemon
pseudospectabilis*

Utah Penstemon
Penstemon utahensis

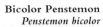

Bicolor Penstemon   **Arizona Scarlet-Bugler**
Penstemon bicolor   *Penstemon subulatus*

FLAX FAMILY

Linaceae

Linaceae is a small family of little ecological consequence, particularly in desert eco-systems. Here only one genus, *Linum* (flax) is represented, and the few species show up only sporadically. The center of distribution of *Linum* is the Mediterranean area, which also gives us cultivated flax and linseed. In general, the family is characterized by the flowers, which are radially symmetrical with five sepals, five petals, five or ten stamens, and a five-compartmented, superior ovary. The flowers are attractive, but if picked the petals promptly fall off.

Broom Flax
Linum aristatum

Annual **herb,** up to 18 inches tall, **stems** branched, most notably near the base, the branches stiffly erect, thin, and broomlike. **Leaves** alternate, up to ½ inch long, nar-rowly lance-shaped, flattened against the stem. **Flowers** solitary at branch tips, ½ to 1 inch across; sepals tipped with a bristle; petals lemon yellow to orangish; stamens 5. **Fruit** a small, elliptical, 10-seeded capsule.

Broom flax grows in sandy areas, often on dunes, ranging from the Painted Desert through the Sonoran Desert of Arizona and into the Chihuahuan Desert of New Mexico and western Texas. A related species with a similar range is **orange flax** *(Linum puberulum).* This species differs from broom flax in having pubescent stems (thus the specific epithet) and orange or salmon-colored petals with a reddish base. It, too, prefers sandy soils and tolerates alkalinity.

Blue Flax
Linum perenne

Perennial **herb,** 12 to 30 inches tall; **stems** erect and unbranched, clustered from a branched root crown. **Leaves** alternate but very numerous and overlapping, particu-larly on the lower half of the stem, ¼ to 1 inch long, narrowly elliptical, ascending rather than spreading. **Flowers** in branched clusters at the tip of stems, about 1½ inches across; sepals elliptical; petals beautifully sky blue, sometimes with a whitish base, stamens 10, 5 of them rudimentary and sterile. **Fruit** a roundish, 10-seeded capsule.

This is a complex species, and the desert form is usually placed in the var. *lewisii* or treated as a distinct species, *Linum lewisii*. It is closely allied with cultivated flax, an annual. Blue flax ranges throughout western North America, in many habitats. It can be found in all our deserts, sometimes forming dense, colorful populations. It prefers sandy or gravelly soils.

Broom Flax *Linum aristatum*   **Blue Flax** *Linum perenne*

Orange Flax *Linum puberulum*

FOUR-O'CLOCK FAMILY   Nyctaginaceae

The four-o'clock family is primarily tropical, perhaps best known for the often cultivated, brilliantly colored bougainvilleas. Although woody species are common in the tropics, only herbaceous forms grow in North American deserts. The most unusual characteristics of the family relate to the flowers. There is only one set of sepals or petals (perianth segments), and these are fused at the base, usually into a tube that tightly surrounds the ovary. Several green, sepal-like bracts form at the base of the flowers, creating the illusion of a flower with both sepals and petals. The stems characteristically have enlarged nodes and opposite leaves, the two leaves of a pair generally unequal in size.

Sand Verbenas   *Abronia* species

Annual or perennial **herbs; stems** succulent and generally spreading. **Leaves** thick and leathery, stalked. **Flowers** borne in heads or umbels surrounded by (involucral) bracts; perianth trumpet-shaped, tubular at the base with flaring lobes generally heart-shaped. **Fruit** a 1-seeded, winged achene.

Several species of sand verbena grow in North American deserts, usually in sandy flats and dunes, as the common name suggests. The best known and most widely photographed is **sticky sand verbena *(Abronia villosa).*** It is not uncommon to see vast expanses of sandy flats of the Mojave and Sonoran Deserts covered and brightly colored by this plant, which often grows in association with lupines and phacelias. These sandy habitats are difficult to match for sheer beauty. Sticky sand verbena is an annual, glandular-hairy herb with several stems that spread across the sand. The perianth tube is about 1 inch long, pink to purple, and glandular-sticky; the heart-shaped perianth lobes are bright pink to magenta, about ½ inch across. The fruit is a leathery achene with 3 to 5 wings. In the Chihuahuan Desert, sticky sand verbena is replaced by the pink- to purple-flowered **winged sand verbena *(A. carnea),*** which is characterized by 3-winged achenes; the wings, also purplish, are membranaceous and completely surround the achene.

Among several white-flowered species, **fragrant sand verbena *(A. fragrans)*** is the most common. It is a perennial herb, with especially sweet-smelling flowers. The perianth tube is greenish to reddish and about 1 inch long; the perianth is white, ragged along the edges, and about ⅓ inch across. The achene has 5 ribs (narrow wings). It ranges from the Great Basin and Painted Deserts southward through the Sonoran Desert of Arizona and into the Chihuahuan Desert. In California it is replaced by the similar but usually smaller *Abronia turbinella.*

Sticky Sand Verbena *Abronia villosa*

Winged Sand Verbena *Abronia carnea*

Fragrant Sand Verbena *Abronia fragrans*

Windmills
Allionia incarnata

Annual or short-lived perennial **herb,** covered with short, glandular-sticky hairs to which small grains of sand typically adhere; **stems** up to 2 feet long, sparsely branched, prostrate and trailing over the ground. **Leaves** narrowly egg-shaped, 1 to 2 inches long and ⅔ as wide. **Flowers** borne in clusters of 3 resembling a single flower, each cluster subtended by 3 bracts; perianth reddish purple, tubular at the base with a petal-like, 3-lobed "limb"; the illusion, then, is that the flowers have 3 petals, each with 3 lobes. **Fruit** a 2-sided, sculpted and glandular achene.

This attractive, sand-loving herb is the most widespread desert species in the four-o'clock family, present in all North American deserts and ranging south into South America.

Wishbone Four-O'clock
Mirabilis bigelovii

Rounded, perennial **herb; stems** erect to spreading, 2-branched (thus the common name "wishbone"), 12 to 30 inches long, covered with glandular-sticky hairs. **Leaves** egg-shaped to round, ⅓ to 2 inches long, glandular-hairy. **Flowers** borne in clusters from leaf axils and stem tips, each flower surrounded by 5 sepal-like bracts; perianth white, ½ to 1 inch long, funnel-shaped, with a narrow tubular base and flaring, 10-lobed top; stamens 3 to 5, extending beyond the perianth. **Fruit** a small, leathery, roundish achene.

Wishbone four-o'clock grows in gravelly soils in washes and along arroyos of the Mojave and Sonoran Deserts. Although it is an attractive herb, with dark green leaves and snow-white flowers, it does not tolerate being picked; the perianth is thin and fragile and almost instantly collapses when the stem is broken.

Large Four-O'clock
Mirabilis multiflora

Mound-shaped perennial **herb,** 12 to 30 inches tall; **stems** clustered from a branched root crown, freely branched, forming a dense clump. **Leaves** rubbery, glandular-sticky, up to ½ inch long. **Flowers** borne in small clusters from axils of upper leaves, each cluster surrounded by 5 fused bracts; perianth magenta, about 2 inches long, trumpet-shaped, with a basal tube and a flaring, shallowly lobed, pleated top; stamens 5 to 10, extending slightly beyond the perianth. **Fruit** a small, elliptical achene.

This variable species is present in all North American deserts. It grows in sandy and rocky habitats and is spectacular in full bloom.

Although several other *Mirabilis* species grow in North American deserts, ranging in color from white to red, none combine the abundance and beauty of the two species described here.

Scarlet Muskflower
Nyctaginia capitata

Perennial **herb** from a woody, branched root crown; **stems** stout, 6 to 15 inches long, freely branched, erect or sprawling, glandular-sticky. **Leaves** triangular, up to 4 inches long, thick and leathery, mottled (white on green); leaf margins wavy and lined with sticky hairs. **Flowers** borne in heads (capitula) surrounded by bracts (involucral); perianth pink to scarlet, 1 to 2 inches long, with 5 pleated lobes and a long narrow, glandular-sticky tube; stamens 5 to 8, extending beyond the perianth. **Fruit** a ribbed achene.

This is a strikingly beautiful plant with its numerous, musky, brilliant scarlet flowers. It shows up sporadically in the plains of the Chihuahuan Desert, growing in sandy and gravelly soils.

Windmills   **Wishbone Four-O'clock**
Allionia incarnata   *Mirabilis bigelovii*

**Large Four-
O'clock** *Mirabilis
multiflora* var.
pubescens

Scarlet Muskflower
Nyctaginia capitata

GERANIUM FAMILY
Geraniaceae

The geranium family is characterized by its fruit, a five-lobed or segmented ovary, and a long, beaklike style. The "beak" is responsible for such common names as storksbill and cranesbill. The single-seeded basal segments separate from each other from the bottom up at maturity. The wiry portion of the beak that remains attached to a segment forms a coil that aids in seed dissemination and "screws" the seed into the soil in response to moisture.

Few members of the geranium family are adapted to deal with drought, and only two species grow in North American deserts, **Texas storksbill** *(Erodium texanum)*, a native, and **filaree** *(Erodium cicutarium)*, a weed introduced from Eurasia. The two species are easily distinguished by their leaves: Texas storksbill leaves are only lobed, and filaree leaves are twice pinnately compound. Not surprisingly, the weed is the more successful species and is more widespread and abundant, often covering the desert landscape.

GOOSEFOOT FAMILY
Chenopodiaceae

The goosefoot family is one of the most important North American desert families, with several community dominants. It includes an assortment of shrubs and herbs adapted for wind pollination. The following characteristics are associated with wind pollination: small, inconspicuous flowers typically clustered in leafy or bracteate spikes; petals absent; sepals small and bractlike; and flowers generally unisexual. The fruit is a leathery, one-seeded achene (technically a utricle).

The plants are not particularly pretty to look at, but they are beautifully adapted to the desert environment. Most have hairy or scaly coverings over the leaves to protect against water loss. Many have exceptionally deep root systems, drawing water from underground reservoirs. Many are succulents, storing water to see them through droughty periods. Most of the shrubs are drought-deciduous. And almost all these species are tolerant to salty soils. Besides the dominant species described below, conspicuous desert plants include other species of *Atriplex*—for example, **desert holly** *(A. hymenelytra)*, easily recognized by its hollylike leaves, and several succulent roadside weeds. In particularly saline areas, **Utah pickleweed** *(Salicornia utahensis)*, recognized by its succulent, jointed stems, can forms impenetrable thickets.

Filaree *Erodium cicutarium*

(I ' S   A N   A R T)

Desert Holly *Atriplex hymenelytra*

Utah Pickleweed *Salicornia utahensis*

✵ Four-Wing Saltbush
Atriplex canescens

Unisexual **shrub** (2 to 6 feet), rounded to irregular in outline; **stems** many with spine-tipped branches; bark typically shredding on the older stems. **Leaves** alternate and evergreen, narrowly elliptical to linear, 1 to 2 inches long, clothed with whitish scales (scurfy). **Flowers** inconspicuous, lacking petals, and unisexual; male flowers borne in congested spikes in leaf axils and branch tips, stamens usually 5, sepals 5, often reddish, scurfy like the leaves; female flowers borne in leafy clusters along the branches, the ovary wrapped inside 2 bracts that are fused at the center (around the ovary) with 4 free, winglike ends that become enlarged as the ovary matures, the **fruit** thus a prominently 4-winged achene. The condition of inconspicuous, clustered, unisexual flowers is an adaptation for wind pollination.

Four-wing saltbush has the widest distribution of all true desert shrubs (thus excluding sagebrush) in North American grasslands, steppes, and deserts. Often it is a community dominant, especially in the Great Basin, Painted, and Chihuahuan Deserts. It tolerates a variety of soil conditions, from moderately alkaline slopes and plains to sand dunes. Its ecological success relates to its variability; several taxonomic varieties have been recognized, all well adapted to droughty conditions. It is a valuable forage species, both for wild animals and range livestock. All parts of the plant are palatable and nutritious. Native Americans have traditionally gathered the large, winged fruits for grinding into meal.

✵ Shadscale
Atriplex confertifolia

Low, rounded **shrub,** 1 to 3 feet tall; **stems** extensively branched, the branches stiffly spreading, becoming modified into spines. **Leaves** alternate, more or less winter-deciduous, roundish to elliptical, about ½ inch long, often sharp-pointed, densely covered with gray scales (scurfy). **Flowers** small and inconspicuous, unisexual, male (staminate) and female (pistillate) flowers borne in leafy clusters on separate plants; petals none; sepals 5; ovary sandwiched between 2 bracts that become enlarged, fan-shaped, and fleshy as the **fruit** matures into an achene.

Shadscale is the most widely distributed and dominant plant in the southern, more arid area of the Great Basin. Because of this, the region has been called the Shadscale Desert. The species is also a frequent dominant in the Painted Desert. It is both drought and salt tolerant and often grows in pure stands in areas unsuited for other species. It ranges from eastern Oregon to South Dakota and south into the hot deserts, where it shows up only sporadically. In much of its range, it grows with four-wing saltbush, and the two species have been reported to hybridize.

Like four-wing saltbush, shadscale is a valuable browse plant for livestock. The young, nonspiny, leafy branches and clusters of fruits are particularly susceptible to heavy browsing.

Four-Wing Saltbush community *Atriplex canescens*
Inset: Four-Wing Saltbush male flower *Atriplex canescens*

Shadscale *Atriplex confertifolia*   Inset: Shadscale *Atriplex confertifolia*

 **Mat Saltbush** *Atriplex corrugata*

Low, spreading, mat-forming, unisexual **shrub** or subshrub, seldom more than 6 inches high but up to several feet in diameter. **Leaves** more or less persistent (evergreen), alternate on the upper part of the stems, opposite below, club-shaped, up to ½ inch long, covered with mealy scales (scurfy). **Flowers** lack petals and are small and inconspicuous; male flowers yellow or brownish with 5 sepals, clustered along the stem tips; female flowers borne in leafy spikes as much as 6 inches long, sepals replaced by 2 bracts roughened by prominent bumps (tubercules). **Fruit** an achene sandwiched between the 2 tuberculate, fan-shaped bracts about ⅙ inch long and wide.

Although this saltbush is primarily limited to southeastern Utah, its ecological importance cannot be overstated. It is a major if not the sole dominant over thousands of acres of fine-textured (clayey), saline soils of the Painted Desert. In much of its range it is the only woody plant present, and even herbs tend to be few and far between. It is important as a forage species, too, partly because little else is available. The young, leafy stems and fruits are nutritious. The plants can withstand heavy grazing pressure.

Frequently, the range of mat saltbush overlaps with the more widespread and variable **Gardner saltbush (*Atriplex gardneri*).** The two species are similar, but Gardner saltbush has somewhat larger, broadly elliptical leaves, and the plants are taller and less matlike. It, too, prefers fine-textured, saline soils but is distributed more or less throughout the Colorado Plateau and Great Basin, ranging through the intermountain plains all the way into Canada.

 **Winterfat** *Ceratoides (Eurotia) lanata*

Low, rounded **subshrub**, woody only at the base, seldom more than 2 feet tall; **stems** several, whitish from a mixture of short, branched (star-shaped) hair and long, tangled, woolly hair. **Leaves** alternate, deciduous, linear or lance-shaped, about 1 inch long, the margins typically rolled under, like the branches, densely covered with a mixture of star-shaped and woolly (lanate) white hair. **Flowers** small and inconspicuous, unisexual, male (staminate) and female (pistillate) flowers borne on the same plant in dense clusters at or near the stem tips; petals none; sepals 4 in male flowers, absent in female flowers but replaced by 2 hairy, lance-shaped bracts that are united around the pistil, which matures into a 1-seeded achene.

Winterfat is widely distributed, sometimes covering thousands of acres in pure or nearly pure stands. It tolerates or prefers moderately alkaline, fine-textured soils that are unsuitable for most desert species, including blackbrush and sagebrush. The dense covering of white hair greatly restricts water loss and acts as a shield, protecting the plant from gnawing insects.

Winterfat is rich in protein and has been touted as the most valuable forage plant of the region, particularly in winter, when few herbaceous plants are available, thus the common name. It tolerates moderate grazing pressure, but heavy grazing by sheep has eliminated it from some of its natural habitat.

Mat Saltbush community *Atriplex corrugata*
Inset: Mat Saltbush male flower branch *Atriplex corrugata*

Gardner Saltbush male flower branch *Atriplex gardneri* var. *cuneata*

Winterfat community *Ceratoides (Eurotia) lanata*
Inset: Winterfat *Ceratoides (Eurotia) lanata*

✳ Hopsage

Grayia spinosa

Medium-size **shrub,** 2 to 4 feet tall, with stiff, dark gray to brown, scaly (scurfy) and hairy branches that eventually become spinelike; bark typically peels from the stems in long strips. **Leaves** alternate, deciduous, spatula-shaped and rounded at the tip, ½ to 1½ inches long, pubescent with branched hairs. **Flowers** small and inconspicuous, unisexual, male (staminate) and female (pistillate) flowers borne in separate spikes at the tips of branches; petals none, sepals 4 in male flowers, none in female flowers but replaced by 2 bracts. **Fruit** a 1-seeded achene enclosed within the 2 bracts that are fused side to side, the entire structure resembling a disk. As the fruit matures the bracts enlarge and become pigmented, ranging from yellowish green to brilliant red or even purplish.

Hopsage seems to prefer moderately alkaline soils, but it has deep roots that draw water from well below the salty surface. It is widely distributed and often grows in nearly pure stands. The fruits and young leafy branches are nutritious and highly palatable, making hopsage an important forage plant for livestock as well as deer, antelope, and elk. The abundance of the pigmented fruit also makes hopsage one of the more colorful plants of the desert landscape.

✳ Greasewood

Sarcobatus vermiculatus

Freely branched, rounded **shrub,** up to 6 feet tall; **stems** whitish to tan, the spreading branches rigid and spine tipped. **Leaves** dark green and succulent, opposite below and alternate above, ¼ to 1 inch long, narrowly cylindrical to linear. **Flowers** inconspicuous and unisexual; male flowers borne in a dense catkinlike spike, each flower with no sepals or petals and 2 to 4 stamens positioned above a roundish bract; female flowers usually solitary in leaf axils, consisting of an ovary surrounded by and fused to a papery, shield-shaped disk that enlarges and persists as a wing on the mature ovary; the **fruit** thus a winged achene.

Greasewood is widespread in western North America, dominating large expanses of desert landscape, most notably where the soil is slightly to strongly alkaline. It has a deep root system, tapping groundwater at depths of between 25 and 40 feet. Greasewood resprouts vigorously, and range fires help promote it by burning off shrubs, such as sagebrush. Greasewood's strongest claim to fame is salt tolerance. Throughout its distribution the plant grows in salt flats (playas), often in pure stands. The plant tissues accumulate salt, allowing the plant to absorb water from salty soils. The salty flavor may contribute to its palatability, but the plant can be poisonous if consumed in large quantities. The generic name is derived from the Greek *sarco,* "fleshy," and *batus,* "bramble."

Hopsage community *Grayia spinosa*
Inset: Hopsage *Grayia spinosa*

Greasewood community *Sarcobatus vermiculatus*

Greasewood female flower *Sarcobatus vermiculatus*
Inset: Greasewood male flower *Sarcobatus vermiculatus*

GOURD FAMILY   Cucurbitaceae

Cucurbitaceae is primarily a tropical family, with many cultivated species, including an assortment of gourds and squashes, cucumbers, pumpkins, cantaloupe, and watermelon. It is a family of trailing or climbing herbs with tendrils. The flowers are large, radially symmetrical, unisexual, and have parts in fives—five sepals, five petals, and usually five stamens. The ovary is inferior.

Among the desert cucurbits, the most spectacular is **buffalo gourd** *(Cucurbita foetidissima),* a perennial herb with large, tuberous roots and thick, branched stems that spread over the ground forming an extensive, rank mat. The leaves are alternate, narrowly triangular, sometimes shallowly lobed, up to 1 foot long, gray green, and foul smelling, particularly when crushed, thus the Latin name *(foetid,* "evil smelling"). The flowers are yellow, funnel-shaped, and up to 4 inches long. The fruit is a roundish, hard-shelled, 2- to 4-inch gourd, green with whitish stripes, becoming lemon yellow when ripe. Buffalo gourd is common in sandy desert flats and waste areas, most notably in the Chihuahuan Desert. It is particularly conspicuous in winter, when the leaves die and the yellow fruits become fully exposed.

Another interesting desert species is **globe-berry** *(Ibervillea tenuisecta),* a vine with palmately divided leaves and greenish yellow flowers. The fruit is a globose, green, white-striped berry, becoming bright red when ripe. It grows on rocky slopes and along canyon walls, using its tendrils to climb over rocks and shrubs. It is primarily a Chihuahuan Desert vine, ranging west into Arizona.

GRASS FAMILY   Poaceae (Gramineae)

Arguably, grasses constitute the third largest plant family in the world. They grow on all continents and in nearly every type of ecosystem, from the arctic tundra to tropical forests, from marshlands to the driest of deserts. They rank number one as a food source for humankind and many other animal species. They are often major dominants in the plant communities where they grow, including deserts. Unfortunately, the grass family has more than its share of invasive weeds, and many habitats have been taken over by invader species.

Grasses combine several characteristics that enable them to deal with drought. The root system is extensive, about twice the mass of the aboveground (shoot) system, effectively trapping and absorbing water in the upper 12 inches of soil. Under conditions of water stress, the leaves roll or fold, greatly decreasing the leaf surface area and reducing water evaporation (transpiration). The leaves and stems have an abundance of supporting tissue, which prevents excessive wilting that would tear and disrupt the fragile photosynthetic tissue. Most desert grasses utilize a highly efficient photosynthetic system (C_4 system) by which they rapidly make hay while the sun shines. This allows annual grasses to complete their life cycle between pulses of rain. Perennial grasses die down to the ground as the drought deepens, awaiting the next rainy period to get on with their life.

To the untrained person, grasses look alike, and the "If you've seen one grass you've seen 'em all" mentality applies. They have long linear or narrowly lanceshaped (grasslike) leaves borne on round stems with swollen nodes. The inflorescence is usually diffuse, sometimes a spike. The flowers are wind pollinated and have

Buffalo Gourd *Cucurbita foetidissima*

Globe-Berry *Ibervillea tenuisecta*

Desert grassland with mesquite near Ajo, Arizona

adapted accordingly. They are small and inconspicuous, with no sepals or petals. The anthers are large and hang from associated bracts on threadlike filaments, rattling in the breeze and releasing massive amounts of pollen. The stigmas are feathery, combing the wind for pollen. The fruit is a grain.

Because grasses look alike, grass taxonomy is a science in itself, agrostology. Separation into species requires a good microscope and familiarity with reproductive structures; grass keys are necessarily highly technical. In this book, grasses are shortchanged, not because they are unimportant in the ecology of deserts, but because they are difficult to deal with. The few species described below are among the most important natives. Because of their palatability, they frequently are overgrazed and replaced by weedy annual grasses.

Blue Grama Grass   *Bouteloua gracilis*

Perennial, rhizomatous, sod-forming grass, **stems** 6 to 24 inches tall, erect or spreading at the base but abruptly erect from lower elbowlike nodes. **Leaves** restricted to the lower part of the stem, linear, flat or rolled up, 2 to 5 inches long, covered with short hair with a tuft of longer hair at the leaf base. **Inflorescence** a one-sided, dense, spikelike, arched panicle, 1 to 2 inches long.

This is one of the dominant grasses of desert grasslands. The border between the desert grassland and desert biomes is not always clearly delineated, and it is not unusual to find blue grama growing alongside creosote bush.

Fluffgrass   *Erioneuron pulchellum*

Perennial or sometimes annual, often spreading by runners (stolons); **stems** densely tufted, only 1 to 6 inches tall. **Leaves** clustered at the nodes, rolled up, rigid and wiry with a pointed tip, about 2 inches long, generally with a tuft of hair at the base. **Inflorescence** headlike, surrounded by leaves.

This is an attractive little package of fluff (*pulchellum,* "beautiful") locally abundant on sandy flats and rocky slopes of all North American Deserts.

Desert grassland in
upper Chihuahua

Desert grassland
in Santa Catalina
Mountains near
Tucson

Blue Grama Grass *Bouteloua gracilis*   Fluffgrass *Erioneuron pulchellum*

Galleta
Hilaria (Pleuraphis) jamesii

Perennial, rhizomatous grass, **stems** tufted or borne in lines from spreading rhizomes, erect, 4 to 18 inches tall, hairy, particularly at the nodes. **Leaves** linear, often curled downward, flat to rolled, up to 6 inches long. **Inflorescence** a purplish spike with tufts of white hair regularly spaced along its length.

Galleta is truly a desert grass although it ranges upward into piñon-juniper woodlands. It is common in all North American deserts except the Chihuahuan, where it is replaced by **tobosa *(Hilaria mutica).*** When **big galleta *(H. rigida),*** a more robust grass, overlaps in distribution with galleta, the two species hybridize.

Indian Ricegrass
Oryzopsis (Stipa) hymenoides

Densely tufted perennial, **stems** erect, up to 30 inches tall. **Leaves** up to 10 inches long, rolled and wiry, remains of old leaves persistent around the base of the tufted stems. **Inflorescence** an open, diffuse panicle with flexuous, threadlike branches.

This attractive grass is widespread, found in all our deserts. It prefers sandy flats, where it is often a major dominant. The common name is derived from its large (ricelike) grains, which in times past were gathered by Indians and used for food.

JOJOBA FAMILY
Simmondsiaceae

Jojoba is a small family, with a single species in North American deserts.

Jojoba
Simmondsia chinensis

Low to medium-size, mound-shaped, unisexual **shrub,** 3 to 6 feet tall; **stems** freely branched, the branches rigid and pubescent. **Leaves** opposite, evergreen and leathery, broadly elliptical, 1 to 2 inches long and half as wide, bluish green, neither toothed nor lobed (entire). **Flowers** unisexual, borne in clusters (male) or singly (female) from leaf axils of different plants; sepals 5, greenish, ⅓ to ⅔ inch long, smaller in male flowers; petals none; stamens 10 to 12 in male flowers; ovary superior, with 3 feathery stigmas in female flowers. **Fruit** a 1-seeded leathery capsule resembling an acorn.

Jojoba grows along rocky slopes and gravelly washes of the Sonoran Desert, often associated with saguaro cactus. Occasionally, it is a community dominant. It is considered to be one of the best browse plants in its range, both for domestic and wild animals. The seeds are unusually rich in a liquid wax similar to sperm whale oil with a multitude of uses and potential uses, including a coffeelike, medicinal beverage. Because of its many uses and its drought tolerance, the plant is now being cultivated on Indian reservations. The species has a variety of common names, including goat nut, deer nut, wild hazel, coffeebush, and quinine plant.

Galleta
Hilaria (Pleuraphis) jamesii

Indian Ricegrass
Oryzopsis (Stipa) hymenoides

Jojoba *Simmondsia chinensis*   **Inset: Jojoba** *Simmondsia chinensis*

LEGUME FAMILY   Fabaceae (Leguminosae)

Fabaceae is large and diverse and is often divided into three separate families. The most unifying characteristic is the fruit, a legume, a one-chambered (pea) pod that typically splits along two sutures. In most genera, the flowers are sweetpea-shaped (as typified by the largest genus in the family, *Astragalus*) with parts in fives—five sepals, five petals, and ten stamens. The leaves are usually compound and alternate. The plants vary in habit from small annuals to large trees. Ecologically the family is very important, both as a source of high-protein food and through representation in most natural ecosystems, often as community dominants. Members of the family are cultivated for food (the family is second only to grasses in importance to humans), for forage (pasture and hay), soil enrichment (because of nitrogen fixation), and for use as ornamentals.

Acacias   *Acacia* species

This is a genus of spiny (usually) shrubs and small trees with twice pinnate leaves and small flowers densely clustered in round heads or spikes. The sepals and petals are inconspicuous, but the many stamens are colorful and extend outward, giving the inflorescence a bristly appearance. Several species grow in our deserts, usually along waterways and washes, where they are often dominants. The greatest concentration of species is in the Chihuahuan Desert, which has locally been called the thorn desert because of acacias and such other spiny shrubs as **mesquite (*Prosopis* species).**

One of the most unusual species is **fern acacia *(A. angustissima),*** combining white flower heads with a lack of spines and prickles. It is usually less than 6 feet tall and grows on gravelly hillsides and mesas in southern Arizona and the Chihuahuan Desert.

A highly variable and widespread shrub that is often cultivated and frequently invasive is **huisache *(A. farnesiana).*** It apparently is native to the high deserts of Arizona, Texas, and Mexico and has been introduced in California. It is a large shrub with multiple, freely branched trunks armed with pinlike spines, 2 at each node. The twice pinnate leaves have 3 to 6 pairs of primary leaflets and 10 to 20 pairs of elliptical secondary leaflets. It has bright yellow, stalked, ball-shaped heads about ½ inch in diameter. The fruit is a dark brown to purplish or black, leathery pod, 1 to 3 inches long. Like other acacias, it grows along rocky hillsides and canyon walls and in gravelly washes. Despite its weedy tendencies, it is a useful shrub. The fragrant flowers have been used in the manufacture of perfumes; tannin and mucilage have been extracted from the bark; the wood is durable and has many uses; and the leaves make good forage.

Another important species of acacia is **catclaw *(A. greggii),*** a large shrub or small tree, up to 20 feet tall. It has curved spines, similar to the claws of a cat, scattered irregularly along the branches. The twice pinnate leaves have 2 to 3 pairs of primary leaflets and 4 to 8 pairs of elliptical secondary leaflets. The flowers are pale yellow or greenish yellow and are borne in cylindrical spikes, 1½ to 2 inches long. The fruit is a flattened, ribbonlike pod up to 5 inches long. Catclaw is locally dominant along desert washes and sandy flats and often forms impenetrable, spiny thickets. It grows in all our deserts except the Painted Desert and provides valuable habitat for desert animals. The dark wood has been used extensively for manufacture of "collectibles."

Fern Acacia *Acacia angustissima*

Huisache *Acacia farnesiana*   Inset: Huisache *Acacia farnesiana*

Catclaw *Acacia greggii*

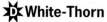 # White-Thorn

Acacia constricta

Large, spreading **shrub,** up to 10 feet tall, the **stems** branched from the ground up; spines straight, stout, sharp, 1 to 2 inches long, borne in pairs at the nodes and usually white, particularly on young branches. **Leaves** alternate, deciduous, twice pinnate (bipinnate); primary leaflets (pinnae) 1 to 7 pairs; secondary leaflets several pairs, tiny, less than ⅛ inch long and half as wide. **Flowers** tiny, congested in round, golden yellow heads ½ inch wide on 1-inch stalks; sepals and petals both yellow and both fused into a tube with 5 teeth; stamens numerous, also golden yellow, extended outward well beyond the petals, giving the head a brushlike appearance. **Fruit** a narrow, arched, reddish brown pod, 2 to 5 inches long, constricted between the seeds.

White-thorn is a wide-ranging, variable species that grows in washes and on gravelly desert slopes. It is important as a habitat for wildlife, but it has little forage value, because of its thorns. Herbivores eat the pods, and Indians and Mexicans have gathered the seeds to grind into pinole flour.

White-Thorn *Acacia constricta* var. *vernicosa*

White-Thorn *Acacia constricta* var. *constricta*

Locoweeds (Milk Vetches) _Astragalus_ species

Astragalus has the greatest number of species of any genus in western North America, most growing in dry areas. As would be expected in such a large genus, there is much variation among the species, coupled with overlap of characteristics that are used to separate the species. Thus distinction of species is often difficult and may require microscopic examination to answer such questions as, are the hairs simple or 2-branched?—making the proverbial argument of "splitting hairs" an actuality. The most important diagnostic characteristics relate to color, size, and shape of the flowers and fruits; and to the size, shape, and number of leaflets of the pinnately compound leaves.

The flowers are sweetpealike, with 5 sepals, 5 petals, and 10 stamens. The conspicuous upper petal, the banner, functions as a flag in attracting insect pollinators, typically bumblebees. Two side petals are called wings, and the lower 2 petals, which are at least partially fused, are shaped like and termed a keel. The 10 stamens, 9 with fused filaments, and the style are retained in the keel until it is depressed by a visiting bee. The sepals (calyx) are generally fused into a tube with 5 narrow lobes. The fruit is variously shaped from nearly round to linear, straight to coiled, and thin to greatly inflated.

Many species of _Astragalus_ are as poisonous as they are beautiful and are responsible for the often fatal condition in livestock known as loco disease. The toxic agent is an alkaloid called "locine." Some species absorb selenium, and when these plants are eaten, the selenium interferes with calcium metabolism, which can also result in death. Thus the locoweeds are not to be trifled with. Fortunately, the most poisonous plants are not particularly palatable. Of the many desert species of locoweed, only a few of the most common and/or attractive have been included in this book. A treatment of all species would be a book in itself.

Crescent Milk Vetch _Astragalus amphioxys_

Short-lived perennial **herb,** 2 to 12 inches tall. **Leaves** primarily basal, up to 6 inches long, clothed with grayish white pubescence, with 5 to 21 elliptical leaflets, ¼ to 1 inch long and half as wide. **Flowers,** 2 to 12 per raceme, are about ½ inch long; the calyx is brownish purple, and the corolla is lavender and very showy. **Fruit** a curved (crescent-shaped) pod, somewhat flattened ("squashed"), ½ to 2 inches long, and often purple-spotted.

Crescent milk vetch grows primarily in sandy flats, ranging from southern Utah into the Chihuahuan Desert of Texas. It is especially common in the Painted Desert, where it often forms dense, colorful populations.

Clay Locoweed _Astragalus argillosus_

Perennial **herb,** 2 to 12 inches tall; **stems** erect, tufted from a branched root crown. **Leaves** alternate, 2 to 6 inches long; leaflets 9 to 21, narrowly elliptical to linear, ¼ to 1 inch long, clothed with silvery pubescence. **Flowers** ⅔ inch long, numerous in dense, headlike racemes; calyx ⅓ inch long, densely covered with long white hairs, giving the inflorescence a shaggy appearance; corolla pinkish purple, twice as long as the calyx. **Fruit** an erect, straight, elliptical, somewhat squashed pod, ⅓ to ½ inch long.

Sometimes this plant is treated as a variety of the yellow-flowered species _A. flavus,_ exemplifying taxonomic uncertainties. It grows in clayey, often saline soils of the Painted Desert. It accumulates selenium, which gives it a bad odor and makes it potentially toxic to herbivores.

Crescent Milk Vetch *Astragalus amphioxys* var. *vespertinus*

Crescent Milk Vetch *Astragalus amphioxys*
Inset: Crescent Milk Vetch *Astragalus amphioxys*

Clay Locoweed *Astragalus argillosus*

Scarlet Locoweed
Astragalus coccineus

Perennial **herb,** only a few inches tall, densely clothed with grayish white hair; **stems** erect to spreading, tufted from a branched root crown. **Leaves** basal, 2 to 4 inches long; leaflets 7 to 15, elliptical, less than ½ inch long. **Flowers** more than 2 inches long, 3 to 10 in a raceme on a leafless stem; calyx ⅔ to 1 inch long, covered with tangled white hair; corolla brilliant scarlet, twice as long as the calyx, the banner marked with whitish lines. **Fruit** an egg-shaped, slightly curved, somewhat flattened (squashed), leathery, hairy, single-compartmented pod, 1 to 2 inches long.

With its silvery leaves and brilliant, bilaterally symmetrical flowers, this is a strikingly attractive plant. It grows in gravelly soil of desert mountains ranging from southern Nevada and western Arizona through the Sonoran Desert of California.

Layne Locoweed
Astragalus layneae

Perennial **herb** spreading by rhizomes; **stems** erect, 3 to 15 inches tall. **Leaves** alternate, 2 to 6 inches long; leaflets 11 to 21, broadly elliptical to nearly round, up to 1 inch long. **Flowers** ⅔ inch long, numerous in a narrow, dense raceme; calyx ⅓ inch long, covered with blackish hair; corolla cream-colored, the keel and wing tips sometimes purple-tipped. **Fruit** a 1- to 2-inch, 2-compartmented, leathery pod that coils inward, sometimes forming a full circle.

This is a Mojave Desert species, growing on sandy flats and along desert washes. In the absence of the coiled pods, it is difficult to distinguish from some varieties of *A. lentiginosus.*

Freckled Milk Vetch
Astragalus lentiginosus

Perennial **herb,** up to 2 feet tall; **stems** mainly erect and tufted from a branched root crown. **Leaves** alternate, up to 6 inches long; leaflets 7 to 15, narrowly to broadly elliptical, ¼ to ¾ inch long. **Flowers** few to numerous in an open to congested raceme, ⅓ to ⅔ inch long; calyx reddish purple; corolla varying in color from whitish to lavender purple, about twice as long as the calyx. **Fruit** a slightly curved, inflated, prominently beaked, 2-compartmented pod, ¼ to ⅓ inch long. The common and Latin names (*lentig,* "freckled") relate to the often purple-spotted pods.

This is the most widespread and variable desert species of *Astragalus,* with more than twenty recognized varieties. It seems to me that this species is a dump for any plant that cannot be placed in another recognized species. The only consistent characteristic of the species is the bladdery, 2-compartmented pod, usually freckled. The species is as wide ranging as variable, present in all our deserts in one form or another. All that can be said of its habitat preference is that it grows in dry areas.

Scarlet Locoweed
Astragalus coccineus

Freckled Milk Vetch
Astragalus lentiginosus
var. *variabilis*

Layne Locoweed
Astragalus layneae

Freckled Milk Vetch
Astragalus lentiginosus var. *araneosus*

Sand-Flat Locoweed
Astragalus insularis var. *harwoodii*

Annual **herb**, 2 to 14 inches tall, silvery gray from short, stiff hairs; **stems** solitary to several, from a taproot. **Leaves** alternate, 1 to 4 inches long; leaflets 9 to 21, elliptical, up to ⅔ inch long. **Flowers** 4 to 9 in a narrow, open raceme, small, less than ½ inch long; calyx purple; corolla pinkish lavender. **Fruit** an egg-shaped, inflated, bladderlike yellow to purplish pod with a conspicuous beaky tip; the pod is ½ to 1 inch long and nearly as wide, deeply grooved on the top and bottom but with a single compartment.

As the common name suggests, this locoweed prefers sandy flats and dunes but also grows on gravelly plains. It is found in the Sonoran Desert of California and western Arizona.

Woolly Locoweed
Astragalus mollissimus

Woolly, perennial **herb,** up to 15 inches tall; **stems** erect, tufted from a branched root crown. **Leaves** basal, 3 to 10 inches long, silvery gray from the woolly pubescence; leaflets 15 to 30, broadly elliptical, up to ½ inch long and nearly as wide. **Flowers** 7 to 20 in a tight raceme at the top of a leafless stem, ⅔ to 1 inch long; calyx pale lavender purple, ½ inch long; corolla lavender purple, the banner with a white face, twice as long as the calyx. **Fruit** an elliptical, 2-compartmented, woolly pod, up to an inch long.

This is a widespread and variable desert species, ranging from the Great Basin and Painted Deserts southward through Arizona into the Chihuahuan Desert. This attractive, early flowering plant is highly poisonous. It prefers gravelly soils.

Stinky Milk Vetch
Astragalus praelongus

Robust perennial **herb,** often exceeding 2 feet in height; **stems** erect, clumped from a branched root crown. **Leaves** alternate, up to 8 inches long; leaflets 7 to 30, narrowly elliptical, up to 2 inches long and about ⅓ as wide. **Flowers** numerous in a congested raceme, spreading outward and downward, ⅔ to 1 inch long; calyx whitish, ⅓ to ½ inch long; corolla cream-colored, twice as long as the calyx. **Fruit** a broadly elliptical to nearly round, inflated but leathery, 1- but nearly 2-compartmented pod, about 1 inch long.

The common name of this milk vetch relates to its strong, unpleasant selenium odor. It ranges across southern Utah and northern Arizona and south into the Chihuahuan Desert, growing in clayey soils, apparently where the selenium content is high.

Sand-Flat Locoweed *Astragalus insularis* var. *harwoodii*

Woolly Locoweed *Astragalus mollissimus*

Stinky Milk Vetch *Astragalus praelongus*

Desert Milk Vetch
Astragalus preussii

Perennial or annual **herb,** up to 15 inches tall; **stems** erect to spreading, forming clumps from a branched root crown. **Leaves** alternate, up to 5 inches long; leaflets 7 to 23, usually narrowly elliptical, up to 1 inch long. **Flowers** 3 to 20 in a tight raceme, ⅔ to 1 inch long; calyx dark purple to nearly black, ¼ to ½ inch long; corolla mainly pale lavender and fading to yellowish—contrasting sharply with the dark-colored sepals. **Fruit** a broadly elliptical, somewhat inflated, leathery, 1-compartmented, purplish pod, about 1 inch long. Like stinky milk vetch, described above, this species accumulates selenium and is ill smelling. It grows in selenium-rich clays and alkaline soils of the Mojave and Painted Deserts.

Pursh Locoweed
Astragalus purshii

Perennial **herb,** only a few inches high, silvery from dense pubescence; **stems** several from a branched root crown, spreading, more or less matted. **Leaves** mainly basal, up to 6 inches long; leaflets 5 to 17, elliptical, up to ½ inch long. **Flowers** 1 to few in open racemes, 1 inch long; calyx reddish purple, hairy, ½ inch long; corolla lavender purple, twice as long as the calyx. **Fruit** an egg-shaped but curved, woolly pod, ⅔ inch long.

Pursh locoweed combines a cushion habit, beautiful flowers, and white-woolly pods to make it one of the most attractive and unusual of desert locoweeds. It is also one of the most poisonous. It grows in sandy or gravelly soils, most commonly in the Great Basin Desert but also in the Mojave and Painted Deserts.

Fairy Duster
Calliandra eriophylla

Low, unarmed **shrub,** usually less than 3 feet tall; **stems** rigid, extensively branched, clothed with short, white hair. **Leaves** alternate, deciduous, twice pinnately compound, primary leaflets 2 to 4 pairs; secondary leaflets 7 to 13 pairs, about ¼ inch long, elliptical, gray green from pubescence. **Flowers** few to several in heads; sepals and petals small and inconspicuous; stamens about 20, pink to red, extending well beyond the sepals and petals, filaments fused near their base. **Fruit** a flat pod, 2 inches long, with prominent red ridges around the margins and white, woolly pubescence on the two sides.

The generic and common names describe the flowers of this straggly shrub; *calliandra* means "beautiful stamens," and the flowers are delicate (fairylike), with soft dusterlike "bristles" (the stamens). *Eriophylla* means "woolly leaves." Fairy duster grows along sandy washes and rocky slopes of the Sonoran Desert, primarily in Arizona. In the Chihuahuan Desert it is replaced by the very similar **false mesquite (*Calliandra conferta*),** which has only 1 or 2 pairs of primary leaflets.

Desert Milk Vetch *Astragalus preussii*

Pursh Locoweed *Astragalus purshii*

Fairy Duster *Calliandra eriophylla*

✳ Palo Verde   *Cercidium* species

Extended Range of Blue Palo
Combined Range of Blue and Littleleaf Palo Verde

Small **tree** or large **shrub,** 10 to 25 feet tall, **stems** up to 20 inches in diameter, branches spiny; bark smooth, green, and photosynthetic. **Leaves** alternate, drought-deciduous, twice pinnate, with 1 pair of primary leaflets and 1 to 8 pairs of small secondary leaflets usually less than ⅛ inch long and half as wide. **Flowers** borne in open clusters (racemes) along the branch tips, ½ to ¾ inch in diameter, somewhat bilaterally symmetrical; petals 5, pale to bright yellow; sepals 5, reflexed backward; stamens 10. **Fruit** a pod, constricted between the seeds.

Two palo verde species are important and often dominant in the Sonoran Desert. **Blue palo verde** *(Cercidium floridum)* grows mainly along washes and sandy plains, depending on an underground water supply; it is particularly abundant in the Colorado Desert. **Littleleaf palo verde** *(C. microphyllum),* primarily an Arizona species, prefers the rocky slopes of desert mountains, where it is a codominant with saguaro cactus. The two palo verdes are similar in appearance, but blue palo verde has blue-green stems with solitary thorns at the nodes; flowers are golden yellow; and the leaves have only 1 to 3 pairs of secondary leaflets. Littleleaf palo verde has yellow-green stems with rigid branch tips that are modified into spines; flowers are lemon yellow; the leaves usually have 4 to 8 pairs of secondary leaflets; and the plants are smaller, often shrublike in particularly droughty sites.

The palo verdes are very attractive, especially when in bloom, decorating the desert landscape over broad expanses. The pods with their seeds (beans) are important as food for desert inhabitants, including humans. The common name, of Spanish derivation, means "green stick," relating to the photosynthetic trunk and branches.

Navajo Prairie Clover   *Dalea (Petalostemon) flavescens*

Perennial **herb** from a woody, branched root crown; **stems** several, erect, 8 to 24 inches tall. **Leaves** alternate, pinnately compound, lustrous green, up to 2 inches long; leaflets 3 to 7, narrowly elliptical, ¼ to 1 inch long, usually folded along the midvein, marked with small, glandular dots and sparsely clothed with white hair. **Flowers** ⅓ inch long, borne in dense spikes, 1 to 4 inches long, at the stem tips; calyx fused at the base with 5 lobes; corolla white to cream-colored, slightly bilaterally symmetrical; stamens 5, extending beyond the corolla. **Fruit** a 1- to 2-seeded, hairy pod, ½ inch long.

Navajo prairie clover is scattered across the sand flats of the Painted Desert of Utah and Arizona. Apparently it grows only in the Navajo Basin. Other prairie clovers grow in North American deserts. Among these, one of the most attractive is **purple prairie clover *(Dalea [Petalostemon] purpurea),*** which ranges from southeastern Utah through Arizona into the Chihuahuan Desert. It differs from Navajo prairie clover in having purple flowers, as the common and Latin names suggest. It, too, prefers sandy soils.

Littleleaf Palo Verde *Cercidium microphyllum*
Inset: Blue Palo Verde *Cercidium floridum*

Navajo Prairie Clover *Dalea (Petalostemon) flavescens* var. *flavescens*

Purple Prairie Clover *Dalea (Petalostemon) purpurea*

Feather-Plume
Dalea formosa

Low, unarmed **shrub,** up to 2 feet tall, extensively branched, dotted with scattered glands. **Leaves** alternate, deciduous, pinnately compound; leaflets 7 to 11, narrowly elliptical, only a small fraction of an inch long, dotted with dark glands. **Flowers** ½ inch long, borne in small, headlike spikes, 2 to 6 flowers per spike; calyx fused at the base into a hairy tube with dark glands, calyx lobes long and featherlike; corolla sweetpealike, the upper petal (banner) yellow, the other petals vibrant rose-colored; stamens 5. **Fruit** a small, egg-shaped 1- to 2-seeded pod, enclosed within the calyx tube.

Although the flowers of feather-plume are small, they are beautiful, as the specific epithet suggests (*formosa,* "beautiful"), with their mix of brilliant yellow and rose colors. The species grows along gravelly or rocky slopes in the Sonoran Desert of Arizona and the Chihuahuan Desert.

Silk Dalea
Dalea mollis

Perennial, mat-forming **herb,** extensively branched from a woody root crown. **Leaves** similar to those of feather-plume but covered with soft, silky hair (*mollis,* "soft"). **Flowers** ¼ inch long, borne in small but dense, headlike spikes; calyx silky-hairy with narrow feathery lobes; corolla white with lavender markings on the banner and wing petals. **Fruit** a small, 1-seeded pod.

Despite its small flowers, silk dalea is an attractive plant; it is also sweet-smelling. It grows on gravelly slopes of the Sonoran Desert. **Gregg dalea *(D. pulchra),*** primarily of the Chihuahuan Desert, is similar but is woodier, has fewer leaflets (5 to 7), and its flowers are uniformly pinkish purple.

Coral Bean
Erythrina flabelliformis

Medium-size **shrub, stems** brittle, armed with short, stout spines. **Leaves** alternate, drought-deciduous, compound with 3 large, triangular leaflets, 2 to 4 inches long and broad. **Flowers** 2 inches long, borne in dense racemes at the tips of branches; calyx fused into a narrow tube without lobes; corolla brilliant red, long, narrowly tubular, and only slightly bilaterally symmetrical; stamens 10. **Fruit** a 5- to 10-inch pod with coral-colored seeds (beans).

Coral bean is an occasional shrub in the Sonoran Desert of southern Arizona and adjacent New Mexico. It grows in rocky sites along desert mountains and canyon walls, where it is conspicuous because of its brilliant hummingbird flowers, which normally appear after the leaves have fallen. The brightly colored beans, reported to be poisonous, have been used to make beads.

Creeping Rush-Pea
Hoffmanseggia repens

Perennial **herbs** only a few inches tall, spreading by creeping (*repens,* "creeping") rhizomes; **stems** prostrate. **Leaves** alternate, silvery pubescent, twice pinnately compound with 3 to 7 primary leaflets and 6 to 14 egg-shaped secondary leaflets ¼ to ½ inch long. **Flowers** 1 to 2 inches across, crowded in dense racemes at the tip of erect branches; calyx fused into a tube with 5 lobes; petals 5, golden yellow, the upper petal shorter and broader than the others and marked with red; stamens 10, yellow and showy. **Fruit** a pendent, membranaceous pod, 1 to 2 inches long.

This is a colorful plant in sandy flats of the Painted Desert, often forming mats from the creeping rhizomes.

Feather-Plume *Dalea formosa*   **Silk Dalea** *Dalea mollis*

Coral Bean
Erythrina flabelliformis

Creeping Rush-Pea
Hoffmanseggia repens

Bush Trefoil
Lotus rigidus

Perennial **subshrub** 10 to 30 inches tall; **stems** woody at the base, stiffly erect (rigid). **Leaves** alternate, pinnately compound, reduced to bracts upward on the stem; leaflets 3 to 5, elliptical, ¼ to 1 inch long, typically folded. **Flowers** ½ to 1 inch long, solitary or few on long stalks from leaf axils; calyx fused into a tube with 5 lobes, purplish, becoming enlarged in fruit; corolla yellow, tinted with red, especially with age; stamens 10, concealed by the lower petals (the keel). **Fruit** an erect, narrowly elliptical, brownish red pod about 2 inches long.

Bush trefoil grows in sandy flats and washes and gravelly foothills of the Mojave and Sonoran Deserts. Several other species of *Lotus* grow in the deserts, varying from small-flowered, prostrate annuals to shrubs. Most have yellow flowers.

LUPINES (BLUEBONNETS)
Lupinus species

Like the genus *Astragalus* (locoweeds) discussed above, *Lupinus* is large and taxonomically difficult, with nomenclature disagreements. Although there are not nearly as many species of lupines as there are locoweeds, the taxonomic problems are more visible because of the more frequent dominance of lupines, such as the **Mojave lupine** *(Lupinus sparsiflorus),* across the desert landscape.

As with most legumes, the flowers of lupines are sweetpealike, with an upper, flaglike petal (banner), 2 lateral petals (wings), and 2 partially fused lower petals that form the keel. The 10 stamens and style are retained inside the keel until it is depressed, usually by a bumblebee foraging for pollen. The leaves are palmately compound.

Also like locoweeds, lupines are often poisonous and although less toxic than their aptly named cousins, they are potentially more dangerous because of their greater abundance.

Silver Lupine
Lupinus argenteus

Perennial **herb,** 8 to 30 inches tall, the foliage and stems clothed with silvery hair; **stems** erect, clustered from a woody, branched root crown. **Leaflets** 6 to 9, often folded, generally narrow, ½ to 3 inches long and ⅙ to ⅓ inch wide, widest near the tip. **Flowers** about ½ inch long, numerous in racemes several inches long; calyx fused with an upper lip and a lower lip; corolla blue or bluish purple with a white or yellow spot on the banner.

Lupinus argenteus is the most variable and taxonomically difficult of all our species. Many varieties are recognized, and taxonomic "lumpers" include additional forms, such as the common **tailcup lupine** *(L. caudatus),* that are regarded as distinct species by taxonomic "splitters." It is also the most widespread and abundant lupine in the Great Basin and Painted Deserts. It prefers well-drained, sandy soils and ranges from the desert to the forests above. It is known to be poisonous to livestock, sheep in particular.

Bush Trefoil *Lotus rigidus*

Mojave Lupine with creosote bush *Lupinus sparsiflorus*

Silver Lupine *Lupinus argenteus* var. *heteranthus*

Arizona Lupine
Lupinus arizonicus

Annual **herb,** up to 20 inches tall; **stems** hairy, solitary but sometimes branched from the base. **Leaflets** 6 to 10, elliptical, ½ to 2 inches long and ⅓ as wide, pointed and usually folded. **Flowers** ⅓ to ½ inch long, fairly dense in a narrow, elongate raceme; calyx fused with an upper and lower lip, the upper lip deeply lobed; corolla dark pink to lavender purple, banner spot yellowish. **Fruit** a few-seeded, hairy pod, ½ to 1 inch long.

Arizona lupine prefers gravelly soils and often grows in profusion along roadsides, helping to make a drive through the desert a pleasant experience. The reddish flowers differentiate it from most other lupines. It grows in the Mojave and, particularly, the Sonoran Deserts.

Miniature Lupine
Lupinus bicolor

Small annual **herb,** 2 to 6 inches tall; **stems** solitary, unbranched, hairy; the cotyledons are persistent at the stem base. **Leaflets** 5 to 7, narrowly elliptical, ½ to 2 inches long, usually folded, silky hairy, at least on the lower surface. **Flowers** about ⅓ inch long in a short raceme; calyx 2-lipped, the upper lip deeply divided; corolla purplish blue, banner spot white, becoming reddish after pollination. **Fruit** a small, few-seeded, hairy pod.

This little charmer is locally abundant in sandy soils and disturbed areas, ranging from southern Canada through California.

Short-Stem Lupine
Lupinus brevicaulis

Annual **herb,** 2 to 6 inches tall; **stems** short or none (*brevi*, "short"; *caulis*, "stem"), the flowers clustered at the end of one or few nodeless/leafless, erect or prostrate stalks clothed with long, silky hair. **Leaves** basal; leaflets 5 to 9, elliptical, usually folded, ¼ to ¾ inch long, the lower surface covered with long, silky hair; leaf stalks ½ to 3 inches long. **Flowers** ½ to 1 inch long, borne in a congested raceme; calyx 2-lipped, the upper lip very short; corolla dark bluish purple, banner spot bright yellow. **Fruit** a 1- to 3-seeded, hairy, egg-shaped pod, ½ inch long.

Sometimes called "sand lupine," this species grows in sand flats and washes, ranging from the Great Basin and Painted Deserts into the Mojave Desert. The plants are small and strikingly attractive, with silky-hairy foliage and bright, contrasting flower colors.

Dwarf Lupine
Lupinus pusillus

Annual **herb,** up to 10 inches tall; **stems** solitary or few from a taproot, hairy; cotyledons persistent on the stem base; **Leaves** alternate; leaflets 3 to 9, elliptical, often folded, ½ to 2 inches long, hairy on the lower surface; leaf stalks up to 3 inches long, shorter upward on the stem. **Flowers** ½ inch long, borne in dense, elongate racemes; calyx 2-lipped, hairy; corolla pale blue to lavender, banner spot white, becoming reddish following pollination. **Fruit** a 2-seeded, hairy, pod, ½ inch long.

This is the most common lupine in the Painted Desert, often forming colorful displays across broad expanses of sandy plains. It also grows in the Great Basin and Mojave Deserts.

Arizona Lupine *Lupinus arizonicus*   **Short-Stem Lupine** *Lupinus brevicaulis*

Miniature Lupine
Lupinus bicolor

Dwarf Lupine
Lupinus pusillus

Mojave Lupine
Lupinus sparsiflorus

Annual **herb,** up to 18 inches tall; **stems** usually branched, hairy; cotyledons usually persistent at the stem base; **Leaves** alternate; leaflets 5 to 9, narrowly elliptical to linear, ⅓ to 1½ inches long, clothed with short, silky hair; leaf stalks up to 3 inches long, shorter upward on the stem. **Flowers** about ½ inch long, fairly sparse along a narrow, elongate raceme; calyx 2-lipped, the upper lip deeply divided; corolla pale blue to lavender, occasionally white, banner spot white, becoming reddish after pollination. **Fruit** a few-seeded, hairy pod, ½ to 1 inch long.

This is the most common lupine in the Mojave and Sonoran Deserts. It prefers sandy soils, where it often grows in dense populations over large areas. Frequently it is a codominant with sand verbena on sand flats and dunes. It is also a common associate of creosote bush.

Cat's-Claw Mimosa
Mimosa biuncifera

Medium-size, rounded, spiny **shrub,** 2 to 6 feet tall; **stems** freely branched, with vicious, curved spines borne singly or in pairs at the nodes. **Leaves** alternate, twice pinnately compound, with 4 to 8 pairs of primary leaflets and up to 12 pairs of secondary leaflets, the latter a small fraction of an inch long. **Flowers** borne in white to pinkish, ¾-inch, ball-like heads, emerging from leaf axils on short stalks; perianth segments (sepals and petals) small, brown to greenish, and inconspicuous; stamens white, 10 per flower, extending well beyond the perianth. **Fruit** a narrowly elliptical, inch-long pod that is often spiny along one margin and at maturity breaks up, releasing its seeds.

This is a common shrub in rocky areas along hillsides and in canyons of the Sonoran Desert of Arizona and the Chihuahuan Desert. Several other species of *Mimosa* grow in similar habitats, particularly in the Chihuahuan Desert, but none are as abundant.

Velvet-Pod Mimosa
Mimosa dysocarpa

Low, sprawling, spiny **shrub,** usually less than 3 feet tall; **stems** freely branched, with vicious, curved spines at nodes and scattered irregularly along the branches. **Leaves** alternate, twice pinnately compound, 5 to 9 pairs of primary leaflets and 6 to 12 pairs of secondary leaflets, the latter only a small fraction of an inch long. **Flowers** borne in very showy pink to purple, inch-long spikes that fade to white; perianth segments purple to greenish but small and inconspicuous; stamens purple or white, 10 per flower, extending well beyond the perianth. **Fruit** a flat, 2-inch pod, densely clothed with velvety, white pubescence.

The velvet-pod mimosa is a plant best admired from a distance; the curved spines are sharp and grasping, seemingly reaching out to grab the unwary photographer trying to capture the elegance of the purple-and-white spikes. Its range is similar to cat's-claw mimosa, noted above, but it is much less common.

Three genera of spiny desert shrubs, *Acacia, Mimosa,* and *Prosopis,* resemble each other and can easily be confused. They all have twice pinnate leaves and an inflorescence that is a spike or head. The flowers are similar in having an inconspicuous perianth and extended, colorful stamens. The acacias usually have yellow, but sometimes white, ball-like heads, and the individual flowers have about 20 stamens. The mesquites *(Prosopis)* have only one or two pairs of primary leaflets, and the inflorescence is an elongate spike of yellow or white flowers, each with 10 stamens. Finally, the mimosas have several pairs of primary leaflets, and the inflorescence is a ball-like head, or occasionally an elongate spike, of white or purplish flowers with 10 stamens.

Mojave Lupine *Lupinus sparsiflorus*   Velvet-Pod Mimosa *Mimosa dysocarpa*

Cat's-Claw Mimosa *Mimosa biuncifera*   Inset: Cat's-Claw Mimosa flowers *Mimosa biuncifera*

Ironwood

Olneya tesota

Low-stature **tree** or large **shrub,** up to 30 feet tall, the crown about as wide as the tree is tall, branches spiny, spines paired at the nodes (stipular spines); bark gray green, stringy or scaly. **Leaves** alternate, more or less winter-deciduous, pinnately compound; leaflets 2 to 10 pairs, elliptical to egg-shaped, ⅓ inch long, pubescent. **Flowers** about ½ inch long, 2 to 5 in racemes arising from leaf axils; calyx fused with 5 teeth, covered with gray hair; corolla mainly lavender purple, the upper petal (banner) generally yellow or white; stamens 10, 9 of which are fused by their filaments. **Fruit** a thick-walled, few-seeded cylindrical pod, 1 to 3 inches long, constricted between the seeds.

This species is aptly named; the wood is extremely hard, with a specific gravity exceeding that of water—it will not float. Unfortunately, the trees have been used so extensively for firewood that few large specimens remain. In earlier times, the seeds provided an important food source for Indians. Ironwood grows primarily in sandy washes in the Sonoran Desert, often in abundance. It is well equipped to deal with drought but cannot tolerate frost.

An attractive plant overlapping in distribution, at least in Arizona, and sharing many characteristics with ironwood is **coursetia *(Coursetia glandulosa).*** This is a large shrub or small tree, up to 20 feet tall. It, too, has pinnately compound leaves with 2 to 10 pairs of leaflets, and the flowers are similar to ironwood in shape and size. Coursetia lacks spines, though, and the flowers are yellow with a white banner. It grows in rocky canyons and sandy washes.

D Mesquite

***Prosopsis* species**

Small, bushy **tree** up to 50 feet tall and 3 feet in diameter but usually much smaller; branches armed with stout, straight spines borne singly or in pairs at the base of leaves. **Leaves** alternate, deciduous, twice pinnate with 1 or 2 pairs of primary leaflets and 7 to 30 pairs of linear to narrowly elliptical secondary leaflets ⅓ to 2 inches long. **Flowers** yellowish, small, but densely clustered in a 2- to 5-inch spike; sepals 5, fused at the base; petals 5; stamens 10, extending beyond the sepals and petals. **Fruit** a linear pod several inches long, constricted between the seeds.

Mesquite is known as a phreatophyte: it has deep roots that penetrate 60 feet or more into the soil, drawing water from aquifers. It most commonly inhabits washes and sandy flats. In dune areas, sand is blown around and over the plants, forming huge mounds. In one form or another it is distributed throughout the hot deserts of North America and is ecologically important. Often it forms impenetrable thickets that are home to many species of birds and mammals, and the flowers provide nectar and pollen for bees. Cattle and other herbivores feed on the young twigs and fruits, but it is invasive in overgrazed desert grasslands. Indians and Mexicans historically made flour or a beverage from the beans. Because the wood is hard and resilient, mesquite has been used for fence posts and lumber to the extent that few large trees remain today.

Prosopsis is taxonomically difficult. Some botanists place all the mesquites in a single species, *P. juliflora.* Others recognize two species, ***P. glandulosa* (honey mesquite)** and ***P. velutina* (velvet mesquite),** each with additional varieties.

Ironwood
Olneya tesota
Inset: Ironwood
Olneya tesota

Honey Mesquite
in red dune
community
Prosopsis glandulosa
Inset: Honey
Mesquite seed pods
Prosopsis glandulosa

Coursetia
Coursetia glandulosa

Honey Mesquite flowers
Prosopsis glandulosa

INDIGOBUSH   *Psorothamnus (Dalea)* species

Intricately branched **shrubs** or small **trees,** generally thorny and gland-dotted. **Leaves** alternate, pinnately compound or simple. **Flowers** sweetpealike but small; sepals (calyx) fused at the base with 5 lobes, generally hairy and gland-dotted; corolla deep violet (indigo) to blue or lavender purple; stamens 10. **Fruit** a 1-seeded, indehiscent, gland-spotted pod.

Several species of indigobush grow in the deserts, most of them strikingly handsome when in bloom. The flowers are small, profuse, and individually beautiful.

When the leaves or stems of some indigobushes are rubbed, they emit a pleasant scent, probably from the glands. When the inflorescences are crushed, they yield a yellow pigment, which has been used as a dye by Indians.

Mojave Indigobush   *Psorothamnus arborescens*

Medium-size **shrub,** 2 to 3 feet tall; **stems** generally spiny, hairy, often densely so. **Leaves** pinnately compound, with 5 to 7 linear leaflets ¼ to ½ inch long. **Flowers** about ⅓ inch long, several in elongate spikes at the tips of branches; corolla uniformly dark blue purple (indigo). **Fruit** an egg-shaped pod ⅓ inch long.

The specific epithet *arborescens* is a misnomer, because the plants never approach tree status. The common name is appropriate, though, since the range of the species, including its three recognized varieties, is centered in the Mojave Desert of California and southern Nevada. It grows in rocky sites in the desert mountains.

White Indigobush   *Psorothamnus emoryi*

Low, mound-shaped, unarmed **shrub,** 1 to 2 feet tall and up to 3 feet across; **stems** densely clothed with white, felty pubescence that hides the scattered, orangish glands. **Leaves** also covered with white, felty pubescence; leaflets 5 to 9, elliptical, generally folded along the midvein, up to ⅓ inch long, the terminal leaflet the longest. **Flowers** small, ¼ to ⅓ inch long, densely clustered in heads at the tips of branches; corolla lavender with white markings, not much longer than the calyx. **Fruit** a small pod that remains concealed inside the calyx tube.

This indigobush grows in sandy desert flats and along washes, occasionally forming dense populations. It ranges from the Mojave Desert into the Sonoran Desert, primarily in California.

Nevada Indigobush   *Psorothamnus polydenius*

Medium-size, mound-shaped **shrub,** 2 to 4 feet tall and wide; **stems** velvety hairy and conspicuously dotted with red-orange glands (*polydenius,* "many glands"); many of the branches end in weak spines. **Leaves** pinnately compound; leaflets 7 to 13, only a small fraction of an inch long and roundish in outline, pubescent and dotted with glands. **Flowers** about ⅓ inch long, borne in dense spikes at the tips of branches; corolla light lavender purple, the upper petal (banner) sometimes with a small, basal yellow spot. **Fruit** a small pod that remains concealed inside the calyx tube.

As the common name suggests, this is primarily a Nevada plant. It is widely distributed in the Great Basin and ranges southward into the Mojave Desert of California. It grows in sandy and gravelly soils of desert plains and foothills and is locally abundant, forming strikingly attractive populations when in bloom.

Mojave Indigobush *Psorothamnus arborescens* var. *simplicifolius*

White Indigobush *Psorothamnus emoryi*

Nevada Indigobush *Psorothamnus polydenius*

Fremont Indigobush

Psorothamnus fremontii

Medium-size, mound-shaped **shrub,** 2 to 5 feet tall and wide, **stems** not conspicuously gland-dotted; branches sometimes ending in weak spines. **Leaves** pinnately compound; leaflets 3 to 9, narrowly elliptical to linear, up to ½ inch long, densely pubescent, glandular on the lower surface. **Flowers** ⅓ to ½ inch long, numerous in narrow, elongate spikes at the tips of branches; corolla uniformly dark bluish purple (indigo). **Fruit** an egg-shaped, 2-seeded, somewhat flattened pod, ⅓ to ½ inch long.

The flowers of this plant are handsomely sculpted and strikingly colored. When in bloom, the plants are particularly showy, with numerous indigo flowers contrasting with the grayish white foliage. The species grows along rocky slopes and canyons ranging from the Painted Desert to the Sonoran Desert of California.

Smoke Tree

Psorothamnus spinosa

Gray-hairy **tree** of low stature, up to 25 feet tall, with an equally wide crown; tips of branches ending in a sharp spine; bark greenish, becoming nearly black with age. **Leaves** simple rather than pinnately compound (unusual in the genus), sparse, spoon-shaped, gland-dotted, only about ⅓ inch long. **Flowers** ⅓ to ½ inch long, congested in short racemes at the tips of branches; calyx with a ring of conspicuous reddish glands at the bottom of the lobes; corolla uniformly dark bluish purple (indigo), resembling the flowers of Fremont indigobush in size and color. **Fruit** an egg-shaped, few-seeded pod, largely concealed by the calyx.

Smoke tree is attractive in all seasons. When in bloom, it is spectacular, with a multitude of indigo flowers; the entire crown comes alive with color. At other times of year the tree is ashy gray, its diffuse branches resembling a cloud of smoke. It grows along sandy washes, often forming dense colonies. It ranges across the Sonoran Desert of California into Arizona.

Mesa Indigobush

Psorothamnus schottii

Medium-size **shrub,** 2 to 6 feet tall; branches thin, green and shiny, some modified into weak spines. **Leaves** more or less evergreen, simple, neither lobed nor divided, narrowly elliptical to linear, the margins rolled under, ½ to 2 inches long, dotted with glands. **Flowers** ½ inch long, numerous but not crowded in narrow, elongate racemes at branch tips; calyx reddish brown, varnished in appearance, gland-dotted; corolla uniformly bright bluish purple. **Fruit** an elliptical pod, ⅓ to ½ inch long.

This species inhabits gravelly mesas, foothills, and washes in the Sonoran Desert of California and adjacent Arizona.

Fremont Indigobush *Psorothamnus fremontii*
Inset: Fremont Indigobush *Psorothamnus fremontii*

Smoke Tree *Psorothamnus spinosa*

Mesa Indigobush *Psorothamnus schottii*

Broom Indigobush

Psorothamnus scoparius

Low, mound-shaped, grayish white (felty) **shrub,** 1 to 3 feet tall and usually much wider; **stems**/branches many, stiffly erect, broomlike, conspicuously gland-dotted. **Leaves** simple, neither lobed nor divided, sparse, somewhat rubbery, linear, ¼ to ½ inch long, gland-dotted. **Flowers** about ⅓ inch long, congested in headlike spikes at the tip of branches; calyx white-hairy, each of the 5 short lobes tipped by a gland; corolla dark bluish purple (indigo), the upper petal (banner) sometimes with a central, basal white stripe. **Fruit** a tiny, 1-seeded, densely hairy pod remaining concealed by the calyx tube.

This may be the most common of the Chihuahuan Desert indigobushes; it undoubtedly is one of the most beautiful, with its grayish white branches and bluish purple flowers. It grows in sandy soils, often on dunes.

Spiny Senna

Senna (Cassia) armata

Low **shrub,** 1 to 3 feet tall; **stems** clustered, more or less erect, green and photosynthetic, branches often ending in spines. **Leaves** alternate, pinnately compound, drought-deciduous (the plants are leafless most of the year); leaflets 2 to 4 pairs, tiny, roundish but asymmetrical; the leaf axis is sharp-pointed and remains on the stem as a weak spine after the leaflets fall off. **Flowers** only slightly bilaterally symmetrical, ½ to 1 inch across, borne in elongate racemes at the stem tips; sepals 5, not fused; petals 5, golden yellow to reddish tinged, strongly veined, narrowed at the base, thus appearing stalked; stamens 10, the 3 upper ones sterile, the anthers of the 7 fertile ones arched upward toward the style. **Fruit** a straight, cylindrical, few-seeded, erect pod.

Spiny senna is locally abundant in gravelly flats and washes of the Mojave and Sonoran Deserts, particularly in California. It is an interesting species in that it exemplifies evolutionary changes plants undergo in adapting to a desert environment. *Senna* is a large genus of primarily unarmed tropical trees and shrubs with large evergreen leaves. In this species the leaflets are deciduous, falling at the onset of drought, and the stems have assumed the major responsibility of photosynthesis. This greatly reduces water loss through transpiration. Also, the young branches are covered with scalelike hairs that further reduce water loss. Finally, the plants are innovative in the development of spines, a common trait among desert plants. Both the stem tips and leaf axils are modified into weak spines. Presumably, these will become stronger and sharper as the species persists in the millennia to come. The specific epithet *(armata)* relates to the armament of the stems. Desert plants can also avoid or escape drought through the herbaceous habit. Although spiny senna is a shrub, most desert species of *Senna* are subshrubs or herbs, an adaptation from the more primitive woody habit of their tropical ancestors.

Broom Indigobush *Psorothamnus scoparius*
Inset: Broom Indigobush *Psorothamnus scoparius*

Spiny Senna *Senna (Cassia) armata*   Spiny Senna *Senna (Cassia) armata*

Coues' Senna — *Senna (Cassia) covesii*

Subshrub, 1 to 2 feet tall; **stems** erect, woody at the base, sparingly branched, clothed with white, felty pubescence. **Leaves** alternate, pinnately compound, pubescent; leaflets 2 to 4 pairs, broadly elliptical, ½ to 1 inch long and at least half as wide. **Flowers** similar to those of spiny senna, described above. **Fruit** a straight, erect, several-seeded pod, 1 to 2 inches long.

This species has a range similar to that of spiny senna but is much less common. It is named in honor of Dr. Elliot Coues, a government ornithologist.

Two-Leaved Senna — *Senna (Cassia) durangensis*

Perennial, grayish pubescent **herb,** 8 to 30 inches tall; **stems** erect to spreading, few to several from a branched root crown. **Leaves** alternate, pinnately compound; leaflets 2 (one pair), egg-shaped, 1 to 2 inches long and nearly as wide. **Flowers** only slightly bilaterally symmetrical, about 1 inch across, borne in stalked racemes from leaf axils, 2 to several per raceme; sepals 5, nonfused, greenish; petals 5, yellow with darker veins, narrowed at the base into a stalk (claw); stamens 10, 3 sterile and 7 fertile, the latter with anthers curved upward. **Fruit** an erect, densely hairy, many-seeded pod, 1 to 2 inches long.

Two-leaved senna, named for its pair of leaflets, grows on limestone soils in the Chihuahuan Desert of Texas.

Chihuahua Senna — *Senna (Cassia) lindheimeriana*

Robust, perennial **herb,** up to 5 feet tall; **stems** clothed with white, felty pubescence, erect, usually several from a woody root crown. **Leaves** alternate, pinnately compound; leaflets 5 to 8 pairs, elliptical, 1 to 2 inches long and half as wide, finely pubescent, tipped with a short bristle. **Flowers** only slightly if at all bilaterally symmetrical, about 1 inch across, borne in stalked racemes from leaf axils, several flowers per raceme; sepals 5, not fused, densely pubescent; petals golden yellow with prominent veins; stamen 10, the 7 fertile ones brown and curved upward. **Fruit** a narrow, somewhat flattened, hairy, many-seeded pod, 2 to 3 inches long.

This is the most common senna of the Chihuahuan Desert, ranging west into Arizona. It grows primarily on limestone soils.

Texas Senna — *Senna (Cassia) roemeriana*

Robust, perennial **herb,** up to 5 feet tall; **stems** clothed with white, felty pubescence, erect or spreading, clumped from a thick, woody root crown. **Leaves** alternate, pinnately compound; leaflets 2 (one pair), narrowly lance-shaped to linear, 1 to 2½ inches long, finely pubescent. **Flowers** only slightly if at all bilaterally symmetrical, about 1 inch across, 2 to 5 in stalked racemes from leaf axils. Sepals 5, not fused, slightly pubescent; petals 5, golden yellow; stamens 10, the 7 fertile ones brown and curved upward. **Fruit** a narrow, somewhat flattened, many-seeded pod, about 1 inch long.

The most common senna of Texas, this species grows in sandy plains, especially in limestone soils. It ranges west into New Mexico and south into Mexico.

Coues' Senna
Senna (Cassia) covesii

Two-Leaved Senna
Senna (Cassia) durangensis

Chihuahua Senna
Senna (Cassia)
lindheimeriana

Texas Senna *Senna*
(Cassia) roemeriana

LILY FAMILY Liliaceae

Liliaceae is a large family, with worldwide distribution. In the broad sense it includes Agavaceae, Amaryllidaceae, and some other smaller "families." Taxonomic "lumpers" regard the overlap among the plant groups too great to warrant placing them in separate families, while "splitters" emphasize differences rather than similarities. The composition of the family thus becomes a judgment call; I have sided with the lumpers.

In the broad sense, the family includes woody plants as well as herbaceous perennials. The flower parts generally are in threes: three sepals, three petals, six stamens, and a three-compartmented ovary. Usually the sepals and petals (perianth segments) are similar in shape and color, and the flowers are radially symmetrical and showy. The ovary may be either superior or inferior and matures into a berry or capsule. The herbaceous representatives usually have modified underground stems, either bulbs, tubers, or rhizomes. Many plants have succulent stems or leaves or both. In deserts the family is particularly important, with some species being community dominants. Beyond that, some species are cultivated for food, many for their horticultural attributes. A few species are poisonous.

AGAVES (CENTURY PLANTS) *Agave* species

The nobility of agaves was recognized by Linneus when he formally established the generic name in the eighteenth century; *Agave* is a Greek term meaning "noble." The common name "century plant" has been applied because of the mistaken belief that the plants bloom after about 100 years. Actually, they flower after remaining 10 to 20 years in the rosette stage. When a rosette has matured sufficiently, it responds to an environmental signal and genetic trigger, rapidly developing an impressive flowering stalk and producing thousands of seeds. Then it dies—its moment of glory is brief. Most agaves have rhizomes, from which several rosettes may develop; thus they do not have a finite life-span. A rosetted individual dies, but the plant lives on.

The rosette of persistent leaves is attractive on its own and continues to expand as the plant matures. The individual leaves are succulent and stiff, bearing vicious spines at their tip and often having sawlike spines along their margins. The leaves have more than aesthetic value—they are a source of fiber used for making ropes, baskets, sacks, and brushes. Indians prepared mescal using the stem crown from the center of the rosette. The national drink of Mexico, pulque, is made from fermented sap collected from leaf bases and the hollowed-out center of the stem crown. Tequila and industrial alcohol is also made from the plant sap.

The agaves are distinct from other members of the lily family because they have succulent leaves and an inferior ovary and yellow or greenish perianth segments that are fused into a tube with 6 narrow lobes. Only the genera *Yucca* and *Nolina* share the woody trait with agaves. Several *Agave* species grow in North American deserts, all in rocky or gravelly soils.

An important agave species in the Sonoran Desert is **desert agave (*A. deserti*).** It has gray-green, lance-shaped leaves 10 to 20 inches long and 2 to 4 inches wide, with small, widely spaced marginal spines. The terminal spine is 1 to 2 inches long. The flowering stalk is up to 18 feet tall, with branches bearing umbel-like flower clusters along the upper third. The flowers are pale yellow and 2 to 3 inches long.

Desert Agave *Agave deserti*   **Big Bend Agave** *Agave havardiana*

Big Bend Agave *Agave havardiana*

Two agave species of the Chihuahuan Desert are **Big Bend agave** *(A. havardiana)* and **Parry agave** *(A. parryi)*. The leaves of these agaves are bluish green, broadly lance-shaped to triangular, up to 2 feet long and half as wide. They have prominent marginal spines, and a 1- to 2-inch terminal spine. The flowering stalks are up to 18 feet tall, with branches bearing umbel-shaped flower clusters along the upper half. The flowers, golden yellow to reddish, are about 3 inches long. Big Bend agave is endemic to the desert mountains of the Big Bend country of Texas. Parry agave, more widespread, ranges west into Arizona. The cabbagelike rosettes of Parry agave are often clustered from spreading rhizomes.

The most widely used agave is **mescal** or **Palmer agave** *(A. palmeri)*. It has bright green to bluish, narrowly lance-shaped leaves up to 3 feet long and 6 inches wide. Marginal spines are prominent, and the terminal spine is 1 to 2 inches long. The flowering stalk can be as tall as 18 feet. It grows in the southeastern corner of Arizona, ranging east into New Mexico.

A petite species is **Utah agave** *(A. utahensis),* which has bright green, narrowly lance-shaped leaves only 6 to 15 inches long and 1 to 2 inches wide with marginal spines. The terminal spine is 1 to 2 inches long. The flowering stalk is only up to 12 feet tall, and the yellow, ½- to 1-inch flowers are borne in a narrow panicle along the upper half of the stalk. This unusual agave grows in the desert where Utah, Arizona, and Nevada come together, often forming dense populations.

✹ Lechuguilla (leh-choo-*ghee*-yuh)   *Agave lechuguilla*

Succulent **shrub** bearing a long (6- to 12-foot), narrow, un-branched stem (flowering stalk). **Leaves** produced in a ground-level, inward-curving cluster (rosette) of about 10 to 30; they are 8 to 15 inches long, 1- to 2-inches wide at the base, narrowly lance-shaped, and armed with a very sharp 1- to 2-inch spine; leaf margins also armed, with shorter spines that point downward. **Flowers** 1 to 2 inches long, borne on short pedicels, often in groups of 2 to 4, along the upper half of the flowering stalk; sepals and petals similar in appearance, greenish or yellowish white or sometimes purplish tinged, fused at the base into a short, funnel-shaped tube bearing the 6 stamens. **Fruit** a 3-chambered, woody capsule bearing numerous flattened seeds, 2 rows in each chamber.

Lechuguilla typically grows in large colonies, spreading from underground root stalks. It is a dominant species over much of western Texas and southeastern New Mexico, preferring limestone soils. More than any other species, lechuguilla typifies the United States component of the Chihuahuan Desert. Although it is an attractive plant, the daggerlike leaves create a hazard for horses and other animals, including humans. The leaves are said to be poisonous, although browsers eat them (carefully!) when other forage plants become unavailable because of overgrazing or severe drought. The leaves have been used as a source of fiber for ropes and baskets. In recent years the plant has become a popular ornamental in succulent gardens. *Lechuguilla* is the Spanish diminutive for lettuce ("little lettuce"), relating to the dense, headlike growth habit of the relatively small leaves.

Parry Agave *Agave parryi*

Mescal Agave *Agave palmeri*

Lechuguilla *Agave lechuguilla*   **Inset: Lechuguilla** *Agave lechuguilla*

Desert Wild Onion
Allium macropetalum

Perennial **herb,** up to 6 inches tall, derived from a roundish, garlic-flavored, under-ground bulb, ½ to 1 inch thick. **Leaves** basal, linear, succulent, usually 2 per flowering stem, nearly round in cross section and only a fraction of an inch wide, exceeding the flowering stem in length. **Flowers** few to many in a dense umbel at the top of the stem, the umbel subtended by 2 to 3 papery bracts; perianth segments white to pinkish with pinkish purple midveins, lance-shaped, ⅓ to ½ inch long; stamens not extending beyond the perianth. **Fruit** a many-seeded capsule with 6 conspicuous crests on top.

This is the most common and widespread of several wild onions that grow in our deserts. It usually grows in clayey soils, often in alkaline areas. Sometimes it grows in such profusion that the desert landscape looks like reddish tinged snow. It ranges from the Painted Desert through Arizona and into the Chihuahuan Desert of Texas.

Small-Flowered Hyacinth
Androstephium breviflorum

Perennial **herb,** 4 to 12 inches tall, derived from a roundish, fibrous-coated bulb, ½ to 1 inch thick. **Leaves** basal, linear, folded or rolled, 1 to 3 per flowering stem and about as long as the stem. **Flowers** 3 to 7 in an umbel at the top of the stem; perianth segments white to pale purplish with a bluish purple midvein, narrowly lance-shaped, ½ to 1 inch long, fused at the base. The 6 stamen filaments are fused into a crown (*andro,* "stamens"; *stephium,* "crown") around the ovary. **Fruit** a several-seeded, 3-lobed capsule, ½ inch long.

This is primarily a Great Basin and Painted Desert species. It prefers well-drained soils and is often associated with blackbrush.

Desert Mariposa Lily
Calochortus kennedyi

Perennial, bluish green (glaucous) **herb,** 4 to 30 inches tall, growing from a roundish bulb; **stems** erect, solitary. **Leaves** 2 to 4, alternate, narrowly lance-shaped to linear, 4 to 8 inches long. **Flowers** bell-shaped, 2 to 4 inches across, solitary or a few in an umbel subtended by 2 leaflike bracts; sepals 3, lance-shaped, greenish purple, about 1 inch long; petals 3, wedge-shaped, 1 to 2 inches long, brilliant reddish orange with a hairy, purplish black, glandular base; anthers deep purple; stigma lobes 3, yellow-orange, shaped like a grappling hook. **Fruit** a 3-angled, many-seeded capsule.

Of the many beautiful desert wildflowers none is more eye-catching than this charmer. It is striking from afar, looking like patches of flame scattered across the desert landscape. Up close its splendor is unsurpassed, combining brilliance with an unusual mix of colors. The plants are usually scattered but may form dense populations. The species ranges from the southern limits of the Mojave Desert into the Sonoran Desert of Arizona. Farther north, in the Great Basin and Painted Deserts, desert mariposa lily is replaced by **sego lily *(Calochortus nuttallii),*** which has pale lavender petals with a yellow or purplish base.

Desert Wild Onion *Allium macropetalum*

Small-Flowered Hyacinth *Androstephium breviflorum*

Desert Mariposa Lily *Calochortus kennedyi*

✵ Sotol (Desert Spoon)   *Dasylirion wheeleri*

Small **tree,** trunk 1 to 3 feet long, bearing a dense rosette of leaves, flowering stem (above the leaves) 10 to 15 feet tall, including an elongate inflorescence. **Leaves** linear, about 3 feet long and 1 to 2 inches wide, not spine-tipped but with sawlike teeth along the margin, bluish green. The base of the leaves is spoonlike, a characteristic responsible for the alternate common name. **Flowers** unisexual, male (staminate) and female (pistillate) on separate plants, small (about ⅛ inch), densely congested in a branched inflorescence (panicle) that is 5 to 8 feet long and about 10 inches thick; sepals and petals 3 each, similar in color (whitish) and size; stamens 6, extended beyond the sepals and petals. **Fruit** leathery, 1-seeded, about ⅓ inch long, triangular, with a thin extension (wing) on each angle.

Sotol is a locally abundant, conspicuous, and attractive plant on rocky and gravelly slopes of the Sonoran and Chihuahuan Deserts, often growing on limestone. It is most common in southeastern Arizona, adjacent New Mexico, and the El Paso area of Texas. In the Chihuahuan Desert it overlaps with other species, most commonly **Chihuahuan sotol *(Dasylirion leiophyllum),*** a smaller plant with dark green rather than bluish green leaves.

Many uses have been made of *Dasylirion* species. The tough leaves have been used by Native Americans for roof thatching and for weaving mats and baskets. The spoonlike leaf bases and spongy interior of the stem, rich in sugar, are eaten by humans and have been used as food for cattle. The stem base (trunk) can be roasted and then fermented to produce an intoxicating beverage known as sotol.

Blue Dicks   *Dichelostemma (Brodiaea) capitatum*
(Desert Hyacinth)

Perennial **herb,** 1 to 2 feet tall, growing from a broadly cylindrical, fibrous bulb; **stems** erect, wiry, and often contorted, unbranched, leafless. **Leaves** 2 to 5, all basal, linear, spreading or erect, 4 to 15 inches long, withering about the time the flowers appear. **Flowers** bell-shaped, ½ to 1 inch long, few to several in a head or tight umbel surrounded by purple bracts; perianth segments pale to dark lavender with a purple midvein, fused about half their length into a tube; stamens derived from the perianth tube and associated with deeply lobed scales. **Fruit** a 3-lobed, few-seeded, small capsule about ¼ inch long.

This species is widely distributed though seldom abundant. It ranges from the Great Basin into California, Arizona, and New Mexico. It prefers gravelly soils and typically grows up through the branches of desert shrubs. Sometimes **few-flowered hyacinth *(Dichelostemma pauciflorum)*** is treated as a variety or subspecies in this species. It differs in having fewer flowers (2 to 5) per inflorescence (*pauciflorum,* "few flowers"), and the bracts that surround the inflorescence are pale lavender rather than purple.

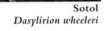

Sotol   **Blue Dicks (Desert Hyacinth)**
Dasylirion wheeleri   *Dichelostemma (Brodiaea) capitatum*

Few-Flowered Hyacinth   *Dichelostemma pauciflorum*

Sand Lily
Eremocrinum albomarginatum

Perennial **herb,** up to 12 inches high, derived from a tuberous root system. **Leaves** mainly basal, linear, 8 to 12 inches long, usually folded with a whitish margin *(albomarginatum),* generally spreading rather than erect. **Flowers** numerous in a narrow, bracteate raceme; perianth segments white with green midveins prominent on the back of the segments, broadly lance-shaped, ⅓ to ½ inch long, fused at the base; stamens about as long as the perianth segments. **Fruit** a small, few-seeded capsule.

Sand lily is endemic to the Painted Desert. It grows in sandy areas, as the common name suggests, often in abundance.

Desert Lily
Hesperocallis undulata

Perennial **herb,** growing from a bulb 2 inches in diameter; **stems** unbranched, from a few inches to more than 3 feet tall. **Leaves** mainly basal, narrowly lance-shaped to linear, flat, wavy along the margin *(undulata,* "wavy"). **Flowers** 2 to 3 inches long, funnel-shaped, opening from the bottom up in a narrow, bracteate raceme; perianth segments white with green stripes along the midveins, fused at the base into a narrow tube, the lobes flaring outward; stamens fused to the perianth. **Fruit** a 3-lobed, few-seeded capsule.

This large-flowered western *(hespero)* beauty *(callis)* seems out of place in the desert and is indeed unforgettable to anyone lucky enough to find it. It grows in sandy flats and dunes, where it achieves its greatest height, and in compacted gravelly sites, where it may be only a few inches high. It ranges from the Mojave Desert of California to western Arizona. Historically, Indians and Spanish settlers dug up and ate the onion-flavored bulbs.

Bigelow Nolina
Nolina bigelovii

Shrub or small **tree,** up to 15 feet tall, including the flowering stalk; **stems** (trunks) only 2 to 6 feet high, sometimes branched. **Leaves** flat and daggerlike but flexuous, 2 to 5 feet long and up to 4 inches wide at the base; young leaves many, erect and spreading at the top of the trunk; the lower, older leaves are persistent, brownish, and hang down, clothing the trunk; margins of young leaves at first have small, sawlike teeth but eventually shred into fibers. **Flowers** whitish, only ⅙ inch long, very numerous in a plumelike panicle at the top of the long stalk. **Fruit** a small, papery, 1- to 3-seeded capsule.

This species grows on rocky and gravelly slopes of the Sonoran and Mojave Deserts, frequently extending upward into juniper woodlands, particularly around the Grand Canyon of Arizona. **Parry nolina (N. parryi),** a closely related species with a similar range, is sometimes treated as a variety of *N. bigelovii.* It is somewhat smaller and the leaf margins do not shred.

In the Chihuahuan Desert two species called **bear grass (Nolina erumpens and N. microcarpa)** grow along limestone slopes and in gravelly arroyos. These shrubs or subshrubs grow to 6 feet tall, including the flowering stalk. The many leaves are basal, linear, less than an inch wide at the base, 2 to 6 feet long, fairly thick, and channeled or grooved along the midvein; the leaf margin has sharp, sawlike teeth, and the leaf tip eventually deteriorates into a soft, ribbonlike fiber. The flowers, tiny and numerous, form an elongate panicle more or less concealed by the leaves. Indians used leaf fibers of these species to weave baskets and mats.

Sand Lily *Eremocrinum albomarginatum*   **Bigelow Nolina** *Nolina bigelovii*

Desert Lily
Hesperocallis undulata

Bear Grass
Nolina erumpens

YUCCAS (SPANISH BAYONETS) *Yucca* species

Yuccas are almost as much a part of the North American deserts as cacti. They have large flowers and stiff, spine-tipped, bayonet-like leaves. Some yuccas grow into large trees, but most are small to medium-size shrubs.

✸ Joshua Tree   *Yucca brevifolia*

Tree, up to 40 feet tall and 4 feet in diameter at the base; **stems** sometimes clumped by emergence of shoots from short rhizomes, freely branched above; bark corky and furrowed, shaggy above from persistent, dead leaves. Roots penetrate deep in the soil and spread widely at shallow depths, providing for effective anchorage and efficient water absorption. **Leaves** 6 to 15 inches long, narrowly lance-shaped and spine-tipped, with small teeth along the margin. **Flowers** 2 to 3 inches long, white to greenish, sometimes purplish tinged, bell-shaped, borne in dense cone-shaped clusters at stem tips; sepals and petals thick and succulent, 3 each, similar in size and color; stamens 6. **Fruit** leathery and spongy at maturity, about 3 inches long and 2 inches wide.

Joshua tree grows almost exclusively in the Mojave Desert, ranging from the gravelly plains up to high elevations in the mountains, where it is often associated with sagebrush and junipers. In some areas, notably Joshua Tree National Monument, the species forms dense, expansive populations. It is a variable species, with two or more recognized varieties.

With the exception of the saguaro cactus, Joshua tree is the best-known and most widely photographed desert plant. Its unusual appearance and large flower clusters catch the eye and the interest of even the most preoccupied desert travelers. But its value transcends its attractiveness. Many desert birds use the trees as nesting sites; rodents and lizards seek food, shade, and shelter among its branches; and most important, as a dominant member of its community, it has a major ecological impact on all other associated plants.

Joshua Tree community *Yucca brevifolia*   Inset: Joshua Tree *Yucca brevifolia*

Joshua Tree and blackbrush community *Yucca brevifolia*

Banana Yucca *Yucca baccata*

Low **shrub,** 1 to 3 feet tall; **stems** (flowering stalks) 1 to few, erect or spreading. **Leaves** in basal rosettes, linear to saber-shaped, stiff, widest in the middle, 15 to 30 inches long, 1 to 2 inches wide, bluish green; leaf margin soon shredding into fibers. **Flowers** 2 to 3 inches long, bell-shaped, pendent, borne in dense panicles largely hidden by the leaves; perianth cream-colored, sometimes purple-fringed. **Fruit** banana-like, 4 to 7 inches long.

Banana yucca grows on rocky hillsides and plains of the Great Basin, Mojave, and Painted Deserts, extending south into the Chihuahuan Desert. It extends upward into grasslands and juniper woodlands. The sweet, fleshy fruit, either raw or dried, is eaten by Indians. The leaves are also used as a fiber source.

Navajo yucca *(Y. navajoa = Y. baileyi),* a Painted Desert species, is similar to banana yucca but has yellowish green leaves, the flowers are borne in a narrow raceme, and the fruit is a 2- to 3-inch, woody capsule. **Narrow-leaved yucca *(Y. angustissima)*** resembles Navajo yucca but grows primarily in the Great Basin and Mojave Deserts. Both prefer sandy soils. The **Great Plains yucca *(Y. glauca),*** which reaches into the deserts of New Mexico and Texas, has a similar growth form, but the inflorescence is a panicle.

D Palmilla (Soaptree) *Yucca elata*

Small **tree,** trunk up to 15 feet tall, often branched, shaggy in appearance from old, drooping leaves; the naked (leafless) flowering stalk 3 to 10 feet long, thus the entire plant up to 25 feet tall. **Leaves** very narrow, 1 to 3 feet long and less than ½ inch wide, flexible, not toothed but sharp-pointed, bearing fine fibers along their whitish margins. New leaves are borne in a rosette at the base of the flowering stalk and at the top of the shaggy trunk. **Flowers** bell-shaped, white, borne in a panicle at the top of the flower stalk; sepals and petals 3 each, similar in size and appearance, elliptical, up to 2 inches long and half as wide; stamens 6. **Fruit** a many-seeded, woody capsule, 2 to 3 inches long.

Palmilla grows primarily in the Chihuahuan Desert, where it is often a major dominant. It is the state flower of New Mexico and one of the few plants that can tolerate the gypsum "sand" in and around White Sands National Monument. Historically, it has been important for Native Americans. The young stems and roots contain large quantities of soapy material, from which the common name "soaptree" derives. The leaves have been used in making baskets, and fibers from the leaves for weaving and making brushes. Young flowering stalks and inflorescences provide forage for large herbivores when other food is scarce. *Palmilla* means "little palm" and *elata* means "high" or "tall," a bit of a contradiction.

Banana Yucca *Yucca baccata*

Navajo Yucca *Yucca navajoa* **Palmilla** *Yucca elata*

❊D Harriman Yucca *Yucca harrimaniae*

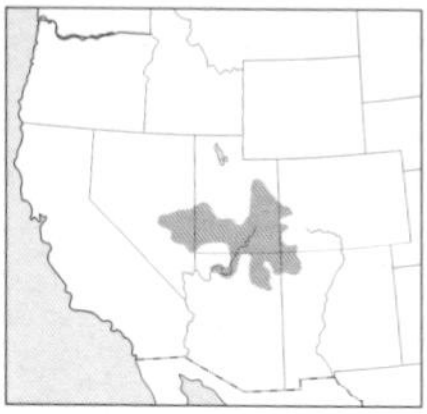

Low **shrub** (1 to 2 feet), often growing in large clumps from spreading rhizomes; **stem** lacking except for the inflorescence. **Leaves** numerous in basal rosettes, spreading in all directions, generally straight, stiff, narrowly lance-shaped, 5 to 18 inches long and up to 2 inches wide at the base, spine-tipped; leaf margins eventually shredding into curly, white fibers. **Flowers** bell-shaped or urn-shaped, pendent, about 2 inches long and two-thirds as wide, crowded in a raceme that extends from the leaf rosette; sepals and petals 3 each, all alike, cream-colored, sometimes with a purple tinge, broadly egg-shaped with a prominent point; stamens 6, about as long as the sepals and petals. **Fruit** a cylindrical, woody, many-seeded capsule that falls from the woody stalk after the seeds have been released.

This is the most common and widely distributed yucca of the Painted Desert. It also ranges westward into the Great Basin, where it is more robust and perhaps should be treated as a separate variety. In southeastern Utah, where it is most abundant, it often extends over vast areas, adding to the appeal of the attractive red desert landscape. It prefers sandy soils and often grows on dunes.

❊D Mojave Yucca (Spanish Dagger) *Yucca schidigera*

Shrub or small tree, up to 15 feet tall; **stem** sometimes branched from near the base, bearing a rosette of leaves at the tip. **Leaves** yellowish green, 1 to 4 feet long and about 1 inch wide, grooved along the midvein, swordlike or daggerlike with a stout spine tip; leaf margins with loose, shredding fibers. Dead leaves persist on the stem, hanging down and giving the plant a shaggy appearance. **Flowers** 1 to 2 inches long, more or less bell-shaped, cream-colored, numerous in a branching, terminal inflorescence up to 2 feet long and nearly as wide; sepals and petals 3 each, similar in size and color; stamens 6. **Fruit** fleshy, 2 to 3 inches long and half as wide.

This is the most common yucca of North American deserts, particularly in the southern part of the Mojave Desert and the Colorado (Sonoran) Desert of southern California. It also grows in some California chaparral communities. It prefers well-drained slopes of desert mountains and is often associated with creosote bush, sometimes as a codominant.

Mojave yucca was important to California Indians, who gathered and roasted the fruits or ate them raw. They also used the fiber extracted from the leaves for weaving blankets, baskets, and ropes. The nutritious fruits are important as a food source for birds and rodents.

Harriman Yucca community, Painted Desert *Yucca harrimaniae*
Inset: Harriman Yucca *Yucca harrimaniae*

Mojave Yucca *Yucca schidigera*

Whipple Yucca

Yucca whipplei

Shrub, up to 10 feet tall; **stems** (flowering stalks) 1 to few, several times longer than the leaves, dying soon after the fruits mature. **Leaves** many in a basal rosette, linear, 1 to 3 feet long, 2 to 3 inches wide at the base; leaf margins lined with minute, sawlike teeth. **Flowers** 1 to 2 inches long, bell-shaped, many, in enlarged, elliptical panicles; perianth segments creamy white. **Fruit** a woody capsule, 1 to 2 inches long.

Another common name, Our Lord's candle, is suggestive of the nobility of this yucca. It grows on rocky slopes and plains of the Mojave Desert, primarily in California.

LOASA FAMILY

Loasaceae

One of the outstanding characteristics of plants in the loasa family is the presence of stiff, often needlelike, sometimes stinging, hairs. The flowers are radially symmetrical with parts in fives—five sepals (usually persistent on the fruit), five petals, and five (or many) stamens. The ovary is inferior. The species vary in habit from diminutive annuals to large shrubs. The stems are often white and the flowers are usually yellow.

Cevallia

Cevallia sinuata

Perennial **herb,** up to 2 feet tall; **stems** erect, woody at the base, freely branched above, clothed with white wool and armed with long, stinging hairs. **Leaves** alternate, 1 to 2 inches long, pinnately lobed or divided, white-woolly and also armed with stinging hairs. **Flowers** borne in heads on long stalks arising from upper leaf axils; sepals and petals similar, yellow, at least on the inner surface, about ⅓ inch long, covered with long, white hair, giving them a feathery appearance. The stamens have a papery appendage that extends beyond the anthers. **Fruit** a 1-seeded, hard-shelled nutlet. The feathery sepals and petals are persistent on the fruit, allowing the fruit/seed to be disseminated in the wind.

This is an unusual and distinctive plant with its woolly pubescence, stinging hairs, and feathery perianth. It prefers gravelly soils, often growing along roadsides. It ranges across the Chihuahuan Desert into southeastern Arizona.

Rock Nettle

Eucnide urens

Perennial **herb,** 12 to 30 inches tall; **stems** erect or spreading, clumped from a branched, woody root crown, long-hairy. **Leaves** alternate but crowded, egg-shaped, toothed, 1 to 2 inches long and about as broad, densely covered with barbed, stinging hairs. **Flowers** numerous in leafy clusters at the tips of branches, 1 to 2 inches long; sepals green with a silvery sheen from the dense covering of stinging hairs; petals lemon yellow, showy; stamens pale yellow, numerous, the filaments fused at the base. **Fruit** a many-seeded, club-shaped capsule, ½ to 1 inch long.

The aptly named rock nettle is deceptively malevolent. The unwary admirer of this attractive plant will not soon forget the handful of tiny stinging hairs resulting from an aborted attempt to collect the plant or pick the flowers. The Latin name also relates to the burning or stinging hairs. The species grows in rocky habitats, primarily in the Mojave Desert.

Whipple Yucca *Yucca whipplei*   **Cevallia** *Cevallia sinuata* —Rocky Taylor photo

Cevallia
Cevallia sinuata

Rock Nettle
Eucnide urens

Small-Flowered Blazing Star   *Mentzelia veatchiana*

Annual **herb** with short, stiff, sandpaper-like hairs; **stems** generally erect but with spreading branches, 4 to 15 inches tall. **Leaves** basal and alternate, dark green, pinnately divided, ½ to 5 inches long, the lower leaves the longest. **Flowers** only ¼ to ⅓ inch long, borne in small clusters at the tips of leafy branches; sepals green, persistent on the ovary; petals yellow orange to bright yellow; stamens numerous. **Fruit** a 1-seeded, club-shaped nutlet.

Several species of small-flowered blazing stars inhabit the deserts of North America; the most common is **white-stemmed blazing star *(M. albicaulis).*** This is an extremely variable species, which grows in all our deserts. Some authorities place *M. veatchiana* in *M. albicaulis* as a variety. A major distinction between the two forms is that the upper leaves (bracts) of *M. veatchiana* are pinnately lobed or divided. Another common small-flowered, white-stemmed desert species sometimes placed in *M. albicaulis* is **Venus blazing star *(M. nitens),*** which has somewhat larger flowers (⅓ to ½ inch) than the other species noted above. **Desert blazing star *(M. desertorum)*** also closely resembles *M. albicaulis,* differing on technicalities. These and other small-flowered species prefer sandy soils, where they are sometimes very abundant.

Sand Blazing Star   *Mentzelia involucrata*

Annual **herb** with short, stiff, sandpaper-like hairs; **stems** generally erect with spreading branches, 3 to 12 inches tall. **Leaves** basal and alternate, toothed, 1 to 6 inches long, the upper leaves reduced and bractlike. **Flowers** large and showy, funnel-shaped, 1 to 2 inches long, usually solitary at the tip of branches and surrounded by bracts (the bracts collectively termed an *involucre,* thus the specific epithet); sepals largely hidden by the bracts; petals creamy yellow with orange veins, fragile and somewhat transparent; stamens numerous, shorter than the petals. **Fruit** a 1-seeded, club-shaped nutlet, ½ to 1 inch long.

This is the most attractive of our desert blazing stars. It grows in sandy washes and on loose-gravelly slopes of the Sonoran Desert. Another species with showy, large flowers is **spiny-haired blazing star *(M. tricuspis).*** Its equally fragile flowers are creamy white to pale yellow without orange veins. It grows in similar sandy and gravelly habitats in the Sonoran and Mojave Deserts.

Small-Flowered Blazing Star
Mentzelia veatchiana

Sand Blazing Star *Mentzelia involucrata*

Venus Blazing Star *Mentzelia nitens*

Spiny-Haired Blazing Star
Mentzelia tricuspis

Sandpaper Plant

Petalonyx thurberi

Low, mound-shaped **shrub,** 12 to 30 inches tall; branches grayish with stiff hairs; bark shredding. **Leaves** alternate, lance-shaped to narrowly triangular, up to 2 inches long, clasping the stem, clothed with short, stiff, barbed, sandpaper-like hairs. **Flowers** less than ¼ inch long, in dense spikes at the tips of branches; sepals not persistent on the ovary; petals creamy white; stamens 5, extending beyond the petals. **Fruit** a 1-seeded achene, ¼ inch long.

This is one of about four similar species of *Petalonyx* that grows in the Mojave and Sonoran Deserts. All prefer sandy or gravelly soils of plains and foothills, sometimes growing on dunes. All have the sandpapery leaves.

MADDER FAMILY

Rubiaceae

The madder family is large and mainly tropical, varying from small annuals to trees, with only a few desert species. Unifying characteristics include opposite or whorled leaves, and flower parts in fours—four sepals, four petals, and four stamens—and an inferior ovary.

Scarlet Trumpet

Bouvardia ternifolia

Low, extensively branched **shrub,** up to 3 feet tall. **Leaves** in whorls of 3 *(ternifolia)* or 4, narrowly elliptical, ½ to 2 inches long, usually covered with short hairs. **Flowers** in clusters at the branch tips; sepals fused at the base, with linear to lance-shaped lobes; corolla bright scarlet, fused into an inch-long tube with 4 short triangular lobes; stamens included within the corolla tube; style and stigma white, extending beyond the mouth of the corolla tube. **Fruit** a roundish, many-seeded capsule, about ¼ inch wide.

This is a strikingly attractive shrub, with scarlet, trumpet-shaped, stereotype hummingbird flowers. It inhabits rocky sites in the Chihuahuan Desert mountains.

Needle-Leaf Hedyotis

Hedyotis (Houstonia) acerosa

Low, cushionlike **shrub,** 2 to 10 inches tall; **stems** many, from a branched root crown. **Leaves** opposite or sometimes whorled, needlelike (acerose), ¼ to ½ inch long; leaf margins rolled under. **Flowers** ⅓ to ½ inch long, solitary in leaf axils and at the tips of branches; corolla usually white, tubular, with 4 curled, pointed lobes. **Fruit** a round, many-seeded capsule.

This and other species of *Hedyotis* grow along rocky slopes of the Chihuahuan Desert. Some (bluets) have showy blue flowers.

Sandpaper Plant *Petalonyx thurberi*

Scarlet Trumpet *Bouvardia ternifolia*

Needle-Leaf Hedyotis *Hedyotis (Houstonia) acerosa*

MALLOW FAMILY   Malvaceae

Most species of the mallow family are herbs or subshrubs, characterized primarily by the reproductive structures, particularly the stamens and the pistil. The stamens are numerous, with the filaments fused at the base into a tube that surrounds the ovary. The ovary is superior and has five or more compartments, which generally separate at maturity, the fruit thus consisting of five or more pie-shaped segments typified by the familiar hollyhock. Otherwise, the flowers are radially symmetrical with parts in fives—five sepals and five petals. Another family characteristic is the clothing of star-shaped (stellate) hair.

Malvaceae enjoys worldwide distribution, with many important cultivated forms, including cotton, okra, and the long list of beautiful hybiscus species. In North American deserts, far and away the best-represented members of the family are the globemallows.

Desert Rose Mallow   *Hybiscus coulteri*

Perennial **shrub** or subshrub, **stems** erect, woody, at least at the base, solitary or few, covered with stellate hair, up to 3 feet tall. **Leaves** alternate, lower ones broadly egg-shaped and only toothed, about 1 inch long, the upper ones divided into 3 to 5 narrow segments. **Flowers** bowl-shaped, about 2 inches across, solitary or few per stem; sepals not stellate; petals showy, lemon yellow to reddish; stamens many, with fused filaments; anthers yellowish orange. **Fruit** a 5-compartmented, several-seeded capsule.

Several species of *Hybiscus* grow in western North America; this is the most common desert form. It is primarily a Chihuahuan Desert species, ranging west into Arizona. It prefers gravelly soils in plains and along hillsides. Species of **Indian mallow (*Arbutilon* species)** also inhabit North American deserts and resemble rose mallow *(Hybiscus)* species, differing primarily by having segmented rather than capsular fruits.

Desert Five-Spot   *Malvastrum (Erimalche) rotundifolium*

Annual, hairy **herb,** 3 to 24 inches tall, sometimes branched from the base. **Leaves** alternate; leaf blades roundish *(rotundifolium),* 1 to 2 inches wide, smaller high on the stem, coarsely toothed; leaf stalks generally longer than the blades. **Flowers** bowl-shaped, about 1 inch across, few to several in a cluster at the stem tip; sepals narrow; petals showy, pinkish purple to lavender, each petal with a conspicuous, fringed bright purple spot; stamens many, with fused filaments. **Fruit** a round disk with 25 to 35 thin-walled, 1-seeded segments.

The unusual flower color makes this mallow one of our most beautiful and un-forgettable desert wildflowers. It grows in sandy washes and gravelly plains of the Mojave and Sonoran Deserts, often associated with creosote bush.

Apricot Globemallow   *Sphaeralcea ambigua*

Perennial **herb** from a woody, branched root crown; **stems** usually several, erect, sparingly branched above, up to 3 feet tall, densely clothed with stellate hair. **Leaves** alternate; leaf blades generally palmately lobed or divided, roundish or triangular in outline, conspicuously veined, particularly on the lower surface, 1 to 2 inches long; the margin of the leaf blade is typically wavy. **Flowers** bowl-shaped, about 1 inch across, borne in racemes or panicles along the upper half of the stems; sepals green,

Desert Rose Mallow *Hybiscus coulteri* —Rocky Taylor photo

Desert Five-Spot *Malvastrum (Erimalche) rotundifolium*

Apricot Globemallow *Sphaeralcea ambigua* **var.** *ambigua*

densely clothed with stellate hairs; petals unusually showy, reddish orange to apricot or lavender pink depending on the variety, often with a yellow base; stamens numerous with fused filaments, anthers bright yellow. **Fruit** a round (*sphaer,* "globe") disk consisting of 8 to 16 1-seeded, pie-shaped segments.

As the specific epithet suggests, this is a complex, variable, and taxonomically difficult species. Three varieties grow in our deserts, *ambigua, rugosa,* and *rosacea,* separated mainly on the basis of leaf shape and flower color. The species is widely distributed and locally abundant in the Mojave and Sonoran Deserts, where it is highly conspicuous, with showy orangish flowers. It grows in a variety of habitats, often in "desert pavement" where little else can grow.

In the Great Basin and sagebrush steppe, apricot globemallow is replaced by **orange globemallow *(S. munroana),*** which is not so densely pubescent and has leaves only slightly lobed.

Scarlet Globemallow *Sphaeralcea coccinea*

Perennial **herb** from a woody, branched root crown; **stems** erect, usually several, up to 15 inches tall, clothed with stellate hairs. **Leaves** alternate, gray green from dense, stellate pubescence; leaf blades about 1 inch long, roundish in outline but deeply divided into 3 to 5 lobes, these often further divided or lobed. The **flowers** resemble those of apricot globemallow but are redder. **Fruit** roundish, separating into 8 to 14, 1-seeded, pie-shaped segments.

This is the most widespread *Sphaeralcea* species in North American deserts, ranging from the Great Basin and Painted Deserts into the Chihuahuan Desert. It grows in a variety of habitats, from the hot deserts into piñon-juniper woodlands.

MILKWEED FAMILY Asclepiadaceae

Two characteristics in combination identify the milkweed family: milky juice and unusually sculpted stamens. Milky juice is present in other families, but nowhere else are the stamens modified as they are here. The filaments are fused into a thick tube (the column), and the anthers are fused into a head. An elaborate appendage (hood) is on the outside of each of the five anthers and alongside the column. Sometimes the appendage has a elongate projection (horn) attached to its inside. Otherwise, the flowers are radially symmetrical with parts in fives—five sepals, five petals, and five stamens.

Rusby Milkweed *Asclepias rusbyi*

Perennial, hairless (glabrous) **herb,** up to 3 feet tall; **stems** erect, clustered from a branched root crown. **Leaves** opposite, linear, 5 to 8 inches long, flexuous. **Flowers** small, borne in umbels; petals white to pale greenish, reflexed backward; hoods and horns white; anther head purplish. **Fruit** a narrowly lance-shaped pod 3 to 5 inches long; seeds numerous, each with a tuft of hair.

This milkweed grows in sandy soils of the Painted Desert.

Apricot Globemallow
Sphaeralcea ambigua var. *rugosa*

Apricot Globemallow
Sphaeralcea ambigua var. *rosacea*

Scarlet Globemallow
Sphaeralcea coccinea

Rusby Milkweed
Asclepias rusbyi

Pallid Milkweed
Asclepias cryptoceras

Perennial, hairless (glabrous) **herb; stems** usually prostrate over the ground, about 1 foot long. **Leaves** opposite, broadly egg-shaped to nearly round, 2 to 4 inches long, bluish green. **Flowers** about ¾ inch across, borne in umbels at the stem tips; petals cream-colored to greenish yellow, spreading to reflexed backward; hoods saclike, pinkish purple; horns lacking. **Fruit** a lance-shaped pod 2 to 3 inches long; seeds numerous, each tufted with hair.

Pallid milkweed, named for its pale flowers, is primarily a Painted Desert species. It grows on gravelly slopes, often associated with blackbrush.

Two other desert species with similarly large cream-colored to greenish flowers are **desert milkweed (*A. erosa*)** and **Mojave milkweed (*A. nyctaginifolia*).** Both are robust plants with large, triangular leaves. Desert milkweed has erect stems and grows in the Mojave and Sonoran Deserts. Mojave milkweed has sprawling stems and is primarily a Mojave Desert species, as the common name suggests.

Short-Crowned Milkweed
Asclepias brachystephana

Perennial, white-woolly **herb,** up to 20 inches tall; **stems** clustered, erect. **Leaves** opposite but crowded, narrowly lance-shaped, 3 to 5 inches long, more or less trough-shaped. **Flowers** only about ¼ inch long, borne in umbels from leaf axils; petals reddish purple; hoods saclike with tonguelike horns; anther head tiny (*brachystephana,* "short crown"). **Fruit** a lance-shaped, white-striped pod (follicle), 2 to 4 inches long; seeds many, each with a small tuft of hair.

This is primarily a Chihuahuan Desert species, growing in sandy plains and washes. It is also invasive, taking advantage of disturbed areas, particularly along roadsides.

Climbing Milkweed
Sarcostemma cynanchoides ssp. *hartwegii*

Shrubby **vine,** clothed with fine, stiff hairs; **stems** twining, often several of them coiled together to form ropes. **Leaves** opposite, varying from narrowly lance-shaped to arrowhead-shaped, 1 to 3 inches long. **Flowers** showy, ½ inch across, borne in umbels from leaf axils; petals pinkish purple, spreading to form a star; hoods white. **Fruit** a narrowly lance-shaped, grooved, 2- to 3-inch pod.

This milkweed usually grows in sandy washes and arroyos, where it clambers over and through the crowns of desert shrubs and trees. It is scattered across all our North American deserts.

Pallid Milkweed
Asclepias cryptoceras

Short-Crowned Milkweed
Asclepias brachystephana

Mojave Milkweed
Asclepias nyctaginifolia

Climbing Milkweed
Sarcostemma cynanchoides
ssp. *hartwegii*

MILKWORT FAMILY   Polygalaceae

Polygalaceae is a large family, with worldwide distribution, but only the type genus, *Polygala,* is found in North American deserts.

Milkwort   *Polygala* species

Several species of milkwort grow in North American deserts, varying from small **herbs** to spiny **shrubs**. The **leaves** are usually alternate but may be opposite or even whorled and are neither lobed nor toothed. The pealike **flowers** are unique: sepals 5, the 2 lower ones (wings) much the largest; petals 3, fused at the base, the lower petal resembling the keel of a boat; stamens 8, filaments united. The **fruit** is a 1-seeded capsule or nut.

Although *polygala* means "many (much) milk," milkworts (milk plants) do not have milky juice. The name originated in Europe, where farmers credited the plants with increasing milk production.

The two most common desert species are **spiny milkwort** *(P. subspinosa),* a subshrub with pink and yellow flowers that grows in the Great Basin and Painted Deserts; and **gland-spotted milkwort** *(P. macradenia).* The latter is a matted perennial herb with gland-spotted leaves and delicate flowers that combine blue, white, and yellow colors. It grows on rocky slopes of the Chihuahuan Desert.

MINT FAMILY   Lamiaceae (Labiatae)

The mint family is large and has worldwide distribution, and is unambiguously united by a combination of characteristics: the sepals (calyx) and petals (corolla) both are fused, and the corolla is two-lipped—the basis for the classical family name Labiatae. The superior ovary is typically 4-lobed, each lobe maturing into a single-seeded nutlet. The stems are generally square, although this is not always apparent in woody plants, and the leaves are opposite. Finally, the family is rich in oils, responsible for the characteristic minty odor and taste.

The mint family is particularly well represented in the chaparral biome, but several species grow in deserts, sometimes as community dominants. The most striking desert mint is **scarlet betony (Stachys coccinea),** a distinctive herb with strongly two-lipped, brilliant scarlet flowers. It grows in rock crevasses and along canyon walls in the Sonoran Desert of Arizona and in the Chihuahuan Desert. The family is best known for its cultivated herbs and ornamentals.

Desert Lavender   *Hyptis emoryi*

Medium-size, grayish **shrub,** up to 9 feet tall, clothed with branched (stellate) hairs; **stems** extensively branched. **Leaves** egg-shaped, toothed, ½ to 1 inch long, gray from a dense coat of branched and woolly hairs. **Flowers** small, only ¼ inch long, borne in clusters (verticels) in leaf axils along the branches; calyx fused with 5 similar, linear lobes, densely pubescent; corolla pale, the upper lip 2-lobed, the lower 3-lobed; stamens 4, derived from the corolla tube and slightly extending from the corolla mouth. **Fruit** 4 smooth nutlets.

Although desert lavender flowers are small and individually not showy, the plants are eye catching with their general grayish white coloration tinged with lavender. The flowers are rich in nectar, and when in bloom the plants are alive with bees. The plants grow in washes of the Mojave and Sonoran Deserts.

Gland-Spotted Milkwort *Polygala macradenia*

Scarlet Betony *Stachys coccinea*   Desert Lavender *Hyptis emoryi*

Bush Mint
Poliomintha incana

Low, mound-shaped **shrub,** up to 3 feet tall; **stems** densely clothed with felty pubescence, the many branches erect and spreading. **Leaves** narrowly elliptical to linear, ¼ to ½ inch long. **Flowers** ⅓ to ½ inch long, borne in clusters in leaf axils; calyx densely pubescent, the 5 lobes nearly equal; corolla pale blue to lavender, the upper lip 2-lobed, the lower 3-lobed (the central lobe further divided); stamens 2, extending slightly beneath the upper lip. **Fruit** 4 nutlets.

This beautiful, strong-smelling shrub grows in sandy plains and on sand dunes. It is common in the Painted Desert, with isolated populations in the Mojave and Chihuahuan Deserts.

Bladder Sage
Salazaria mexicana

Low, rounded, hairy **shrub,** up to 4 feet tall; **stems** stiffly erect with nearly perpendicular, spreading, spine-tipped branches. **Leaves** elliptical, about ½ inch long, sparse on the branches. **Flowers** about 1 inch long, borne in pairs from the leaf axils near the stem tips; calyx fused into a reddish to purple tube that becomes inflated and bladderlike as the fruit matures; corolla 2-lipped and bicolored, the narrow tube and upper, hoodlike lip white or pale lavender, the lower lip 3-lobed and vibrant violet purple; stamens 4, concealed under the upper lip.

Bladder sage is an occasional plant of sandy and gravelly soils, primarily in washes, in the Mojave and Sonoran Deserts and has a limited range in the Big Bend country of Texas.

Sages
Salvia **species**

Many *Salvia* species, both shrubs and herbs, grace the desert landscapes, with beautifully sculpted, bluish flowers clustered along the branch tips. Both the calyx and corolla are 2-lipped, and the 2 stamens extend well beyond the mouth of the corolla tube. All species emit a strong sage odor when the tissue is crushed, perhaps a defense mechanism against herbivores.

The most common and variable shrub is **purple sage (*Salvia dorrii*),** a low, mound-shaped plant clothed with short, silvery white pubescence. The leaves are spoon-shaped and ½ to 1 inch long. The beautiful sky-blue to purplish flowers are about ½ inch long. The upper lip of the corolla is notched (heart-shaped); the lower lip 3-lobed, the middle lobe much the largest. When in bloom this symmetrical shrub is truly handsome. It is found in one form or another in all of our deserts except the Chihuahuan Desert, growing in sandy or gravelly plains and mountain slopes.

The most common herb is **chia (*Salvia columbariae*),** an annual up to 18 inches tall with erect, grooved stems. The leaves are pinnately divided and the veins are conspicuously sunken, giving the leaf surface an irregular, bumpy appearance. The flowers are about ⅓ inch long and congested in round heads that appear burrlike from the spine-tipped bracts and calyx lobes. The corolla is sky blue. Chia is widespread in the Mojave and Sonoran Deserts, growing in several habitats but preferring sandy and gravelly soils of desert washes. Indians used to gather the abundant seeds (nutlets) for food.

Bush Mint
Poliomintha incana
Inset: Bush Mint
Poliomintha incana

Bladder Sage
Salazaria mexicana

Purple Sage *Salvia dorrii*   **Chia** *Salvia columbariae*

MISTLETOE FAMILY   Viscaceae

Plants in the mistletoe family are parasitic on various shrubs and trees, often forming large, tumerous growths in their crowns. The stems of mistletoe are short, brittle, and profusely branched. The leaves are opposite in four rows, small and sometimes scale-like. The flowers are unisexual and tiny. The fruit is a berry.

Desert mistletoe *(Phoradendron californicum)* is the most serious parasite of desert shrubs, including creosote bush, palo verdes, acacias, and mesquite. It is extensively branched, the reddish branches spreading in all directions, including downward. The leaves are reduced to scales. The flowers are small with only one set of sepals or petals (perianth segments). They are also unisexual, male (staminate) and female (pistillate) flowers on different plants. The fruit is a bright, shiny, red berry.

Another common desert parasite, in the unrelated **dodder family *(Cuscutaceae),*** is *Cuscuta denticulata.* This dodder is like an orange plague, completely covering its hapless host with an intricate, twining network of yellow to orange, threadlike, leafless stems. Its flowers are bell-shaped, whitish, and tiny, only a small fraction of an inch long. It parasitizes both herbs and shrubs and is particularly damaging on bur sage.

MORNING-GLORY FAMILY   Convolvulaceae

Although the morning-glory family is large, it is poorly represented in North American deserts, and only one species is treated here.

Silky Evolvulus   *Evolvulus sericeus*

Low, perennial **herb,** 3 to 10 inches tall; **stems** spreading to prostrate, clumped from a branched, woody root crown. **Leaves** alternate, narrowly lance-shaped, ½ to 1 inch long, silky-pubescent *(sericeus)* on both the upper and lower surface. **Flowers** trumpet-shaped, about ½ inch across; sepals 5, small, fused at the base; corolla (petals) white to lavender tinged, fused, tubular at the base, flaring and saucer-shaped above, the "saucer" with 5 shallow lobes; stamens 5, positioned at the mouth of the corolla tube. **Fruit** a few-seeded capsule.

This is one of 3 species in North American deserts. *Evolvulus arizonicus,* with beautiful sky-blue flowers, grows in the deserts of Arizona; *E. nuttallianus* ranges from the Painted Desert south into the Chihuahuan Desert. It, too, has bluish flowers. Silky evolvulus grows in sandy or clayey soils of the Chihuahuan Desert.

Desert Mistletoe *Phoradendron californicum*

Dodder *Cuscuta denticulata*

Silky Evolvulus *Evolvulus sericeus*

MUSTARD FAMILY   Brassicaceae (Cruciferae)

Brassicaceae is one of those large families readily recognizable on the basis of a unique combination of characteristics. Separating one species from another, though, is often difficult. The outstanding diagnostic features are the flowers and the fruits. The flowers are radially symmetrical with parts in fours—four sepals, four petals, and six stamens (four long and two short). The classical family name (Cruciferae) is descriptive of the cross formed by the four petals. The inflorescence is a raceme. The fruit, developing from a superior ovary, is typically a type of capsule that has two compartments, the walls (valves) of which fall away at maturity leaving a persistent, papery partition on the flower stalk. The seeds are attached to the outer walls adjacent to the partition. Most family members also share the mustard oils responsible for the pungent taste best expressed in horseradish. These oils are nature's chemical warfare—a natural deterrent to herbivory.

The mustards are mainly herbaceous plants of cool temperate regions, although many grow in deserts. The family includes cultivated species, such as cabbage, cauliflower, turnip, and radishes, and several ornamentals. It is best known for the many weed species of garden and field (and desert).

The most conspicuous desert mustard is **prince's plume** *(Stanleya pinnata),* a robust, hairless (glabrous), perennial herb, 1 to 3 feet tall. The stems are generally clustered from a woody, branched root crown. The leaves are both basal and alternate, the larger ones up to 6 inches long, pinnately divided but lance-shaped in outline, and stalked. The upper ones are narrowly lance-shaped and neither lobed nor stalked. The flowers are about 1 inch across and borne in dense, elongate, plumelike racemes. The sepals are pale yellow, spreading or reflexed backward; the petals are lemon yellow, the base narrowed into a hairy "stalk" (claw). The stamens extend well beyond the petals, contributing to the plumelike appearance of the inflorescence.

When in full bloom, prince's plume is strikingly attractive. It frequently grows in abundance where the soil is rich in selenium; it is known as a selenium indicator. The selenium accumulates in the plant tissues and can be toxic, disrupting the calcium metabolism of an unlucky herbivore. It is one of the few mustards that is not edible. It ranges from the Great Basin and Painted Deserts southward into the Mojave Desert of California.

A related species, **desert plume** *(Stanleya elata),* differs in having cabbagelike basal leaves, branched stems, and hairless petals. It is a noble *(elata)* herb that grows in gravelly plains and along rocky slopes of the Great Basin and Mojave Deserts, ranging southward along the Colorado River.

Rockcresses   *Arabis* **species**

Perennial or biennial **herbs**, up to about 30 inches tall; **stems** mainly erect, usually branched, hairy or not. **Flowers** erect or reflexed downward, usually about ½ inch long; sepals tightly enclosing the base of the petals, more or less urn-shaped; petals white to purple, spoon-shaped; **Fruit** a linear, many-seeded pod.

Probably the most widespread and common desert species is **prince's rockcress** *(Arabis pulchra),* a perennial clothed with branched (stellate) hairs. The leaves are basal and alternate, linear or narrowly lance-shaped, generally folded, and 1 to 3 inches long. The petals are pale lavender to reddish purple, and the pod hangs downward. This is a variable species and grows in all our deserts except the Chihuahuan Desert.

Prince's Plume *Stanleya pinnata*　Inset: **Prince's Plume** *Stanleya pinnata*

Desert Plume *Stanleya elata*　**Prince's Rockcress** *Arabis pulchra*

Desert Candle
Caulanthus inflatus

Succulent, annual **herb,** up to 20 inches tall; **stems** strictly erect, usually unbranched, thick and hollow. **Leaves** basal and alternate, clasping the stem with earlike lobes, broadly elliptical to lance-shaped, 1 to 3 inches long. **Flowers** ⅓ to ½ inch long, scattered along the upper part of the stem; sepals purple in bud, becoming white; petals also purple and fading to whitish. **Fruit** a linear, ascending, many-seeded pod, 2 to 4 inches long.

This interesting, cabbagelike plant grows in sandy soils of the Mojave Desert. In the past it was gathered and eaten by Indians. Of the other *Caulanthus* species that grow in our deserts, the most widespread is **chocolate drops *(C. pilosus).*** It is an annual or biennial herb, 6 to 20 inches tall, with erect stems. The leaves are pinnately divided, the lower ones at least. The flowers are only about ⅓ inch long; the sepals are reddish brown (chocolate) and urn-shaped; the petals are white to purplish, barely longer than the sepals. The fruit is a linear, often curved, many-seeded pod, 1 to 6 inches long. This is predominantly a Great Basin species but ranges south into the Mojave Desert of California. It prefers gravelly soils.

Spectacle Pod
Dithyrea wislizenii

Annual or biennial **herb,** clothed with branched (stellate) hairs, up to 20 inches tall; **stems** erect and usually branched. **Leaves** alternate, lance-shaped, varying from smooth margined to deeply toothed, ½ to 4 inches long, smaller upward on the stem. **Flowers** about ⅓ inch long, borne in a narrow raceme; sepals yellowish to purple, covered with stellate hairs, urn-shaped with a saclike base; petals white, twice as long as the sepals, spreading outward. **Fruit** flat and deeply lobed into 2 disk-shaped halves, fancifully resembling a pair of spectacles, even to the point of having frames around the lenses. Each spectacle half has a single, flattened seed.

Spectacle pod ranges from the Great Basin and Painted Deserts south into the Chihuahuan Desert. It prefers sandy soils. In the Sonoran Desert of California it is replaced by **California spectacle pod *(D. californica).*** In this species the flowers are somewhat larger and the petals are cream-colored—with a bit of a yellowish hue. It also grows in sandy desert flats and washes.

Desert Candle *Caulanthus inflatus*

Chocolate Drops *Caulanthus pilosus*

Spectacle Pod *Dithyrea wislizenii*

California Spectacle Pod *Dithyrea californica*

Western Wallflower *Erysimum capitatum*

Biennial or perennial **herb,** 6 to 30 inches tall; **stems** erect, usually branched. **Leaves** basal and alternate, linear to narrowly elliptical, often toothed, 1 to 6 inches long. **Flowers** about 1 inch long, borne in dense racemes at the tips of the stem and branches; sepals pale yellow, urn-shaped; petals golden yellow, showy. **Fruit** an erect, 4-sided, many-seeded pod, 2 to 6 inches long.

This attractive mustard ranges over much of western North America, preferring sandy soils.

Peppergrasses *Lepidium* species

Lepidium is a large genus, comprising herbs and shrubs, characterized by its often winged, 2-seeded fruit, 1 seed per compartment. All species have small yellow or white flowers.

The most noticeable of the yellow-flowered species is **yellow peppergrass (*L. flavum*),** a hairless, annual herb with spreading, prostrate stems. The leaves are spoon-shaped, sometimes toothed, 1 to 2 inches long, and conspicuously shiny. Small, yellow flowers are crowded at the tips of the branches. The fruit has a notched tip and winged sides. In spite of its tiny flowers, this plant does not go unnoticed. The stems and leaves are yellowish green, making it stand out against the greens and gray greens of other plants. Also, it usually grows in somewhat alkaline soils where vegetation is sparse. It blooms earlier than most wildflowers and often carpets the ground; the flowers make up in mass what they lack in size. It ranges from the Great Basin southward into the Mojave and Sonoran Deserts.

Several white-flowered species grow in the deserts, and **bush peppergrass (*L. fremontii*)** is the most important. This is a roundish, hairless, perennial subshrub with intricately branched stems 1 to 2 feet tall. The leaves are linear, up to 4 inches long, and often pinnately lobed. The fruit is roundish to egg-shaped and notched at the tip. This species is a common and often dominant member of desert communities, particularly in the Mojave Desert. It prefers gravelly and sandy soils.

Two of the most common annuals and/or biennials are **Thurber peppergrass (*L. thurberi*)** and **mountain peppergrass (*L. montanum*).**

Thurber peppergrass is locally abundant in slightly alkaline and clayey soils of the Mojave and Sonoran Deserts. It has pinnately divided stem leaves. Mountain peppergrass, an extremely variable species with several recognized varieties, has undivided stem leaves and grows in the Painted Desert, ranging southward into the Chihuahuan Desert. It strongly prefers sandy habitats.

Western Wallflower *Erysimum capitatum*   Yellow Peppergrass *Lepidium flavum*

Thurber Peppergrass *Lepidium thurberi*

Slender Bladderpod
Lesquerella tenella

Annual **herb,** up to 30 inches tall, clothed with branched (stellate) hair; **stems** erect, usually branched. **Leaves** narrowly elliptical, 1 to 3 inches long, reduced in size upward on the stem, sometimes toothed. **Flowers** ½ to ⅔ inch across, borne in open racemes at the tip of the stem and branches; sepals green, pubescent; petals golden yellow. **Fruit** a few-seeded, round, somewhat inflated, pubescent pod, about ¼ inch long.

This is one of the most common, and variable, among several species of *Lesquerella* that grow in our desert regions. It frequently forms dense, showy populations in sandy desert plains.

Twinpods
Physaria **species**

Perennial **herbs,** densely clothed with silvery, stellate pubescence; **stems** usually several from a taproot, 3 to 8 inches long, spreading outward or sprawling over the ground. **Leaves** mainly in a basal rosette, elliptical to spoon-shaped, up to 3 inches long and half as wide; leaf margin often angular or toothed. **Flowers** about ⅔ inch across, borne in tight racemes; petals bright yellow or sometimes purplish. **Fruit** divided into 2 greatly inflated pods, each with a few seeds.

In the absence of mature fruits, twinpods are difficult to distinguish from bladderpods (*Lesquerella* species). Both groups generally have bright, golden yellow flowers, and the stems and leaves are densely clothed with stellate hairs. The fruits of the twinpods, however, have 2 distinct inflated halves, as the common name suggests, while those of bladderpods are more or less round. Two twinpods show up occasionally in our deserts, *P. acutifolia* and *P. chambersii*. The former is primarily a Painted Desert species, growing in rocky soils, often in association with blackbrush. *Physaria chambersii* grows in the desert mountains of Nevada, northeastern California, and northern Arizona.

Linear-Leaf Sisymbrium
Schoencrambe (Sisymbrium) linearifolia

Robust, perennial, hairless **herb,** 1 to 4 feet tall; **stems** clustered, branched. **Leaves** narrowly lance-shaped to linear, folded along the midvein, 1 to 2 inches long. **Flowers** showy, 1 inch across; sepals lavender, the 2 outer with a saclike base; petals lavender with darker veins. **Fruit** an erect, narrowly cylindrical, many-seeded pod, 1 to 3 inches long.

This is one of our most attractive desert mustards. It grows in the desert mountains of Texas, Arizona, and New Mexico.

Long-Beaked Twist-Flower
Streptanthella longirostris

Hairless, annual **herb,** 4 to 30 inches tall; **stems** solitary, erect, branched. **Leaves** elliptical to linear, ½ to 3 inches long, toothed or not; upper leaves much the smallest. **Flowers** about ⅓ inch long, borne in open racemes; sepals dark purple, fading to whitish as the flowers open; petals white with purplish veins; **Fruit** a linear, several-seeded pod that is reflexed downward. The pod has a prominent terminal "beak" (a narrower, sterile structure) from which the common and Latin names derive.

This species is abundant in sandy plains of the Painted Desert, often growing up through the canopy of associated shrubs. It ranges south and east into the Mojave and Sonoran Deserts.

Slender Bladderpod
Lesquerella tenella

Long-Beaked Twist-Flower
Streptanthella longirostris

Twinpod
Physaria acutifolia

**Linear-Leaf
Sisymbrium**
*Schoencrambe
(Sisymbrium)
linearifolia*

Yellow Thelypody   *Thelypodiopsis divaricata*

Biennial **herb,** 8 to 30 inches tall; **stems** solitary, usually branched above. **Leaves** basal and alternate; the basal ones larger and irregularly lobed; the stem leaves lance-shaped with earlike lobes that wrap around the stem. **Flowers** about ⅓ inch long, with sepals and petals pale yellow. **Fruit** an erect, linear, cylindrical, many-seeded pod, 2 to 3 inches long.

This *Thelypodium* look-alike (the definition of *Thelypodiopsis*) is locally abundant in sandy and clayey soils of the Painted Desert, often associated with shadscale.

Howell Thelypody   *Thelypodium howellii*

Biennial **herb,** 6 to 30 inches tall; **stems** solitary, usually branched above. **Leaves** similar to those of yellow thelypody. **Flowers** showy, about ⅔ inch across; sepals purplish, vase-shaped; petals lavender purple. **Fruit** a spreading, linear, cylindrical, many-seeded pod, ½ to 2 inches long; the pod is narrower between the seeds, the seeds thus outlined.

Typically the stems of this plant extend up through the crown of shrubs, with the flowers presented above. The plants prefer the clayey, slightly alkaline soils of the Great Basin.

NIGHTSHADE FAMILY   Solonaceae

Solonaceae is a family with worldwide distribution, best represented in the tropics. It has long been famous (or infamous) for its toxic alkaloids; deadly nightshade is the most notorious species. It is best known for its important cultivated species, including potato, tomato, tobacco, and peppers. Some plants, such as petunias, are cultivated as ornamentals.

Solonaceae, a variable family, includes everything from small annuals to trees. It is loosely held together by a combination of floral characteristics. The flowers are radially symmetrical with parts in fives—five sepals, five petals, and five stamens. Both the sepals (calyx) and petals (corolla) are fused; the stamens are derived from the corolla tube. The superior ovary has two to five chambers.

False Nightshade   *Chamaesaracha coronopus*

Perennial **herb,** 4 to 16 inches tall; **stems** several from a branched root crown, generally prostrate over the ground. **Leaves** alternate, narrowly lance-shaped, ½ to 3 inches long; leaf margins prominently wavy and sometimes lobed. **Flowers** about ½ inch across, borne singly or in small clusters at the tip of leafy branches; calyx tube and lobes densely hairy; corolla greenish white, saucer-shaped, and marked by a prominent, pale green star; the throat of the corolla tube is restricted by 5 white-woolly appendages; stamens barely extend beyond the throat of the corolla tube. **Fruit** a greenish white berry, almost entirely enclosed in the expanded but not inflated calyx.

This is a widespread, variable species that grows in gravelly soils in all our deserts. It and other species of *Chamaesaracha* resemble ground-cherries but differ in not having a bladdery calyx.

Yellow Thelypody *Thelypodiopsis divaricata*   Howell Thelypody *Thelypodium howellii*

False Nightshade *Chamaesaracha coronopus*

Jimsonweed
Datura (meteloides) wrightii

Robust **herb,** 8 to 30 inches tall; **stems** 1 to several, branched, erect to spreading, covered with white, felty pubescence. **Leaves** egg-shaped to lance-shaped, up to 10 inches long, usually toothed, gray-pubescent; leaf veins prominent. **Flowers** 6 to 10 inches long, trumpet-shaped, borne singly from leaf axils near the tips of branches; calyx tube narrow, 3 to 5 inches long with prominent veins and lance-shaped lobes; corolla white to lavender tinged, trumpet-shaped; stamens included within the corolla tube. **Fruit** a roundish, leathery, inch-long capsule that breaks apart at maturity.

Jimsonweed grows in all our deserts, usually in sandy soils and often along roadsides. It is well known for its toxic (hallucinogenic) properties and is sometimes called "angel's-trumpet."

Fremont Desert-Thorn
Lycium fremontii

Medium-size, glandular-hairy, extensively branched and dense, thorny **shrub,** up to 8 feet tall. **Leaves** alternate but crowded, succulent, glandular-sticky, narrowly club-shaped, ½ to 1 inch long. **Flowers** ½ inch long, scattered along the leafy branches; calyx tube short with triangular lobes, glandular-hairy; corolla pale lavender to purple with darker veins, trumpet-shaped with a very narrow tube and short, rounded lobes; stamens included within the corolla tube. **Fruit** a red, juicy berry, about ⅓ inch in diameter.

This is an occasional shrub in sandy plains and alkaline flats of the Sonoran Desert, particularly in Arizona.

Pale Desert-Thorn
Lycium pallidum

Medium-size, extensively branched and dense, very thorny **shrub,** up to 6 feet tall. **Leaves** alternate, crowded, not pubescent, pale green, elliptical to spoon-shaped, ½ to 2 inches long. **Flowers** ⅔ inch long, scattered along the leafy branches; calyx tube equaling the lobes in length; corolla greenish white, tinged with purple, especially on the inside of the lobes, narrowly funnel-shaped; stamens extending beyond the mouth of the corolla tube. **Fruit** a greenish purple to reddish berry, about ⅓ inch thick.

There are two varieties of this species; var. *oligospermum* in the Mojave Desert and var. *pallidum,* which ranges across the other North American deserts. Both varieties grow in gravelly plains and along desert mountain slopes.

Jimsonweed *Datura (meteloides) wrightii*

Fremont Desert-Thorn *Lycium fremontii*

Pale Desert-Thorn *Lycium pallidum* var. *oligospermum*

Torrey Wolfberry (Tomatilla) *Lycium torreyi*

Medium-size, extensively branched, thorny **shrub,** up to 8 feet tall; branches rather flexuous. **Leaves** alternate, not pubescent, spoon-shaped, ½ to 2 inches long, succulent. **Flowers** ½ inch long, scattered along the leafy branches; calyx tube short and cup-shaped, toothed; corolla greenish lavender to purplish, narrowly funnel-shaped, with hairy lobes; stamens extend slightly beyond the mouth of the corolla tube. **Fruit** a bright red or orange-red, juicy berry, ⅓ inch long, more or less egg-shaped.

The berries of *Lycium* species are edible but bland and resemble miniature tomatoes (*tomatilla* is diminutive for "tomato"). Torrey wolfberry is widespread in drainages and washes in all our deserts.

Anderson wolfberry (*L. andersonii*) closely resembles Torrey wolfberry, differing in having smaller, linear leaves and nonhairy corolla lobes. It, too, is widespread, found in all our deserts except the Chihuahuan Desert. It grows in a variety of habitats, and its abundant fruit is often gathered and eaten.

Desert Tobacco *Nicotiana obtusifolia (trigonophylla)*

Perennial **herb,** 8 to 30 inches tall; **stems** single or clumped, glandular-sticky, especially in the inflorescence. **Leaves** basal and alternate, 1 to 3 inches long; basal leaves broadly elliptical, stalked; stem leaves are lance-shaped, clasping the stem with ear-shaped basal lobes. **Flowers** about 1 inch long, borne in panicles; calyx tube with 5 narrowly triangular lobes equaling the tube in length; corolla dull white to greenish, the tube narrow with short, spreading lobes; stamens included within the corolla tube. **Fruit** a many-seeded, angled capsule about ½ inch long.

This is an occasional plant in desert washes and gravelly plains. It grows in all our deserts. **Tree tobacco (*Nicotiana glauca*),** a native of South America, is now also widely distributed in our deserts. It is a small tree with bluish green (glaucus), narrowly egg-shaped leaves and tubular, yellow flowers.

Thick-Leaf Ground-Cherry *Physalis crassifolia*

Perennial **herb** or **subshrub,** 8 to 20 inches tall; **stems** clustered, woody at the base, profusely branched, glandular-sticky. **Leaves** alternate, egg-shaped to broadly lance-shaped, succulent (*crassifolia,* "succulent leaves"), about 1 inch long; margins generally wavy. **Flowers** about ⅔ inch across, borne in small clusters at the tips of leafy branches; corolla dull yellow with brownish markings, saucer-shaped; stamens extending beyond the mouth of the corolla tube. **Fruit** a greenish berry enclosed within the green calyx, which becomes enlarged, grooved, and bladdery (*Physalis* is a Greek term meaning inflated or bladdery).

This is the most common of several desert species of *Physalis,* present in all our deserts except the Chihuahuan Desert. It prefers gravelly soils and even grows in "desert pavement."

Torrey Wolfberry
Lycium torreyi

**Thick-Leaf
Ground-Cherry**
Physalis crassifolia

Desert Tobacco
Nicotiana obtusifolia (trigonophylla)

Tree Tobacco
Nicotiana glauca (trigonophylla)

Lobed Ground-Cherry   *Physalis lobata*

Perennial **herb,** 6 to 15 inches tall; **stems** weak and more or less prostrate over the ground, covered with small, crystalline hairs. **Leaves** alternate, lance-shaped, sometimes lobed or divided, 2 to 4 inches long; leaf margins generally wavy if not lobed. **Flowers** showy, about 1 inch across, borne singly or in small clusters at the tips of leafy stems; corolla bluish purple to rarely white, saucer-shaped and decorated by a prominent purple star; stamens located at the mouth of the corolla tube. **Fruit** a greenish berry enclosed within the bladdery calyx.

This attractive herb grows in gravelly soils and sandy washes of the Painted Desert, ranging southward through the Sonoran Desert of Arizona and eastward into the Chihuahuan Desert.

Silverleaf Nightshade   *Solanum elaeagnifolium*

Perennial **herb,** up to 2 feet tall; **stems** clustered and freely branched, densely clothed by white, stellate hair, and generally bearing small but nasty prickles, particularly in the inflorescence. **Leaves** narrowly elliptical to lance-shaped, occasionally toothed, 1 to 6 inches long, grayish green (silvery) from the dense covering of scurfy stellate hair; the leaves resemble those of Russian olive *(Elaeagnus)* in color and shape, thus the specific epithet. **Flowers** showy, about 1 inch across, borne in open clusters at the tips of branches; calyx stellate pubescent, fused with 5 linear lobes; corolla lavender to dark purple, star-shaped with the lance-shaped lobes spreading from the tube; anthers bright yellow, elongate, spreading forward from the mouth of the corolla tube. **Fruit** a round, yellowish green to eventually blackish berry.

Silverleaf nightshade has recently been introduced from the Plains States into our deserts and is spreading rapidly. It grows mainly in disturbed areas, such as along roadsides, but is invasive. So although it is attractive, it is regarded as a noxious weed. The obscure nettlelike prickles provide a painful wake-up call of how obnoxious it can be.

OAK (BEECH) FAMILY   Fagaceae

The oak family of trees and shrubs is well represented in North American deciduous forests. The leaves are alternate and toothed, lobed, or pinnately divided. The flowers are small and unisexual, both sexes occurring on the same plant. Male (staminate) flowers are produced in hanging catkins, and female (pistillate) flowers are solitary or in groups of two to three along the branches.

There aren't many oaks that can tolerate desert drought; the few that can, tend to grow in rocky sites, where rain penetrates more easily to the depth of the roots, or along arroyos, where the water accumulates and percolates downward.

Of the few oaks that grow within the desert boundaries, **live oak (*Quercus turbinella*)** is the most common and widespread. This is an evergreen shrub or small tree. The twigs are densely clothed in woolly pubescence, which protects against water loss. The stiff, inch-long, leathery leaves are elliptical and have spiny margins. The fruit is a small acorn. This is a dominant tree in the desert chaparral of Arizona and is an important component of oak woodlands in other semiarid regions of the southwest.

Lobed Ground-Cherry *Physalis lobata*

Silverleaf Nightshade *Solanum elaeagnifolium*

Live Oak *Quercus turbinella*

OCOTILLO FAMILY Fouquieriaceae

Only one genus (or two, depending on who you ask) and about ten species are in this family, and only one species, ocotillo, grows in the deserts of the United States, where it is often dominant.

✲ Ocotillo *Fouquieria splendens*

Shrub, up to 20 feet tall, with many unbranched, canelike, crooked, viciously spiny **stems** that spread outward, the plant thus resembling an inverted cone. The plants have a wide-spreading, shallow root system that enables them to absorb water after even light rains, an adaptation shared with cacti. **Leaves** oblong, about 2 inches long and half as wide, neither hairy nor toothed, shed during periods of drought, with new leaves produced after rainy episodes. **Flowers** about 1 inch long, densely clustered toward the stem tips; sepals 5, pinkish red; petals 5, fused at the base into a tube, orangish to bright red; stamens numerous, extending beyond the petal tube. **Fruit** a many-seeded capsule.

Ocotillo prefers rocky slopes and gravelly desert plains and is widely distributed in the hot deserts of North America. In the upper bajadas of the Sonoran Desert it often shares dominance with saguaro cactus and palo verde. In the Chihuahuan Desert it is frequently a codominant with lechuguilla. And in the Mojave Desert it is locally abundant, typically associated with creosote bush.

Ocotillo is an unusual and attractive plant, particularly when in bloom; the specific epithet *splendens* is aptly applied. Even when the stems lack leaves and flowers, they are attractively sculpted with spines from which pale gray bands extend downward over a black background. The plants are useful—the stems are used to build impenetrable fences and to support thatched roofs; the flowers and seeds have been used as a source of food; and a waxy substance is extracted from the stem and used commercially. The species is important as a nectar source for hummingbirds migrating across the desert landscape. The common name is derived from the Aztec word for pine *(ocotle)* with the addition of the Spanish diminutive *(-illo)*. Thus, little pine.

OLIVE FAMILY Oleaceae

The olive family, small but widely distributed, includes olive and several well-known ornamentals, such as lilac and forsythia. The family is variable and held together loosely by floral characteristics. Most important, the petals (corolla) are fused, and there are only two stamens, fused to the corolla tube. Few olive species grow in deserts, and only one genus is described here.

Ground-Thorn *Menodora spinescens*

Low, rounded **shrub,** 1 to 2 feet tall, **stems** freely branched, the tips of the branches modified into stout, sharp spines. **Leaves** mainly alternate, narrowly elliptical to linear, up to ½ inch long. **Flowers** about ⅓ inch across, borne along leafy branches; sepals usually 5; corolla white and funnel-shaped, with 5 or 6 lobes. **Fruit** a 2-lobed, few-seeded capsule that breaks apart at maturity.

This is a vicious, aptly named, ground-loving shrub that grows in rocky habitats in the desert mountains of the Mojave.

Ocotillo *Fouquieria splendens*   Inset: Ocotillo *Fouquieria splendens*

Ocotillo, palo verde, cholla, and saguaro

Ground-Thorn *Menodora spinescens*

Broom Menodora

Menodora scabra

Rough-pubescent (scabrous) **subshrub,** 10 to 30 inches tall; **stems** several, branched, woody at the base, stiffly erect and nearly leafless above, broomlike. **Leaves** mainly alternate, narrowly lance-shaped, ⅓ to 1 inch long. **Flowers** ⅔ inch wide and long, borne in open clusters near the stem and branch tips; sepals 5 or more, rough-hairy; corolla yellow and funnel-shaped, with a narrow tube and 5 spreading lobes; stamens 2, extending beyond the corolla tube. **Fruit** a 2-lobed, few-seeded capsule with a top that separates at maturity, releasing the seeds—like a sugar bowl lid.

This is an occasional species along rocky slopes and canyon walls of hot deserts—the Mojave, Sonoran, and Chihuahuan. It resembles yellow flaxes, but the 2 stamens give it away.

PALM FAMILY

Arecaceae

This is a large family, but most species grow in tropical forests. Many palms are cultivated as ornamentals or for commercial products, including oils, fats, seeds, and fruits. Only one species, described below, is a North American desert native.

Desert Palm (California Fan Palm)

Washingtonia filifera

Unbranched **tree,** up to 60 feet tall and several feet in diameter. **Leaves** produced only at the stem crown but persistent, the older ones hanging down like a skirt over the trunk; leaf stalk (petiole) 2 to 6 feet long, spiny; leaf blade equally long, fan-shaped, palmately divided nearly to the petiole into 40 to 60 segments, the margins of which have threadlike fibers. **Flowers** bisexual, borne in a panicle in the tree crown; sepals 3, white; petals 3, white; stamens 6; ovary superior, 3-chambered. **Fruit** a 1-seeded berry (drupe).

This majestic plant is a desert species only in the sense that it grows within desert boundaries. It is undoubtedly a relict species from a time when the area that is now a desert received abundant rain and was covered by a tropical forest. Today, the desert palm grows only around springs and along streams. Because these oases are becoming fewer and farther between, the palms are becoming less common and more locally distributed. Many of the few remaining palm oases are now under protection. The oases are havens for many birds and other animals, not just for the palms themselves. Whatever the perceived cost, they are worth preserving.

Broom Menodora *Menodora scabra*   **Desert Palm** *Washingtonia filifera*

Desert Palm (old and young plants) *Washingtonia filifera*

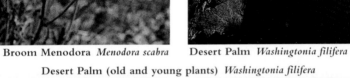

PARSLEY FAMILY   Apiaceae (Umbelliferae)

The umbellate inflorescence, fruit type, and parsleylike leaves make Apiaceae easy to recognize. The umbels may be simple or compound (umbel within umbels). Usually there is a set of bracts (involucre) at the base of the umbels, sometimes with another set surrounding the secondary umbels. The fruit of the family has two, one-seeded halves that separate at maturity. The parsleylike leaves are generally expanded at the base, sheathing the stem. The flowers are radially symmetrical with parts in fives— zero or five sepals, five petals, and five stamens. The ovary is inferior, and the style bases are generally enlarged. Most species are perennial herbs. Some, like carrot, have edible roots; others, such as hemlock, are poisonous.

Cymopteris   *Cymopteris* species

Hairless, perennial **herbs** with an enlarged taproot; **stems** none, the flower stalk(s) and leaves derived from the root crown. **Leaves** basal, somewhat leathery, parsleylike, the leaf segments generally spine-tipped. **Flowers** small, borne in compound umbels surrounded by bracts with papery margins; sepals none; petals variable in color from yellow to purple. **Fruit** halves broadly elliptical to nearly round, flattened with conspicuous ribs.

Probably the most common purple-flowered desert species is **widewing spring-parsley *(Cymopteris purpurascens)*,** named for the prominent, membranaceous "wing" around the margin of the fruit halves. It is an attractive plant, with dense umbels of purple flowers and bluish green (glaucous) leaves. It grows in fine, clayey soils in all our deserts except the Chihuahuan Desert, where it is replaced by the very similar **mountain spring-parsley (C. montanum). Mojave desert-parsley *(Lomatium mohavense),*** which has dark maroon to purple flowers, is similar but densely hairy.

A common, variable, yellow cymopteris is **plains spring-parsley (C. acaulis),** which seems to prefer clayey, slightly alkaline soils and ranges from the Great Basin and Painted Deserts southward into the Chihuahuan Desert. It is distinguished from yellow-flowered desert-parsleys (*Lomatium* species) by technical characteristics.

Mexican Thistle   *Eryngium heterophyllum*

Mexican thistle is one of the most interesting and unusual members of the parsley family. The stems are erect and leafy; the flowers are condensed into cone-shaped heads rather than umbels; the entire plant is silvery though glabrous (not hairy); and the leaf segments and involucral bracts are tipped with sharp, businesslike spines. It grows in sandy plains of the Chihuahuan Desert.

Widewing Spring-Parsley *Cymopteris purpurascens*

Plains Spring-Parsley *Cymopteris acaulis*   Mexican Thistle *Eryngium heterophyllum*

PHLOX FAMILY
Polemoniaceae

The most obvious feature of the phlox family is the trumpet-shaped flowers adapted for pollination by lepidopterans—butterflies and moths. Typically the petals (corolla) are fused into a narrow tube with the nectar concealed at the base. Only a butterfly or moth (or hummingbird) can reach to the bottom of the tube. The corolla has five lobes, which usually spread perpendicular to the tube and form a platform for the butterfly probing for nectar. The single most important diagnostic characteristic of the family is the presence of three (rather than two) stigma lobes or style branches. Otherwise, the flowers are radially symmetrical, with a few exceptions, and have parts in fives—five sepals, five petals, and five stamens. The ovary is superior.

Diffuse Eriastrum
Eriastrum diffusum

Annual **herb,** 2 to 6 inches tall; **stems** solitary but extensively branched from the base (diffuse). **Leaves** alternate, up to 1 inch long, usually trifoliate, the 3 lobes linear with a fine point. **Flowers** ⅓ inch long, clustered in woolly, bracteate heads at the tips of branches; calyx fused into a tube with 5 unequal, spine-tipped lobes; corolla pale blue, the narrow tube yellow-throated; stamens extending beyond the corolla tube. **Fruit** a tiny, few-seeded capsule.

This small annual is found in all our deserts. It is often abundant along sandy, desert washes but is easily overlooked because of its pale, inconspicuous flowers.

Many-flowered eriastrum *(E. pluriflorum)* resembles diffuse eriastrum but generally has more erect, less-branched stems, and the flowers are a bit larger, about ½ inch long. It grows in gravelly soils of the Mojave Desert.

Desert Eriastrum
Eriastrum eremicum

Annual **herb,** 2 to 10 inches tall; **stems** solitary but freely branched. **Leaves** alternate, up to 1½ inches long, entire and linear or pinnately divided with linear segments. **Flowers** about ½ inch long, clustered in woolly, bracteate heads at the tips of branches; calyx glandular-hairy, tubular with 5 spine-tipped lobes; corolla pale bluish violet, slightly bilaterally symmetrical with 3 upper and 2 lower or lateral lobes; the tube very narrow with a white to yellowish throat; stamens extending beyond the corolla tube. **Fruit** a small, few-seeded capsule.

This charming desert annual grows in sandy and gravelly soils of the Great Basin, Mojave, and Sonoran Deserts.

Diffuse Eriastrum *Eriastrum diffusum*

Many-Flowered Eriastrum
Eriastrum pluriflorum

Desert Eriastrum
Eriastrum eremicum

GILIAS   *Gilia* species

Annual or perennial **herbs**; **stems** erect, usually branched from the base, glabrous, hairy, glandular, or woolly, depending on the species. **Leaves** basal and/or alternate, generally toothed or lobed. **Flowers** generally small but sometimes showy; corolla fused into a narrow tube with 5 spreading lobes. **Fruit** a small, egg-shaped, few-seeded capsule. Many species of *Gilia* grow in North American deserts, particularly in California. Only a few are treated here.

Great Basin Gilia   *Gilia brecciarum*

Annual **herb**, 3 to 12 inches tall; **stems** cobwebby below and glandular-hairy above. **Leaves** mainly basal, 1 to 2 inches long, once or twice pinnately compound. **Flowers** about ⅓ inch long, borne singly or in small clusters at the tips of branches; calyx ribbed and densely glandular; corolla lavender purple, the tube with a yellowish throat; stamens extending slightly beyond the corolla tube.

This is a variable species, with several recognized varieties or subspecies. It grows in sandy flats of the Great Basin and Mojave Deserts.

Mojave Gilia   *Gilia cana*

Annual **herb**, 3 to 12 inches tall; **stems** cobwebby below and glandular above. **Leaves** basal in a thick rosette, once or twice pinnately compound with toothed segments. **Flowers** showy, up to 1 inch long, several in open racemes at the tips of branches; calyx glandular to cobwebby; corolla whitish to purple; stamens extending slightly beyond the corolla tube.

The species has several recognized varieties or subspecies, some intergrading with other species. Its distributional range is centered in the Mojave Desert, where it sometimes grows in colorful populations on sandy flats, often associated with rabbitbrush.

Gunnison Gilia   *Gilia gunnisonii*

Annual **herb**, 3 to 10 inches tall; **stems** glandular-hairy above. **Leaves** alternate, linear, sometimes lobed, glandular-hairy. **Flowers** about ⅓ inch long, borne in dense, bracteate clusters at the tips of branches; calyx lobes spine-tipped; corolla white; stamens extending well beyond the corolla tube.

Although this wildflower is not particularly showy, it often grows in profusion in sandy flats of the Painted Desert, where the white flowers contrast with the red sand.

Broad-Flowered Gilia   *Gilia latiflora*

Annual **herb**, 4 to 12 inches tall; **stems** solitary or clustered, branched. **Leaves** basal in a rosette, pinnately divided, woolly-pubescent. **Flowers** showy, an inch or more long and across, borne in open clusters at branch tips; calyx glandular; corolla tube purple at the base, white above; corolla lobes lavender at the tips, white below; stamens extending slightly beyond the throat of the corolla tube.

This is a variable and beautiful species. It grows in sandy soils of the Mojave Desert. A similar but smaller-flowered species is **G. sinuata,** which grows in all our deserts except the Chihuahuan Desert.

Great Basin Gilia
Gilia brecciarum ssp. *brecciarum*

Mojave Gilia
Gilia cana ssp. *tricepts*

Gunnison Gilia   *Gilia gunnisonii*

Broad-Flowered Gilia   *Gilia latiflora*

Broad-Leaf Gilia   *Gilia latifolia*

Glandular-hairy, annual **herb,** 2 to 10 inches tall; **stems** usually solitary and unbranched. **Leaves** alternate, toothed along the margin, hollylike, rather thick and
succulent. **Flowers** about ⅓ inch long, borne in a panicle at the stem tip; calyx
glandular, lobes pointed; corolla tube white, lobes pink; stamens positioned at the
mouth of the corolla tube.

With its unusual leaves, this is our most distinctive gilia. It grows in rocky and
sandy soils along washes of the Mojave and Sonoran Deserts.

Rock Gilia   *Gilia scopulorum*

Glandular-hairy, annual **herb,** 4 to 12 inches tall; **stems** solitary, branched, often
with long, white hair, as well as glandular hair. **Leaves** mainly basal in a rosette,
pinnately divided. **Flowers** about ⅔ inch long, borne in open panicles; calyx
glandular, lobes lance-shaped; corolla tube very narrow, purple below, pale yellow
above, 3 times as long as the calyx; corolla lobes pink to lavender; stamens extending only slightly beyond the mouth of the corolla tube.

As the common name suggests, this gilia grows in rocky sites, generally along
ravines and often in the shade of large shrubs. It is found in the Mojave and
Sonoran Deserts.

Carmine Gilia   *Gilia subnuda*

Glandular-hairy and sometimes skunky-smelling biennial or short-lived perennial **herb,** up to 30 inches tall; **stems** usually solitary, branched. **Leaves** basal in a
rosette, toothed, glandular-sticky. **Flowers** very showy, ¾ inch long, borne in
open clusters at the tips of branches; calyx short with pointed lobes; corolla brilliant carmine-colored, trumpet shaped, the tube narrow and much longer than
the calyx.

This strikingly attractive wildflower grows in sandy to clayey soils in the Painted
Desert.

Long-Flowered Gilia   *Gilia (Ipomopsis) longiflora*

Annual or biennial **herb,** up to 2 feet tall; **stems** usually solitary from a thick
taproot, branched throughout. **Leaves** alternate, pinnately divided into 5 to 7
linear lobes. **Flowers** 1 to 2 inches long, borne in open panicles along the branches;
calyx glandular-hairy, the lobes linear and pointed; corolla white to lavender tinged,
tube very long and narrow, several times longer than the calyx; corolla lobes
generally tilted on one side, propeller-like; stamens extending slightly beyond the
throat of the corolla tube.

Only night-flying hawkmoths and a few butterflies have proboscises long
enough to reach the nectar at the bottom of the narrow corolla tube. The flowers
are strongly fragrant, another adaptation for pollination by moths, which have an
exceptional ability to detect scent. The plants are widely scattered in our deserts
but seldom abundant. They prefer sandy and gravelly soils.

Broad-Leaf Gilia *Gilia latifolia*

Rock Gilia *Gilia scopulorum*

Carmine Gilia *Gilia subnuda*

Long-Flowered Gilia *Gilia (Ipomopsis) longiflora*

Lilac Sunbonnet
Langloisia punctata

Bristly, annual **herb,** only a few inches tall; **stems** solitary or few, branches spreading or prostrate. **Leaves** alternate, ½ to 2 inches long, restricted to the upper part of the stem, more or less wedge-shaped with 3 to 5 bristle-tipped teeth toward the tip; leaf axis and base also prickly ("punctate"). **Flowers** showy, about ⅔ inch long and across, borne in small clusters at the tip of the stem and branches; calyx purple, the 5 lobes bristle-tipped; corolla tube equaling and hidden by the calyx; corolla lobes colorful, white to pale lilac with purple dots; in addition, each lobe has 2 yellow spots in the middle and a dark purple splotch at the base; stamens extend somewhat beyond the corolla tube. **Fruit** an angled, few-seeded capsule, about ⅓ inch long.

Although the flowers are handsomely colored, they are well camouflaged against the backdrop of multicolored gravel. Thus, even though the plants are fairly common, they are seldom noticed. The species grows only in the Mojave Desert.

Bristly Gilia
Langloisia setosissima

This low, tufted annual is similar to the lilac sunbonnet in all aspects except the flower. Because of the close similarity, the two species are sometimes combined as subspecies in *L. setosissima*. The corolla of bristly gilia is more or less uniformly pale blue to lavender, and the corolla tube is much longer than the calyx; the stamens extend well beyond the corolla tube.

Bristly gilia is fairly common in sandy washes and along gravelly slopes of the Great Basin, Mojave, and Sonoran Deserts.

Golden Gilia
Linanthus aureus

Low, annual **herb,** 2 to 6 inches tall; **stems** intricately branched, the branches threadlike and flexuous, spreading in all directions. **Leaves** opposite or alternate above on the stem, sparse, palmately divided into 3 to 7 linear lobes only a small fraction of an inch long. **Flowers** ⅓ to ½ inch long, several borne at the tip of each of the many branches; calyx fused with short, triangular lobes; corolla uniformly bright golden yellow; corolla tube equaling and hidden by the calyx; stamens positioned near the mouth of the corolla tube. **Fruit** a small, few-seeded capsule.

It is always difficult to rank wildflowers by their beauty, but this delicate annual is high on the list. Although it is distributed only sporadically, it is locally abundant, lighting up the desert landscape with golden brilliance. It prefers sandy soils and ranges from the Great Basin south and east into the Mojave, Sonoran, and Chihuahuan Deserts.

Lilac Sunbonnet *Langloisia punctata*

Bristly Gilia *Langloisia setosissima*

Golden Gilia *Linanthus aureus*

Humble Gilia   *Linanthus demissus*

Low, tufted, annual **herb,** 1 to 4 inches tall; **stems** spreading to prostrate on the ground, white-hairy. **Leaves** alternate, hairy, palmately divided into 3 to 5, bristle-tipped lobes. **Flowers** ⅓ inch long, clustered at the tips of branches; calyx fused into a short tube with unequal, bristle-tipped lobes; corolla bell-shaped, white with a yellowish tube and two maroon spots or lines at the base of each corolla lobe; stamens positioned below the mouth of the corolla tube. **Fruit** a small, few-seeded capsule.

Although humble or modest (*demissus,* "humble"), this wildflower is beautiful when observed closely. It grows primarily along sandy washes but is not uncommon in gravelly soils under such shrubs as blackbrush or creosote bush. It is found in the Mojave and Sonoran Deserts.

Desert Calico   *Loeseliastrum (Langloisia) mathewsii*

Bristly, annual **herb,** 2 to 6 inches tall; **stems** covered with white, crinkly hairs, extensively branched, the branches spreading and often prostrate on the ground. **Leaves** alternate, narrow, ½ to 2 inches long, hairy, restricted to the top of the stem and branches, deeply toothed, each tooth tipped with a bristle. **Flowers** bilaterally symmetrical, about ½ inch long, clustered among leaves at the branch tips; calyx pubescent, lobes bristle-tipped; corolla tube pale lavender to white; corolla lobes lavender, with the 2 to 3 lobes that form the upper lip having a bright maroon arch above a white spot; stamens extend well beyond the mouth of the corolla tube. **Fruit** a small, few-seeded capsule.

The floral design of desert calico is exquisite but cannot be fully appreciated without close observation. The species is fairly common in washes and sandy flats of the Mojave and Sonoran Deserts.

Schott Gilia   *Loeseliastrum (Langloisia) schottii*

Bristly, annual **herb,** 1 to 4 inches tall; **stems** pubescent with white, crinkly hairs, branches more or less prostrate over the ground. **Leaves** alternate, narrow, ½ to 2 inches long, hairy, restricted to the top of the stem and branches, deeply toothed, each tooth tipped with a bristle. **Flowers** slightly bilaterally symmetrical, about ½ inch long, clustered among leaves at the branch tips; calyx pubescent, lobes bristle-tipped; corolla white to pale lavender; the 2 to 3 corolla lobes that form the upper lip are generally lightly spotted with purple; stamens extend somewhat beyond the corolla tube. **Fruit** a small, few-seeded capsule.

This small, tufted annual grows in sandy and gravelly soils of the Mojave and Sonoran Deserts.

Humble Gilia *Linanthus demissus*

Desert Calico *Loeseliastrum (Langloisia) mathewsii*

Schott Gilia *Loeseliastrum (Langloisia) schottii*

Long-Leaf Phlox   *Phlox longifolia*

Mat-forming, perennial **herb;** 2 to 12 inches tall; **stems** generally clustered from a woody, branched base. **Leaves** opposite, narrowly lance-shaped to elliptical, glandular-hairy, ½ to 3 inches long. **Flowers** about 1 inch long, clustered among the leaves at the tips of stems; calyx usually glandular-sticky; corolla pink to lavender or white (or a mixture of colors), corolla tube much longer than the calyx; stamens positioned in the throat of the corolla tube. **Fruit** a many-seeded capsule.

Long-leaf phlox is primarily a steppe species, growing in association with sagebrush. Its ecological tolerance, though, allows it to move upward onto high mountain ridges and downward into the Great Basin and Painted Deserts, where it grows along rocky slopes, often with blackbrush.

Dwarf Phlox   *Phlox nana*

Dwarf (*nana,* "dwarf"), glandular-hairy, perennial **herb,** 2 to 6 inches tall; **stems** generally several from a branched root crown. **Leaves** opposite, narrowly lance-shaped to elliptical, 1 to 2 inches long. **Flowers** ⅔ inch long, sparse at the stem tips; calyx glandular; corolla pinkish purple with a conspicuous white band (eye) at the mouth of the tube and base of the lobes; corolla tube about equaling the calyx in length; stamens not extending beyond the corolla tube. **Fruit** a few-seeded capsule.

This captivating wildflower is locally abundant along rocky slopes in the Chihuahuan Desert, ranging eastward into Arizona. It is closely allied with *Phlox mesoleuca,* differing in having a smaller growth form and more glandular stems and leaves. The two species have a similar range.

Slender-Leaf Phlox   *Phlox tenuifolia*

Perennial **herb** or **subshrub,** up to 3 feet tall; **stems** several, branched, woody at the base but flexuous, often growing up through the crown of associated shrubs. **Leaves** opposite, sparse, pubescent, narrowly lance-shaped to elliptical, ½ to 2 inches long. **Flowers** about ⅔ inch long, in open panicles at the tips of spreading branches; calyx clothed with tangled white hair; corolla white, somewhat funnel-shaped, the tube wider at the mouth and about as long as the calyx; stamens positioned at the mouth of the corolla tube. **Fruit** a few-seeded capsule.

This phlox grows in rocky habitats in the Sonoran Desert of Arizona. A more wide-ranging, sometimes white-flowered Sonoran Desert phlox is *P. stansburyi,* differing from slender-leaf phlox in having a corolla tube much longer than the calyx.

Long-Leaf Phlox *Phlox longifolia*

Dwarf Phlox *Phlox nana*

Slender-Leaf Phlox *Phlox tenuifolia*

PLANTAIN FAMILY   Plantaginaceae

This is a small, easily recognized family of herbs, some of them well-known weeds. The leaves are basal and entire (neither toothed nor lobed). The flowers are small with parts in fours (four sepals, four petals, and two or four stamens) and are densely clustered in a narrow, bracteate spike. The ovary is inferior and matures into a several-seeded capsule. Only a few small annuals from this family grow in North American deserts.

Pursh Plantain   *Plantago patagonica (purshii)*

Small, densely hairy, annual **herb**, 2 to 8 inches tall; **stems** erect, 1 to few. **Leaves** basal, narrowly elliptical, 1 to 4 inches long. **Flowers** small in a dense, bracteate, terminal spike; sepals 4, papery in texture; petals (corolla) fused at the base with 4 white, spreading lobes; stamens 4. **Fruit** a small, several-seeded capsule.

This is a weedy and often abundant plant. It prefers sandy or fine-gravelly soils and grows in all our deserts. Another common desert species is **woolly plantain *(P. ovata)*,** which is also a wide-ranging herb. It is easily distinguished from Pursh plantain by its shorter and broader spikes. The specific epithet relates to its egg-shaped (ovate) floral bracts, which in Pursh plantain are linear.

POPPY FAMILY   Papaveraceae

The poppy family is large and variable, especially when treated in the broad sense to include plants traditionally placed in the fumitory family (Fumeriaceae). Generally, the flowers have parts in fours—four (or two) sepals, four (or more) petals, and four (to many) stamens. The ovary is superior. The flowers are radially symmetrical with the exception of the fumitory family group, which has bilaterally symmetrical flowers and is exemplified by **golden corydalis *(Corydalis aurea).*** In this species, the upper of four golden yellow petals is extended into a prominent, neciferous spur, and the lower petal hangs down like a tongue. Golden corydalis is as wide ranging as it is beautiful, throughout western North America from Alaska into Mexico. It also grows in a variety of habitats, from high mountain ridges to gravelly desert plains.

One of the most important unifying characteristics of the poppy family, including the fumitory group, is the presence of colored or milky, sticky, toxic sap, a chemical defense against herbivores. The family is most famous, or infamous, for the opiate alkaloids that are produced by most species. The family also includes a great many prized ornamentals, especially poppies and bleeding-hearts (of the fumitory group). Only a few species grow in North American deserts.

Prickly Poppy (Chicalote)   *Argemone munita*

Coarse, well-armed *(munita)*, perennial **herb** up to 5 feet tall, with yellow-orange sap; **stems** sometimes clustered, branched, spiny. **Leaves** alternate, lobed about halfway to the midvein, 2 to 6 inches long, bluish green, spiny along the midvein and the leaf margins. **Flowers** large and showy, 3 to 5 inches across, borne singly on short stalks along the tips of branches; sepals 2, prickly, with a pointed appendage below the tip; petals 4, white, thin and fragile; stamens numerous; stigma enlarged, lobed, and purple. **Fruit** a tough, leathery, prickly, many-seeded capsule, 1 to 2 inches long.

Pursh Plantain
Plantago patagonica (purshii)

Woolly Plantain
Plantago ovata

Golden Corydalis
Corydalis aurea

Prickly Poppy
Argemone munita

Prickly poppy flowers are indeed beautiful, with snow-white petals, bright yellow anthers, and purple stigma. Even the plants are attractive, with lobed, bluish green leaves and reflective armament. But they are best appreciated from arm's length. The species is widespread in all our deserts except the Chihuahuan Desert and is especially abundant in areas with a grazing history. The poisonous alkaloids and general armament give the plants full protection from herbivores. In the Chihuahuan Desert, prickly poppy is replaced by **rough prickly poppy (*A. squarrosa*)** (*squarrosa*, "rough"), which is similar in nearly all respects but has pale yellow sap and, perhaps, even more vicious spines.

Parish Poppy *Eschscholzia parishii*

Annual **herb,** 2 to 12 inches tall; **stems** erect, usually clustered. **Leaves** basal and alternate, dissected into several linear segments. **Flowers** bowl-shaped, 1 to 2 inches across, solitary on long stalks; sepals 2, fused together and shed as the flower opens; petals 4, golden yellow; stamens several. **Fruit** a narrowly cylindrical, many-seeded capsule, 2 to 3 inches long.

Parish poppy resembles desert poppy, described above, but the flowers are more golden colored and the stems are leafy below. It grows on gravelly slopes of the Mojave and Sonoran Deserts.

Mexican Poppy *Eschscholzia mexicana*

Annual or biennial **herb,** up to 12 inches tall; **stems** usually several, fanning outward from a branched root crown. **Leaves** mainly basal, 1 to 2 inches long, bluish green, dissected into narrow segments. **Flowers** showy, bowl-shaped, 2 to 3 inches across, solitary on long, leafless stalks; sepals 2, fused together and shed as the flower opens; petals 4, bright golden yellow with a prominent orange spot at the base; stamens several; style branches 4.

This poppy frequently puts on spectacular golden displays across the desert landscape. It grows in the Mojave, Sonoran, and Chihuahuan Deserts. In less arid regions, it is replaced by **California poppy (*E. californica*),** which is generally taller and less orangish. The two species are similar in appearance, and some authorities place *E. mexicana* in *E. californica* as a variety or subspecies.

Desert Poppy *Eschscholzia glyptosperma*

Annual **herb,** 2 to 10 inches tall; **stems** 1 to several, erect. **Leaves** basal, 1 to 3 inches long, bluish green, dissected into several, linear segments. **Flowers** showy, bowl-shaped, 1 to 2 inches across, solitary on long, leafless stalks; sepals 2, fused together and shed as the flower opens; petals 4, bright yellow; stamens several. **Fruit** a narrowly cylindrical, many-seeded capsule, 2 to 3 inches long.

The specific epithet *glyptosperma* describes the sculpted (*glypto*, "carved") seeds, which are strikingly ornate under high magnification. The flowers don't have to be magnified, though, to be appreciated; the leaves, too, contribute to the overall beauty of the plant. It grows in gravelly flats and sandy washes of the Mojave Desert, ranging south along the Colorado River drainage into the Sonoran Desert.

Prickly Poppy
Argemone munita

Mexican Poppy
Eschscholzia mexicana

Parish Poppy *Eschscholzia parishii*

Desert Poppy *Eschscholzia glyptosperma*

Creamcups
Platystemon californicus

Annual **herb,** 4 to 12 inches tall; **stems** 1 to many, erect, leafless above, clothed with tangled hairs. **Leaves** basal (mainly) and opposite, linear to narrowly lance-shaped, 1 to 3 inches long, pubescent. **Flowers** bowl-shaped (or cup-shaped), about 1 inch across, solitary on long, leafless stalks; sepals 3, hairy; petals 6, white to yellowish (cream-colored); stamens several, with flattened filaments, thus the generic name (*platy,* "broad, flat"). **Fruit** multisegmented, the segments separating at maturity, each linear and 1-seeded.

This is an occasional plant in the Great Basin, Mojave, and Sonoran Deserts. It prefers the fine, gravelly soils of desert mountains.

RATANY FAMILY
Krameriaceae

A single genus, *Krameria,* represents this small family, with four species in North American deserts; only two, described below, grow in any abundance. The genus traditionally has been placed in the legume family, but the characteristics of the flowers and fruits are sufficiently unusual to warrant a separate family. The flowers are bilaterally symmetrical, with the sepals larger and more colorful than the petals. The upper three sepals are generally erect and narrowly elliptical, while the lower two each generally resemble a cupped hand. The upper three petals look like a diamond on a stalk; the lower two petals are tiny and are more or less glandlike, secreting oils that are collected by bees. The fruit is a 1-seeded burr.

The species of *Krameria* are known to be root parasites, tapping the roots of associated shrubs, such as creosote bush. They are also known to be preferred browse for large herbivores, in spite of the plants' general spininess. The persistent browsing is at least partly responsible for the low growth form and dense branching.

White Ratany
Krameria grayi

Low, mound-shaped **shrub,** 1 to 2 feet tall, densely covered with white, silky hair; **stems** intricately branched, the branches stiff and often spine-tipped. **Leaves** alternate, linear or narrowly lance-shaped, about ½ inch long. **Flowers** showy, ⅔ to ¾ inch across, borne singly or in pairs on short stalks from between 2 leafy bracts; sepals reddish purple, hairy, at least on the back; upper 3 petals purplish with a yellow-green center, lower 2 petals purple; stamens 4. **Fruit** covered with stalked barbs resembling miniature grappling hooks, which facilitate seed dissemination.

White ratany is probably our most common species of *Krameria,* ranging across the hot deserts—the Mojave, Sonoran, and Chihuahuan—where it is locally dominant in rocky soils. **Pima ratany (Krameria [erecta] parvifolia)** closely resembles white ratany in shape, hairiness, and leaves. It has showy flowers ⅔ to ¾ inch across, borne singly or in small clusters along leafy branches. The sepals are pink to reddish purple, broadly lance-shaped, tending to be cupped. The petals are greenish yellow and purple. The burrlike fruits are covered with spines, which are barbed their full length rather than only at the tip, like a grappling hook. The two ratanys have a similar distribution.

Creamcups *Platystemon californicus*   White Ratany *Krameria grayi*

Pima Ratany *Krameria parvifolia*   Inset: Pima Ratany *Krameria parvifolia*

ROSE FAMILY   Rosaceae

Rosaceae is a large family and includes everything from small annuals to large trees. It has been divided into at least four subfamilies, based predominantly on the type of fruit. Despite the considerable variation, two floral characteristics hold the family together: the presence of a hypanthium in combination with numerous stamens. The hypanthium is a saucer-shaped, cup-shaped, or tubular structure from the rim of which the sepals, petals, and stamens are borne. In most genera, the flowers have multiple pistils.

The family includes such well-known fruit-producing plants as strawberry, raspberry, cherry, and apple and many ornamentals, such as roses. Although it is not well represented in the desert, the few species that do grow there are ecologically important.

Dwarf Mountain Mahogany   *Cercocarpus intricatus*

Medium-size, intricately branched **shrub,** 2 to 6 feet tall; **stems** crooked, erect and spreading, branches stiff and spinelike. **Leaves** ¼ inch long, clustered at the nodes, leathery, linear with the margins rolled under. **Flowers** small, borne in clusters along the branches; hypanthium tubular, green to brownish; sepals 5, green to brown, soon deciduous; petals none; pistil 1, enclosed by the hypanthium. **Fruit** a single, 1-seeded achene with a feathery style.

This and other species of mountain mahogany *(Cercocarpus)* frequently grow along rocky slopes of desert mountains, particularly in the Great Basin and Painted Deserts.

▣ Blackbrush   *Coleogyne ramosissima*

Extensively branched, rounded, thorny **shrub,** 1 to 5 feet tall. **Stems** mainly solitary but branched from the base, stiff, dark gray to blackish. **Leaves** in opposite clusters, narrowly oblong to linear, ¼ to ⅔ inch long, gray from a thick coating of hair, somewhat leathery, with the smooth margins rolled under. **Flowers** borne singly or in small clusters on short branches; petals usually absent; sepals 4, yellow on the inside and reddish brown on the outside, about ⅛ inch long, borne on a bell-shaped tube (hypanthium), which is surrounded by 2 or 4 greenish, 3-lobed bracts; stamens numerous; style feathery near the base, borne on the side of the ovary. **Fruit** a small, crescent-shaped achene.

This distinctive shrub gets its name from the dark gray to blackish bark. The Latin name *ramosissima* ("many branches") is also aptly descriptive. Although many of the stiff branches are modified into spines, the species is an important browse plant for domestic sheep and desert bighorn.

Blackbrush is a frequent dominant in areas transitional between the creosote bush–dominated hot deserts and the higher and more northerly sagebrush-dominated steppe. It is particularly prevalent in the Painted Desert of southern Utah. It often forms pure stands over large areas, and the evenly spaced, low, rounded shrubs with a purplish hue add to the scenic beauty of the red desert landscape. In the Great Basin Desert it is often associated with hopsage *(Grayia),* and in the upper bajadas of the Mojave Desert it is often a codominant with Joshua tree.

Dwarf Mountain Mahogany *Cercocarpus intricatus*

Blackbrush community in Painted Desert *Coleogyne ramosissima*
Inset: Blackbrush *Coleogyne ramosissima*

Apache Plume   *Fallugia paradoxa*

Medium-size, densely pubescent **shrub,** 2 to 6 feet tall; **stems** several, extensively branched. **Leaves** alternate or clustered at the nodes, ⅓ to ½ inch long, palmately lobed into narrow segments with the margins rolled under. **Flowers** saucer-shaped, 1 to 2 inches across, solitary or few at the tips of branches; sepals 5, each with a threadlike tip; hypanthium and sepals woolly-hairy; petals 5, white, showy; stamens and pistils numerous, the styles elongating and becoming feathery, aiding in seed dispersal; **fruits** (achenes) thus collectively plumelike, resembling an Apache chief headdress.

Apache plume is locally abundant along rocky or gravelly slopes and in washes. It grows in all our deserts.

Cliff Rose   *Purshia (Cowania) mexicana*

Large, rounded **shrub,** up to 10 feet tall; **stems** glandular-hairy; reddish brown bark. **Leaves** alternate, ¼ to ½ inch long, wedge-shaped with 3 to 5 narrow, gland-dotted lobes. **Flowers** showy, ¾ to 1 inch across, profuse along the branches; hypanthium funnel-shaped, glandular-sticky; petals 5, white to yellowish; pistils 3 to 5. **Fruit** an achene with a persistent feathery style.

Thousands of years ago, *Cowania stansburiana* (cliff rose) and *Purshia tridentata* (bitterbrush) were first brought together on dry mountain slopes of the Great Basin because of climatic changes. These species hybridized, eventually giving rise to the hybrid species *Purshia glandulosa* (antelope brush), which was intermediate between the two parental species and occupied an intermediate habitat (bitterbrush grows in moist areas of the sagebrush steppe, and cliff rose grows on desert mountain slopes). Hybridization between genera is a no-no, so taxonomists in their infinite wisdom placed *Cowania* in the genus *Purshia,* and it became *Purshia mexicana* var. *stansburiana.* That solved the biological problem, but the taxonomic problem persists because hybridization among the *three* species frequently takes place, and hybrid swarms result. Taxonomy aside, the three *Purshia* species are ecologically important; they often dominate in their respective habitats and are among the most important winter browse plants for deer and other herbivores.

Apache Plume *Fallugia paradoxa*   Apache Plume *Fallugia paradoxa*

Cliff Rose *Purshia (Cowania) mexicana* var. *stansburiana*
Inset: Cliff Rose flowers *Purshia (Cowania) mexicana* var. *stansburiana*

RUE (CITRUS) FAMILY   Rutaceae

Rutaceae is a family of aromatic trees and shrubs made famous by its citrus fruits. There is only one fairly common North American desert species.

Turpentine Broom   *Thamnosma montana*

Small, aromatic **shrub**, 1 to 3 feet tall; **stems** yellowish green, covered with blisterlike glands; the stems and branches stiffly erect, giving the plant a broomlike appearance. **Leaves** alternate, ¼ inch long, linear, quickly shed, the stems thus leafless through most of the year. **Flowers** about ⅓ inch long, borne along the branches; sepals 4, greenish; petals 4, bluish purple; stamens 8, 4 long and 4 short. **Fruit** a leathery, 2-lobed (each lobe pea-sized), 1- to few-seeded, yellowish, gland-dotted "capsule."

Like most aromatic plants, turpentine broom has long been thought to have medicinal properties, and in fact the glandular secretions may cause severe skin irritation. Indians used the secretions to promote healing of wounds and made a mind-altering tea from the leaves and stems. The species grows on gravelly slopes in the Mojave and Sonoran Deserts.

SOAPBERRY FAMILY   Sapindaceae

This is a family of woody plants and vines that grow primarily in the tropics, with only a few native species in western North America, two of which are noted below.

Hop Bush   *Dodonaea viscosa*

Medium-size, unisexual **shrub**, 3 to 8 feet tall; **stems** freely branched, conspicuously ridged; bark gray, tending to shred. **Leaves** alternate, narrowly elliptical to linear, 2 to 4 inches long, sticky and appearing varnished. **Flowers** bilaterally symmetrical but small and inconspicuous, borne in leafy clusters at the tips of branches; male (staminate) and female (pistillate) flowers on different plants; sepals generally 5, yellowish green; petals none; stamens 6 to 10. **Fruit** a reddish, showy, few-seeded capsule that develops 3 conspicuous wings as it matures, resembling hops.

Hop bush grows on gravelly or rocky slopes in the Sonoran Desert of Arizona. It is locally abundant and often dominant. The other species worth noting is **western soapberry (Sapindus saponaria),** which has a similar range in Arizona but extends westward into the Chihuahuan Desert. It is a small tree with pinnately compound leaves and bright yellow-orange, poisonous berries that are rich in saponins, making them useful as a laundry soap. It grows along waterways and rocky canyons.

Turpentine Broom   Hop Bush *Dodonaea viscosa*
Thamnosma montana

Hop Bush *(Dodonaea viscosa)* with ocotillo *(Fouquieria splendens)*

Rue (Citrus) Family/Soapberry Family   ❖   **229**

SPURGE FAMILY   Euphorbiaceae

Euphorbiaceae is a large and variable, primarily tropical family. In deserts of Africa and Asia, euphorbs occupy niches similar to cacti in North American deserts. They are also similar in appearance, with succulent, spiny, prominently ribbed stems. Some species, such as *Hevea,* the rubber tree, are economically important. Others, for example, poinsettia, are cultivated as ornamentals. Most species are toxic, particularly the sap, which is often milky. The flowers tend to be difficult to interpret. They are unisexual, generally lack petals, and are often borne inside a cup-shaped structure (involucre) with fleshy glands along the rim and appendages spreading outward from the rim. The appendages, often colorful, easily pass as petals. Apart from the flowers and toxic sap, there is little that holds the family together.

Mouse-Eye   *Bernardia myricifolia*

Medium-size, unisexual, white-barked **shrub,** 3 to 6 feet tall; **stems** erect, freely branched. **Leaves** alternate, elliptical with rounded teeth, ½ to 1 inch long. **Flowers** unisexual, nonshowy; sepals 3 to 5; petals none; male flowers with 3 to several stamens, borne in elongate clusters from leaf axils; female flowers with a 3-lobed ovary, solitary in leaf axils. **Fruit** a 3-lobed capsule, each lobe (compartment) producing a single seed. Mouse-eye grows along rocky canyon walls and in gravelly washes of the Mojave, Sonoran, and Chihuahuan Deserts. The common name, translated from Spanish, probably relates to the lobed fruits with pupil-like scars.

Desert Croton   *Croton californicus*

Perennial, unisexual **herb,** 1 to 2 feet tall, densely clothed by grayish white, stellate (star-shaped) hairs; **stems** clustered, erect and spreading, sparingly branched. **Leaves** alternate, elliptical, 1 to 2 inches long. **Flowers** unisexual and nonshowy; sepals 5; petals none; male flowers with 10 to 15 hairy stamens, borne in clusters at the tips of branches; female flowers with a 3-lobed ovary. **Fruit** a 3-lobed capsule, each lobe (compartment) producing a single seed.

This and other species of *Croton* are strongly aromatic and have long been thought to have medicinal value, particularly when used as a hot poultice to relieve rheumatic pain. The plants are also poisonous, thus protected from grazing. In some sandy areas of the Mojave and Sonoran Deserts, desert croton is abundant. Several species of *Croton* grow in the Chihuahuan Desert, and the most common is probably **leatherleaf (*C. pottsii*).** It has broader leaves than desert croton, and produces male and female flowers on the same plant.

Mouse-Eye *Bernardia myricifolia*

Desert Croton *Croton californicus*

Leatherleaf *Croton pottsii*

Spurge Family ❖ 231

SPURGES   *Euphorbia* species

Flowers of the *Euphorbia* species, the largest genus in this family, are the most difficult spurges to interpret. They are unisexual, on the inside of a cup-shaped involucre. The male (staminate) flowers are reduced to a single stamen with several borne at different levels on the inside wall of the involucre. The single female (pistillate) flower, consisting of only a pistil, emerges on a long, arched stalk from the center of the involucre. There are no sepals or petals. The rim of the involucre generally has 4 glands more or less alternating with 5 petal-like appendages that commonly fork, resembling a pair of horns. The involucre easily passes as a single bisexual flower with several stamens. Milky juice (sap) also characterizes the spurges. Several species grow in North American deserts, most similar and difficult to distinguish.

Black-Gland Spurge   *Euphorbia melanodenia*

Low, matted, perennial **herb,** 2 to 8 inches tall; **stems** many, from a branched root crown, generally woolly-pubescent. **Leaves** opposite, egg-shaped, more or less woolly, ¼ to ½ inch long. **Involucres** rimmed by horizontally elongate black glands *(melanodenia)* that contrast with the snow-white, fused, petal-like appendages. **Fruit** a small, 3-lobed, 3-seeded, stalked capsule.

This is a fairly common, attractive (with close observation) species that grows along rocky and gravelly slopes of the Sonoran Desert. Also growing in the Sonoran Desert, but with a range extending into the Mojave Desert, is the related species **small-seeded spurge (Euphorbia polycarpa).** This, too, is a matted perennial with white, petal-like involucral appendages. Unlike black-gland spurge, it has hairy, reddish stems and reddish brown glands.

Candelilla   *Euphorbia antisyphilitica*

Low **subshrub,** 12 to 30 inches tall; **stems** woody, spreading horizontally over the ground with numerous erect, waxy, grayish green (glaucous) branches, these generally wiry and unbranched. **Leaves** alternate, narrowly cylindrical, only a small fraction of an inch long, early deciduous. **Involucres** with many stamens (staminate flowers), 5 purplish brown glands, and 5 white appendages. **Fruit** a long-stalked, 3-lobed, 3-seeded capsule.

Although ragged looking when not in flower and after the leaves have fallen, candelilla is seasonally attractive. It is abundant in the Chihuahuan Desert, particularly on limestone deposits. The Latin name suggests a medicinal use.

STONECROP FAMILY   Crassulaceae

The stonecrops are succulent herbs with a water-storage capability rivaling cacti. The family is large and enjoys worldwide distribution, representatives growing mainly in dry sites. The flower parts are in fours or fives—four or five sepals, four or five petals, eight or ten stamens, and four or five pistils, each of which matures into a many-seeded pod (follicle). Succulence in combination with the four to five separate pistils generally identifies the family. Many species are cultivated as ornamentals.

Only one genus, *Dudleya* (live-forevers), is well represented in North American deserts. Generally the plants are erect, with a basal rosette of leaves and reduced, often scalelike, stem leaves. Perhaps the most common desert inhabitant is **rock dudleya (Dudleya saxosa),** which grows in rocky habitats *(saxosa,* "of rocks"). It is a variable species of attractive plants with reddish flowers and broadly lance-shaped leaves. It grows on rocky slopes of the Sonoran Desert.

Black-Gland Spurge
Euphorbia melanodenia

Small-Seeded Spurge
Euphorbia polycarpa

Candelilla *Euphorbia antisyphilitica*
—Richard Worthington photo

Rock Dudleya *Dudleya saxosa*

SUMAC FAMILY

Anacardiaceae

The sumacs are a family of trees and shrubs with small, generally unisexual, radially symmetrical flowers with parts in fives—five sepals, five petals, and five or ten stamens (in male flowers). The ovary is superior and the fruit is a one-seeded berry (drupe). Several species cause skin rashes (dermatitis) upon contact, including poison oak and poison ivy. Some species are grown as ornamentals, because the leaves turn brilliant red and orange in the fall. Other species are cultivated for their fruit, including cashew and mango. Some sumacs are ecologically important because of their dominance in plant communities and the edible berries they produce. A few of these grow in deserts.

Evergreen Sumac
Rhus chlorophylla

Large **shrub** or small **tree,** 3 to 10 feet tall; **stems** freely branched, generally pubescent. **Leaves** alternate, evergreen, and pinnately compound; leaflets 3 to 5, broadly elliptical, about 2 inches long, conspicuously veined. **Flowers** about ⅓ inch across, both unisexual and bisexual ones borne in panicles at the tips of branches and from leaf axils; sepals 5, green; petals 5, creamy white; stamens 5. **Fruit** a red, glandular-hairy berry.

Evergreen sumac prefers limestone soils on rocky slopes of the Chihuahuan Desert, ranging into southeastern Arizona. A closely related evergreen species with a similar range is **tobacco sumac (*R. virens*),** which differs in having fewer and smaller inflorescences and pubescent leaflets, at least on the lower surface.

Skunkbush
Rhus trilobata

Medium-size **shrub,** up to 6 feet tall; **stems** freely branched, the branches clothed with soft hair. **Leaves** alternate, deciduous, pubescent (at least on the lower surface), compound; leaflets 3, egg-shaped, irregularly lobed, 1 to 3 inches long, the terminal leaflet the largest. **Flowers** small, congested in narrow spikes at the tips of branches; sepals 5; petals 5, pale yellow; stamens 5. **Fruit** red, glandular-hairy berry.

Skunkbush is a variable and taxonomically confusing species. Some authorities treat it a variety in the species *R. aromatica.* Other taxonomists recognize several varieties in its own species, *R. trilobata.* It goes by several common names, including fragrant sumac, squawbush, and lemonade berry, the latter because of its astringent fruit. It resembles poison oak, but poison oak is not pubescent and has white berries. Skunkbush is widespread and locally abundant in the desert mountains of North America.

Evergreen Sumac *Rhus chlorophylla*

Tobacco Sumac community *Rhus virens*

Skunkbush *Rhus trilobata*

SUNFLOWER FAMILY　　　　　Asteraceae (Compositae)

Asteraceae is arguably the largest family of flowering plants in the world and far and away the largest in North American deserts. It is represented on all continents and in all habitat types. It includes everything from diminutive annuals to trees. Many of our most noxious weeds are composites, as are innumerable ornamentals and a few plants cultivated for food or oils. In our deserts, the composites provide a showcase of color, especially in shades of yellow. It seems that one out of every four wildflowers is a DYC—a damned yellow composite (see page 276). Not all composites produce showy flowers, though; many have adopted a wind pollination strategy.

Despite its size and variability, the family is well defined by floral structure and inflorescence: a head. A few to numerous flowers are congested on an expanded receptacle surrounded by green (involucral) bracts, collectively termed an *involucre*. The flowers may be either disk or ray or a combination of both, in which case the ray flowers, which advertise for pollinators, are on the outside. Disk flowers are radially symmetrical, and the corolla is fused into a tube with five lobes or teeth. Ray flowers are bilaterally symmetrical with the corolla modified into a short basal tube from which a straplike, sometimes toothed, ray protrudes outward. The sepals (calyx) are modified into bristles or scales of some sort, collectively termed the *pappus*, which is persistent on the inferior ovary. In some species the pappus is absent. The ovary matures into a single-seeded achene, and the pappus may assist in its dissemination. There are five stamens, with the filaments fused to and derived from the corolla tube. The sides of the anthers are fused to each other, forming a tube through which the two stigmatic branches of the style grow as the flower opens, pushing the pollen ahead and presenting it to floral visitors. Finally, in some species there are scales (chaff) scattered among the flowers on the receptacle.

Goldenhead　　　　　　　*Acamptopappus shockleyi*

Low, mound-shaped **subshrub,** about 1 foot tall; **stems** many, woody at the base; branches often spinelike. **Leaves** alternate, elliptical, about ½ inch long, somewhat sandpapery with short, stiff hairs. **Heads** about 2 inches across, solitary on leafy branches; involucral bracts overlapping in 2 to 3 series; **ray flowers** yellow, 7 to 14, ½ to ⅔ inch long; **disk flowers** yellow, many. **Achenes** densely hairy with a pappus of several stiff, spreading bristles.　　.

Goldenhead grows in rocky mesas and mountain slopes of the Mojave and Great Basin Deserts. The similar **rayless goldenhead (*A. sphaerocephalus*),** differing in having rayless, clustered, roundish heads, grows in the Mojave and Sonoran Deserts in similar habitats.

Goldenhead *Acamptopappus shockleyi*

Goldenhead *Acamptopappus shockleyi*

Rayless Goldenhead *Acamptopappus sphaerocephalus*

Orange Glandweed — *Adenophyllum (Dyssodia) cooperi*

Low, rounded **subshrub,** 12 to 20 inches tall; **stems** many, branched, woody at the base, roughened by short, stiff hairs. **Leaves** alternate, lance-shaped, about ½ inch long, dotted with oil glands (*Adenophyllum,* "glandular leaf"), the margins with spine-tipped teeth. **Heads** about 1 inch across, solitary on leafless stalks; involucral bracts narrowly lance-shaped, gland-dotted, in 2 to 3 series; **ray flowers** reddish orange to yellow, 5 to 13, ⅓ to ½ inch long; **disk flowers** yellow to orangish, many. **Achenes** brownish with a pappus of flat scales, each dissected into numerous bristles.

This attractive composite is locally abundant in sandy flats and washes of the Mojave and Sonoran Deserts. A related, hairless species, **Sonoran glandweed (A. porophylloides),** with pinnately divided leaves, is abundant in similar habitats of the Sonoran Desert.

Scale-Bud — *Anisocoma acaulis*

Annual **herb** with milky juice (sap), 2 to 8 inches tall; **stems** leafless, unbranched, hairless. **Leaves** basal, 1 to 2 inches long, pinnately lobed, the lobes toothed. **Heads** about 1 inch across, solitary on leafless stems; involucral bracts more or less transparent with a dark green to reddish center and tip, in 2 to 3 series, the outside series much the smallest; **ray flowers** pale yellow, many, about ⅔ inch long; **disk flowers** none. **Achenes** with a pappus of feathery (plumose) bristles of unequal size (*anis,* "unequal"; *coma,* "tufts of hair," relating to the pappus).

Scale-bud is widely distributed in the Sonoran and Mojave Deserts. It prefers sandy soils, especially washes.

Canyon Ragweed — *Ambrosia ambrosioides*

Low, mound-shaped **shrub,** 2 to 3 feet tall; **stems** many, branched, brownish purple, clothed with white hairs. **Leaves** alternate, lance-shaped, 2 to 5 inches long, pubescent, the margins toothed. **Heads** discoid (disk flowers only) unisexual; male (staminate) heads many-flowered, borne in elongate racemes, female (pistillate) heads 2 to 3 flowered, burrlike, borne in small clusters from leaf axils. **Fruit** functionally a burr with 2 to 3 seeds, pappus none.

Canyon ragweed is wind pollinated (and allergenic), and the flowers are accordingly small and nonshowy; the pistillate flowers lack a corolla. This ragweed grows in sandy plains and along rocky canyon walls, primarily in deserts of Arizona.

Orange Glandweed   Scale-Bud
Adenophyllum (Dyssodia) cooperi   *Anisocoma acaulis*

Canyon Ragweed *Ambrosia ambrosioides*

❄ Bur Sage (White Bur Sage) *Ambrosia dumosa*

Low **shrub** (1 to 2 feet), extensively branched from the base and typically dome shaped; **stems**/branches whitened by a dense covering of short hair. **Leaves** alternate, up to an inch long, twice pinnate, the leaf segments irregular in size and shape and often toothed; covered by short, white hairs. **Flowers** small and inconspicuous, unisexual, borne in small, male (staminate) and female (pistillate) heads in elongate woolly clusters (spikes) at the branch tips. **Fruit** an achene but burrlike, enclosed by spiny, protective bracts.

Bur sage is widespread and common in the foothills and basins of the Mojave and Sonoran Deserts, surpassed only by creosote bush in ecological importance. Typically they are codominants, the dark or olive green creosote bush contrasting with the ashy gray of its smaller companion. The two species are equally adapted to the extreme aridity of their desert habitat, but they use different adaptive strategies. Creosote bush has a deep root system and highly varnished evergreen leaves. Bur sage has an extensive shallow root system and white-woolly, drought-deciduous leaves. Creosote bush endures the drought; bur sage avoids the drought.

In the Sonoran Desert of Arizona, bur sage is mainly replaced by or grows along with **triangular-leaved bur sage *(Ambrosia deltoidea)*.** The branches of this bur sage are resinous and sticky, not covered with white hair; the leaves are white pubescent only on the lower surface and are narrowly triangular and toothed rather than pinnately divided. Both species are wind pollinated and like other members of the infamous ragweed genus *(Ambrosia)* are among the worst hay fever plants. Both species produce chemicals that render the leaves and branches bitter. Still, bur sage is said to be a preferred food source of burros and consequently is also known as "burro-bush."

Budsage (Spiny Sagebrush) *Artemisia spinescens*

Low, compact, strongly aromatic **shrub,** 6 to 20 inches tall; **stems** stout, crooked, freely branched; new branches covered with short, white hair, old branches eventually modified into stiff spines; bark furrowed and tending to shred. **Leaves** alternate, clothed with soft, white pubescence, about ½ inch long, palmately divided into 3 to 5 narrow segments. **Heads** unisexual, tiny, borne in leafy clusters along the branch tips; involucral bracts densely covered with soft, woolly hair; **ray flowers** none; **disk flowers** 2 to 10, bell-shaped. **Achenes** hairy, lacking a pappus.

This stout little shrub is a dominant over large areas of the Great Basin, Painted, and Mojave Deserts. It grows in a variety of soil types: gravelly, clayey, and saline.

Bur Sage and creosote bush community *Ambrosia dumosa*
Inset: Bur Sage *Ambrosia dumosa*

Triangular-Leaved Bur Sage
Ambrosia deltoidea

Budsage
Artemisia spinescens

✸ Sagebrush (Tall Sagebrush)   *Artemisia tridentata*

Freely branched and more or less rounded, aromatic **shrub; stems** gray, hairy when young, irregularly furrowed, 2 to 6 feet tall, or occasionally taller when growing in deep soil; bark typically shredding in flat strips. **Leaves** alternate, of two types: (1) persistent, wedge-shaped, 3-lobed or toothed (tridentate), and up to 2 inches long; and (2) drought-deciduous, elliptical, nonlobed (entire), and borne along the stem tips; leaf surfaces are covered with short but dense, silvery white hair. **Flowers** individually minute in elongate clusters of small heads at branch tips; **ray flowers** none, **disk flowers** yellow, 3 to 12 per head; pappus none; involucral bracts surrounding the heads hairy. Plants bloom in late summer and early autumn. **Fruit** a flattened, resinous achene.

Much of the Great Basin and Colorado Plateau has been called a sagebrush desert. Most ecologists, however, regard the advent of sagebrush-dominated communities as the beginning of the sagebrush steppe and a marker of the upper or northern limit of true deserts. But sagebrush ranges well beyond the steppe. It is a frequent understory dominant in piñon-juniper and oak forests and woodlands of the mountainous West. It is regularly one of the most abundant species on dry, rocky, south-facing mountain slopes, ranging from the steppes below to the alpine zone above.

While sagebrush may not be a true desert species, it has drought adaptations: deep roots that draw water from soil reservoirs combined with extensively branched, shallow roots that absorb water barely penetrating the soil; dense, white, light-reflective pubescence; and soft, photosynthetic-efficient leaves produced in early spring and dropped when drought becomes severe combined with tougher, persistent leaves that carry on limited photosynthesis under suitable conditions the year round.

Mark Twain echoed a common mind-set when in one of his famous letters he referred to sagebrush as "the fag-end of vegetable creation." Sagebrush is a major contributor to the stability of the ecosystem where it grows, but cattle ranchers, in particular, generally label it a nuisance because it competes with range grasses. It might not be the stuff of gods (Artemis was the virgin goddess of ancient times), but for some of us it has considerable aesthetic appeal. Many years ago, for example, when I was in the Air Force and stationed in Iceland, my wife asked me by mail what I would most like to have her send to me. My response: a sprig of sagebrush. Years later I selected a large specimen of sagebrush to serve as a Christmas tree. It was an elegant and fragrant addition to our Christmas decor.

Sagebrush community in Painted Desert *Artemisia tridentata*
Inset: Sagebrush *Artemisia tridentata*

Sagebrush Christmas tree *Artemisia tridentata*

Gravel Ghost   *Atrichoseris platyphylla*

Annual **herb** with milky juice (sap), 1 to 3 feet tall; **stems** solitary, branched above, hairless. **Leaves** basal, lying flat on the ground (*platyphylla,* "flat leaves"), egg-shaped, 1 to 4 inches long and nearly as wide, generally finely toothed, often purplish mottled. **Heads** pleasantly fragrant, solitary on branches, 1 to 2 inches across; involucral bracts in 2 to 4 series, lance-shaped, with transparent margins; **ray flowers** 20 to 40, snow white, with 4 to 5 shallow lobes at the tip; **disk flowers** none. **Achenes** ribbed, lacking a pappus.

The common name is appropriately descriptive. The plant grows in gravelly soils of the Mojave Desert where the attractive white heads seemingly float, ghostlike, across the desert landscape and the thin, leafless stems are well camouflaged.

Broom Baccharis   *Baccharis sarothroides*

Medium-size, unisexual, resinous-sticky, aromatic **shrub,** 3 to 8 feet tall; **stems** many, from a branched root crown; the stems and branches green, strongly angled, erect and leafless through much of the year, giving the plants a broomlike appearance. **Leaves** alternate, narrowly lance-shaped, about 1 inch long; margins rolled under. **Heads** borne in open racemes; male and female heads on separate plants; involucral bracts lance-shaped, in several overlapping series; **ray flowers** none; **disk flowers** dull whitish, those of female heads very narrow, threadlike. **Achenes** hairless (glabrous), with a pappus of numerous short bristles.

This is the most common of several species of *Baccharis,* with mainly subtle differences, that grow in North American deserts. It grows in the Sonoran and Mojave Deserts and is best represented and often abundant in Arizona. It prefers gravelly and sandy washes and flats.

Like most aromatic plants, species of *Baccharis* have been used for medicinal purposes. Among other uses, Indians chewed the stems and leaves for relief from toothache. The resins of most (perhaps all) species make them unpalatable to browsers, if not poisonous.

Bahias   *Bahia* **species**

Annual or perennial **herbs,** from a few inches to nearly 3 feet tall; **stems** solitary from a taproot or few. **Leaves** alternate and/or opposite, usually toothed or divided, generally gland-dotted. **Heads** solitary on branches or clustered; involucral bracts in 1 to 3 series; **ray flowers** few to 20, yellow; **disk flowers** many, yellow. **Achenes** 4-angled, wedge-shaped, with a pappus of papery scales or none.

Several species of *Bahia* grow in North American deserts, especially in Arizona, New Mexico, and Texas. The genus is distinguished by the combination of a naked receptacle (no chaff), pappus absent or of scales, and 4-angled achenes.

The most widespread desert species is ***Bahia dissecta,*** an annual herb with divided leaves and a single stem bearing several heads. The showiest species is ***B. absinthifolia,*** a perennial with clustered stems, each with a single or few, rather large heads. The leaves are generally toothed or lobed, and both the stems and leaves are densely covered with soft, white pubescence.

Gravel Ghost *Atrichoseris platyphylla*   **Bahia** *Bahia absinthifolia*

Broom Baccharis *Baccharis sarothroides*

Desert Marigold
Baileya multiradiata

Annual or short-lived perennial **herb,** 8 to 24 inches tall, the entire plant clothed with woolly pubescence, giving it a grayish green appearance; **stems** solitary to several, erect to spreading, branched only at the base. **Leaves** basal and alternate, low on the stem, 1 to 4 inches long, pinnately lobed. **Heads** showy, saucerlike, 2 inches across, solitary at the top of the stems; involucral bracts similar in size, not in series; **ray flowers** bright golden yellow, 3-lobed, numerous in 2 to 4 overlapping series; **disk flowers** numerous, yellow. **Achenes** cylindrical with no pappus.

Desert marigold grows in sandy and gravelly soils in all our deserts but is most abundant in the Mojave. It is said to be poisonous to livestock. A related species with a similar range and habitat preference is **woolly marigold** *(Baileya pleniradiata).* It has somewhat smaller heads, and the stems are branched above the middle and have more leaves. These two wildflowers are known for their roadside beauty. In some areas, roadsides are adorned for miles with solid borders of bright, golden yellow color, a welcome relief from the assortment of weeds that border most roadsides in North America.

Sweetbush
Bebbia juncea

Profusely branched **shrub** or **subshrub,** 2 to 5 feet tall. **Stems** numerous, erect and spreading, brittle. **Leaves** opposite (at least low on the stem), drought-deciduous, about 1 inch long, linear to narrowly triangular, toothed. **Heads** discoid (no ray flowers), yellow, roundish, ½ to ⅔ inch in diameter, borne singly on the many branches; involucral bracts in 3 or more series; receptacle chaffy, each of the chaffy scales wrapped around a disk flower. **Achenes** hairy, club-shaped, with a pappus of white bristles.

"Sweetbush" relates to the pleasant fragrance of the numerous heads, which attract large numbers of bees. The specific epithet relates to the rushlike (*Juncus*-like) appearance of the narrow, generally leafless stems and branches. The plants grow in sandy washes and gravelly slopes of the Mojave and Sonoran Deserts.

Green-Eyes
Berlandiera lyrata

Perennial **herb,** 8 to 30 inches tall, grayish green with velvety pubescence; **stems** several from a branched root stalk. **Leaves** basal and alternate, blades elliptical in outline, pinnately toothed or divided, 1 to 4 inches long. **Heads** showy, about 2 inches across, solitary on long stalks; involucral bracts broad and leaflike, in 3 series, the inner series of smaller bracts wrapped around the achenes of the ray flowers; receptacle with chaffy bracts; **ray flowers** usually 8, yellow, the lower surface with maroon veins; **disk flowers** numerous, maroon. **Achenes** narrow, with no pappus.

The heads of green-eyes are strikingly attractive, with an unusual combination of green bracts, yellow rays, maroon disk flowers, and yellow, pollen-covered style branches. The common name probably relates to the eyelike appearance of the unopened heads. The species grows in gravelly soils of the Chihuahuan Desert, ranging west into southern Arizona.

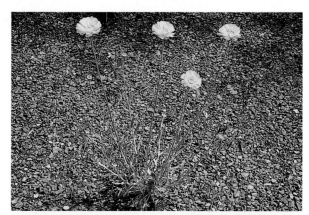

Desert Marigold
Baileya multiradiata

Woolly Marigold
Baileya pleniradiata

Sweetbush *Bebbia juncea*   **Green-Eyes** *Berlandiera lyrata*

White Tack-Stem   *Calycoseris wrightii*

Annual **herb** with milky juice (sap), 6 to 15 inches tall; **stems** solitary but branched; the upper part of the stem is covered by stalked glands that resemble tacks, which, together with the white rays, are the source of the common name. **Leaves** basal and alternate, pinnately divided into long, linear segments. **Heads** showy, 1 to 2 inches across, solitary or few at the tips of branches; involucral bracts in 2 series; receptacle chaffy with bristles; **ray flowers** 15 to 25, white to purplish tinged underneath; **disk flowers** none. **Achenes** bottle-shaped, the top tapering into a narrow beak bearing the pappus of bristles.

This is an attractive inhabitant of gravelly plains and washes of the Mojave, Sonoran, and Chihuahuan Deserts.

Pebble Pincushion   *Chaenactis carphoclinia*

Annual **herb,** up to 2 feet tall; **stems** usually solitary but freely branched, pubescent when young, glandular-hairy just below the heads. **Leaves** basal and alternate, once or twice pinnately divided into linear segments up to 1 inch long; the basal leaves generally wither by the time the flowers open. **Heads** one per branch, discoid (ray flowers absent), about ⅔ inch across; involucral bracts narrowly lance-shaped, equal in length, glandular; **ray flowers** none; **disk flowers** white to pinkish, the outer ones radially symmetrical and only slightly enlarged if at all. **Achenes** club-shaped, hairy, with a pappus of 4 to 6 scales.

As the common name suggests, this plant typically grows in gravelly areas, often on desert pavement and in great abundance. The head fancifully resembles a pincushion. The species ranges from the Great Basin southward through the Mojave and Sonoran Deserts. In most of the Great Basin it is replaced by **Douglas pincushion (C. douglasii),** a biennial with a persistent rosette of basal leaves.

Desert Pincushion   *Chaenactis fremontii*

Annual **herb,** up to 15 inches tall; **stems** 1 to few, branched from near the base, glandular-hairy just below the heads. **Leaves** basal and alternate, 1 to 3 inches long, pinnately divided into fleshy, linear segments; the basal leaves generally wither by the time the flowers open. **Heads** 1 per branch, discoid, about ⅔ inch across; involucral bracts narrowly lance-shaped, equal in length, glandular; **ray flowers** none; **disk flowers** white to pinkish, the outer ones bilaterally symmetrical with the outer lobes greatly enlarged. **Achenes** club-shaped, hairy, with a pappus of 4 scales.

Over vast expanses of gravelly desert landscape, this and the other species of *Chaenactis* described here are the most common annuals. They tend to be particularly abundant under and around the protective umbrella of such desert shrubs as creosote bush. Desert pincushion grows in the Mojave and Sonoran Deserts.

Stevia Pincushion   *Chaenactis stevioides*

This species closely resembles desert pincushion and often goes by the same common name. It differs, though, in several aspects: the **leaves** are divided into smaller and more numerous segments; the **stems** are generally clothed with white, woolly pubescence; the involucral bracts are blunt-tipped; and the outer **disk flowers,** although greatly enlarged, are only slightly bilaterally symmetrical. The two species are equally abundant, but Stevia pincushion has a broader range, extending northward through the Great Basin Desert.

White Tack-Stem
Calycoseris wrightii

Pebble Pincushion
Chaenactis carphoclinia

Desert Pincushion *Chaenactis fremontii*   **Stevia Pincushion** *Chaenactis stevioides*

Damianita
Chrysactinia mexicana

Low, mound-shaped, bright green, aromatic **subshrub,** 6 to 12 inches tall; **stems** several, erect and spreading, woody at the base. **Leaves** both alternate and opposite, linear, more or less fleshy, about ½ inch long, crowded along the branches. **Heads** solitary at the tips of branches, about 1 inch across; involucral bracts linear, equal in length, dotted with small glands; **ray flowers** 8 to 12, bright yellow, narrow; **disk flowers** many, yellow. **Achenes** cylindrical, blackish, with a pappus of unequal, white bristles.

This attractive DYC grows on limestone soils of the Chihuahuan Desert, especially in Mexico.

❄ Rabbitbrush
Chrysothamnus **species**

Shrubs or **subshrubs,** 1 to 5 feet tall, rounded; **stems** many, extensively branched, whitish, sometimes covered with felty wool, sometimes glandular-sticky. **Leaves** alternate, deciduous, linear or narrowly lance-shaped, particularly numerous on the upper branches. **Flowers** borne in narrow heads clustered at branch tips; disk flowers few, yellow or rarely white; ray flowers absent; involucral bracts surrounding the heads keeled on the back and arranged in vertical rows, the heads thus strongly angular, an important diagnostic characteristic of rabbitbrush species. **Fruit** an achene tipped with persistent, threadlike (capillary) bristles (the pappus) that assist in seed dispersal.

Several species of rabbitbrush grow in the deserts, steppes, and prairies of western North America, usually in sandy soils. Several factors contribute to their ecological success: they have deep root systems, an adaptation to dry climates; they resprout following fire; they are not particularly palatable; and wide seed dispersal enables them to readily colonize disturbed soils. The species typically grow in dense populations, where they provide a striking display of golden color when in bloom in late summer and fall; *Chrysothamnus,* "golden shrub."

The most widespread and variable species is **rubber rabbitbrush** *(Chrysothamnus nauseosus),* which is distinctive because the stems and leaves are densely covered with white wool, giving the entire plant a gray-green or grayish blue-green appearance. The densely clustered heads are very small, with only 2 to 6 disk flowers. Including all subspecies and varieties, perhaps as many as 20, this species ranges from Canada to Mexico, inhabiting all the arid and semiarid ecosystems of western North America.

The stems of rubber rabbitbrush contain latex, from which a high-quality rubber can be extracted. The species name may relate to the effect of chewing the stems, which plains Indians did for medicinal purposes, or from the plant's strong odor.

Other desert species include **green rabbitbrush** *(Chrysothamnus greenii)* and **sticky rabbitbrush** *(C. viscidiflorus).* They are similar in appearance and may hybridize. Both grow in sandy soils, often in pure or nearly pure stands, sticky rabbitbrush primarily in the Great Basin and green rabbitbrush in the Painted Desert.

Rabbitbrush is vitally important to the ecology of deserts. It provides shelter for many animals, including the ubiquitous jackrabbit. Bees and other insects forage on the floral rewards. The abundant seeds (achenes) are food for birds and rodents. Herbivores browse the new growth.

Damianita *Chrysactinia mexicana*

Rubber Rabbitbrush *Chrysothamnus nauseosus* var. *bigelovii*
Inset: Rubber Rabbitbrush *Chrysothamnus nauseosus* var. *bigelovii*

Sticky Rabbitbrush (left) and Rubber Rabbitbrush (right)
Chrysothamnus viscidiflorus and *C. nauseosus* var. *bigelovii*

Green Rabbitbrush
Chrysothamnus greenii

Low, mound-shaped **shrubs** or **subshrubs,** up to 15 inches tall; **stems** erect and spreading, profusely branched, with white bark. **Leaves** alternate, about 1 inch long, linear, usually not hairy. **Heads** narrow, clustered at branch tips, discoid, involucral bracts small, keeled on the back, overlapping in vertical rows; **ray flowers** none; **disk flowers** 4 to 6, yellow. **Achenes** hairy, narrowly cylindrical, with a pappus of numerous capillary bristles.

This is one of the most common plants on sandy flats of the Painted Desert, ranging southward and westward. It is similar to and easily confused with *Xanthocephalum (Gutierrezia)* species when not in flower; the heads of *Xanthocephalum* have ray flowers.

Another wide-ranging and variable rabbitbrush species is **sticky rabbitbrush (C. viscidiflorus),** which closely resembles green rabbitbrush and may hybridize with it. Sticky rabbitbrush is larger in all respects and has sticky involucral bracts and leaves. It, too, prefers sandy soils but is most common in the Great Basin, often in pure or nearly pure stands. A common species of the Mojave, Great Basin, and Painted Deserts is **alkali rabbitbrush (C. albidus),** which resembles sticky rabbitbrush but is generally larger, has whitish bark, and grows in alkaline flats. **Desert rabbitbrush (C. paniculatus)** is the largest of the species, growing 6 feet tall. It has green to tan stems, and its heads are loosely clustered in panicles. It prefers washes and gravelly slopes of the Mojave and Sonoran Deserts.

Desert Thistle
Cirsium neomexicanum

Robust, spiny, biennial **herb,** up to 8 feet tall; **stems** solitary, often branched near the top, covered with white, woolly pubescence. **Leaves** alternate, woolly-pubescent on both surfaces, 3 to 10 inches long, elliptical in outline, shallowly lobed, spiny along the margins. **Heads** very showy, creamy white to lavender, about 3 inches across, solitary at the tips of stems and branches; involucral bracts in several series, sparsely hairy, spreading and spine-tipped; **ray flowers** none; **disk flowers** many, corolla modified into a long, narrow tube with 5 linear lobes. **Achenes** egg-shaped, hairless (glabrous), with a pappus of feathery bristles that function like a parachute in spreading the seed.

This is one of few truly desert thistles. It grows on rocky slopes and along canyon walls of all our deserts except the Chihuahuan Desert. Another robust, biennial desert species is **Mojave thistle (Cirsium mohavense).** It, too, is clothed with white, felty wool and has similarly lobed and spiny leaves. The most obvious distinction between the two thistles is that the involucral bracts of Mojave thistle are erect and tightly appressed, but on desert thistle they spread outward and have longer spines.

Green Rabbitbrush community *Chrysothamnus greeni*
Inset: Green Rabbitbrush *Chrysothamnus greeniii*

Desert Thistle *Cirsium neomexicanum*   **Desert Thistle** *Cirsium neomexicanum*

Yellow-Spine Thistle *Cirsium ochrocentrum*

Perennial, spiny **herb,** 12 to 30 inches tall; **stems** white from felty pubescence, generally clumped from short, spreading rhizomes. **Leaves** alternate, green on the upper surface, white-woolly below, 4 to 10 inches long, elliptical to lance-shaped in outline, deeply lobed, the lobes tipped with stiff, yellow spines. **Heads** showy, white or pale lavender to purplish, 2 to 3 inches long, longer than wide; involucral bracts in several series, strictly erect and tightly appressed with short, spreading spines; **ray flowers** none; **disk flowers** numerous, corolla modified into a long, narrow tube with 5 linear lobes. **Achenes** tan, egg-shaped, glabrous, with a pappus of numerous feathery bristles.

This thistle tends to be invasive, often forming dense populations in disturbed areas and along roadsides. It hybridizes with other species, perhaps including **Texas thistle *(C. texanum),*** which is distinct in having heads that are wider than long and less deeply lobed leaves. Texas thistle is less invasive, lacking rhizomes, but grows primarily in disturbed areas in the Chihuahuan Desert.

Bigelow Tickseed *Coreopsis bigelovii*

Annual, glabrous (hairless) **herb,** 4 to 12 inches tall; **stems** 1 to several, erect and generally unbranched, purplish. **Leaves** basal or occasionally 1 to 2 alternate on the lower stem, 1 to 3 inches long, once or twice pinnately divided into linear segments. **Heads** showy, about 2 inches across, solitary at the tip of the stems; involucral bracts in two series, bracts of the outer series much narrower; **ray flowers** 5 to 10, bright yellow, widely spreading, 3-lobed at the tip; **disk flowers** many, yellow. **Achenes** flattened, those of the ray flowers glabrous, those of the disk flowers hairy along the thin edges; pappus of 2 stout, hairy, bristlelike appendages.

The common generic name *tickseed* relates to the ticklike appearance of the flattened, hairy, appendaged achenes. The resemblance is even greater in some species. Bigelow tickseed grows in gravelly or clayey soils in the California deserts.

Showy Tickseed *Coreopsis calliopsidea*

Annual, glabrous (hairless) **herb,** 3 to 12 inches tall; **stems** 1 to several, erect and generally unbranched, greenish purple. **Leaves** basal and alternate, ½ to 2 inches long, once or twice pinnately divided into linear segments. **Heads** showy, 2 to 3 inches across, solitary at the tip of the stems; involucral bracts in two series, bracts of both series more or less similar; **ray flowers** usually 8, bright golden yellow, wedge-shaped; **disk flowers** numerous, golden colored. **Achenes** flattened, those of the ray flowers glabrous, those of the disk flowers hairy; pappus of 2 stout, hairy bristles.

The specific epithet of this species means "most beautiful" *(calli)* in appearance *(opsidea),* and it is aptly applied. Showy tickseed is one of the first plants to bloom in spring and often grows in profusion, turning the desert landscape into a sea of gold. It inhabits sandy and clayey soils across much of the Mojave Desert.

A similar tickseed that barely reaches into the Mojave Desert is **California tickseed *(C. californica).*** It differs in having glabrous achenes, both those of ray and disk flowers, and the achenes have no pappus. It, too, forms dense, spectacular populations.

Yellow-Spine Thistle
Cirsium ochrocentrum

Showy Tickseed
Coreopsis calliopsidea

Bigelow Tickseed *Coreopsis bigelovii*   **Showy Tickseed** *Coreopsis calliopsidea*

✳ Brittlebush

Encelia farinosa

Low, rounded to flat-topped **subshrub,** 1 to 4 feet tall; **stems** many, woody only at the base, freely branched above, white-woolly. **Leaves** alternate, clustered below the flower stalks, egg-shaped to lance-shaped, 1 to 2 inches long, densely covered with tangled white hairs. **Flowers** in heads (sunflower-like) on long leafless stalks; ray flowers bright yellow, 3-lobed, about ½ inch long, 10 to 20 per head; disk flowers numerous, yellow to purplish; pappus none. **Fruit** a flattened achene with straight hairs along the edges and tip.

Along the rocky slopes and gravelly mesas of the Colorado and Mojave Deserts, brittlebush is the most conspicuous of all plants when it is in bloom. It is strikingly attractive because of its abundance, symmetrical shape, grayish leaves and stems, and bright yellow flowers. At first glance, it seems out of place in the harsh desert environment, but its extensive root system and white pubescence, which reduces water loss, adapt it well for dealing with drought. During periods of severe drought it drops its leaves, the major source of water loss.

The stems of brittlebush produce a bitter but pleasantly fragrant resin that helps to protect them from herbivores. When the stems are injured, the clear resin is exuded and can be easily gathered. It is often burned as an incense in Mexican churches and from this use the plant has been given the name *incienso.*

Rayless Encelia

Encelia frutescens

Low, rounded **shrub,** 2 to 4 feet tall; **stems** clustered and branched, grayish white with rough pubescence. **Leaves** alternate, egg-shaped, about 1 inch long, green but covered with short, stiff hair. **Heads** discoid (rayless), roundish, ½ to 1 inch in diameter, solitary at the tips of branches; involucral bracts in 2 series, lance-shaped, glandular-pubescent; **ray flowers** none; **disk flowers** many, yellow. **Achenes** flattened, black, with long hair on the thin edges; pappus of 2 small awns or absent.

Encelia species are notorious for their ability to hybridize, even those that are very different in appearance. For example, *Encelia virginensis,* which has ray flowers and white-woolly leaves, apparently hybridizes with rayless encelia. Both grow on rocky slopes and plains of the Mojave and Sonoran Deserts.

In the Chihuahuan Desert, rayless encelia is replaced by the closely related and common **tarbush (Flourensia cernua).** Most of the characteristics noted above could be applied equally well to tarbush, but its achenes are covered with long hair rather than hairy only on its thin edges, and it has a strong odor of tar.

Brittlebush in Mojave Desert community
Encelia farinosa

Rayless Encelia
Encelia frutescens

Brittlebush *Encelia farinosa*

Naked-Stem Sunray
Enceliopsis nudicaulis

Perennial **herb,** 4 to 20 inches tall; **stems** 1 to several from a woody root crown, leafless (*nudicaulis,* "naked stem"), pubescent, unbranched. **Leaves** basal, silvery gray from woolly pubescence; blades prominently 3-veined, triangular to egg-shaped, 2 to 3 inches long and nearly as wide, the margins generally wavy. **Heads** showy, 2 to 3 inches across, solitary at the tip of the leafless stems; involucral bracts in 2 to 3 series, narrowly lance-shaped; receptacle chaffy, the scales folded around the achenes; **ray flowers** 13 to 21, bright yellow; **disk flowers** numerous, yellow. **Achenes** flattened, black, silky-hairy; pappus of 2 awns separated by tiny scales.

The silvery leaves and large yellow heads make this an attractive plant. It grows on rocky hillsides and canyon walls, ranging from the Great Basin eastward into the Painted Desert and southward into the Mojave Desert.

Painted Desert Sunray
Enceliopsis nutans

Perennial **herb,** 4 to 10 inches tall; **stems** 1 to few, arising from a tuberous root, leafless, pubescent. **Leaves** basal, green but covered with short, stiff hair; blades triangular to egg-shaped, 1 to 3 inches long and nearly as wide. **Heads** similar to those of the naked-stem sunray (described above), but they lack ray flowers and the **achenes** are brown and have no pappus.

This species grows in gravelly soils of the Painted Desert.

Mojave Goldenbush
Ericameria (Haplopappus) linearifolia

Low, rounded to mound-shaped **shrub,** 15 to 36 inches tall; **stems** several, extensively branched, the branches yellowish green and resinous. **Leaves** alternate, linear, ½ to 1½ inches long, shiny and varnished looking. **Heads** showy, solitary at the tips of branches, 1 to 2 inches across; involucral bracts in 2 to 3 series, linear to narrowly elliptical, glandular-hairy; **ray flowers** about 15, bright yellow; **disk flowers** many, yellow. **Fruit** a somewhat flattened achene, densely clothed in white, silky hair; pappus of numerous soft, white, threadlike (capillary) bristles.

Mojave goldenbush is often a dominant species in the desert mountains, especially in the Mojave, and when in bloom it puts on a striking golden yellow display. It ranges from the Great Basin through the Mojave Desert into the Sonoran Desert.

Naked-Stem Sunray
Enceliopsis nudicaulis

**Mojave
Goldenbush**
*Ericameria
(Haplopappus)
linearifolia*

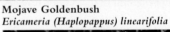

Painted Desert Sunray
Enceliopsis nutans

Mojave Goldenbush
Ericameria (Haplopappus) linearifolia

FLEABANE DAISIES   *Erigeron* species

Fleabane daisies make up a large genus, and many species grow in North American deserts. With few exceptions, the plants have many narrowly elliptical to linear rays that are white or some shade of pink to lavender blue. The species can generally be separated from those of the related genera *Aster* and *Machaeranthera* by their more numerous rays, narrower, green involucral bracts, and double pappus (two rows of bristles).

Rayless Daisy   *Erigeron aphanactis*

Low, more or less cushionlike, perennial **herb,** 3 to 8 inches tall, the entire plant clothed with short, stiff hairs; **stems** erect and spreading, generally several from a branching root crown. **Leaves** alternate, linear to narrowly club-shaped, 1 to 3 inches long, reduced in size upward on the stems. **Heads** discoid (an exceptional condition among daisies), about ½ inch in diameter, flat-topped, usually solitary at the stem tips; involucral bracts narrowly lance-shaped, nearly equal in length, usually glandular-hairy; **ray flowers** none; **disk flowers** numerous, yellow. **Achenes** cylindrical, sparsely hairy, with a double pappus.

Although it lacks ray flowers, rayless daisy is attractive, especially in dense populations. It grows in gravelly soils in the mountains and plains of the Great Basin and Mojave Deserts.

Spreading Daisy   *Erigeron divergens*

Annual or perennial pubescent **herb,** 4 to 20 inches tall; **stems** branched from the base, the many branches spreading and erect. **Leaves** basal and alternate, 1 to 2 inches long, elliptical to club-shaped (wider toward the tip), reduced in size upward on the stem, covered with spreading hairs. **Heads** about 1 inch across, clustered at the branch tips; involucral bracts narrowly lance-shaped, equal in length, glandular-hairy; **ray flowers** numerous, white to pink or lavender blue, narrowly elliptical; **disk flowers** numerous, yellow. **Achenes** sparsely hairy, cylindrical, with a double pappus of bristles, the bristles of the outer ring shorter.

This is a highly variable and widely distributed species, ranging through all North American deserts. It prefers sandy or gravelly soils and often grows in dense, showy populations.

Engelmann Daisy   *Erigeron engelmannii*

Low, perennial, pubescent **herb,** 2 to 10 inches tall; **stems** several from a branching root crown, erect to widely spreading. **Leaves** alternate, 1 to 3 inches long, linear to narrowly club-shaped, reduced in size upward on the stem. **Heads** showy, about 1 inch across, solitary or few per stem; involucral bracts narrowly lance-shaped, hairy and glandular, more or less equal in size; **ray flowers** numerous, white to pale lavender, linear; **disk flowers** numerous, yellow. **Achenes** cylindrical, hairy, with a double pappus. This is one of the more common and widely distributed daisies of the Great Basin. It grows in a variety of habitats, from salt flats to rocky mountain slopes.

Rayless Daisy *Erigeron aphanactis*

Spreading Daisy *Erigeron divergens*

Engelmann Daisy *Erigeron engelmannii*

Utah Daisy
Erigeron utahensis

Low, perennial **herb, up** to 2 feet tall, the entire plant generally covered with tangled hair; **stems** many from a branched root crown, erect and widely spreading, thin and flexuous. **Leaves** alternate, up to 4 inches long, linear, reduced in size upward on the stem. **Heads** showy, an inch or more across, solitary or few per stem; involucral bracts narrow, brownish, glandular, somewhat unequal in size and shape; **ray flowers** many, lavender to white, linear; **disk flowers** numerous, yellow. **Achenes** cylindrical, hairy, with a double pappus, the bristles of the outer row smaller.

Utah daisy is asterlike in being tall, but the *Erigeron* characteristics noted above clearly mark it as a daisy. It grows primarily on sandstone deposits in the Painted Desert.

White-Ray Woolly Sunflower
Eriophyllum lanosum

Small **annual,** 1 to 5 inches tall, unevenly covered with loose, woolly hair; **stems** solitary from a spindly taproot but usually branched. **Leaves** alternate, narrowly club-shaped, about ½ inch long. **Heads** solitary at the tips of branches, about ½ inch across; involucral bracts in one series, lance-shaped; **ray flowers** usually 8, white; **disk flowers** many, yellow. **Achenes** club-shaped, generally hairless (glabrous), with a pappus of 4 to 6, papery, bristle-tipped scales.

This small, woolly annual is fairly common in the Mojave and Sonoran Deserts, generally growing in gravelly soil under and around shrubs such as creosote bush.

Pringle Woolly Sunflower
Eriophyllum pringlei

Diminutive **annual,** up to 3 inches tall, the entire plant covered with cobwebby, white wool; **stems** branched, the branches spreading and prostrate over the ground. **Leaves** alternate, wedge-shaped, 3-lobed at the tip, ¼ to ⅓ inch long. **Heads** discoid, about ¼ inch across, solitary or clustered at branch tips; involucral bracts in one series, elliptical; **ray flowers** none; **disk flowers** about 15, yellow. **Achenes** club-shaped, hairy, with a pappus of 6 to 8 papery, ragged-tipped scales.

The pubescence of this Mojave Desert annual is so dense that the leaves and stems are largely hidden, and the small but bright yellow heads appear to be sitting in a pile of wool; thus the sometimes used common name "golden tuft." The protective role of pubescence is developed to the extreme in this annual.

Wallace Woolly Sunflower (Desert-Gold)
Eriophyllum wallacei

Small, woolly **annual,** 1 to 6 inches high; **stems** solitary from a spindly taproot but freely branched, the plants thus appearing tufted. **Leaves** alternate, spoon-shaped, sometimes 3-lobed at the tip, ⅓ to 1 inch long. **Heads** showy, about ½ inch across, solitary at branch tips; involucral bracts in one series, elliptical; **ray flowers** 6 to 10, golden yellow; **disk flowers** many, golden yellow. **Achenes** narrowly club-shaped, hairy, with a pappus of 6 to 10 tiny papery scales.

This is the most handsome and common of the desert woolly sunflowers. It is locally abundant in gravelly soils of the Mojave and Sonoran Deserts. Another species that is fairly common in the Mojave Desert is **yellow frocks (*E. ambiguum*),** a taller, woolly-pubescent annual with yellow rays that are often paler toward the tips.

Utah Daisy
Erigeron utahensis

**Wallace Woolly
Sunflower**
Eriophyllum wallacei

White-Ray Woolly Sunflower
Eriophyllum lanosum

Pringle Woolly Sunflower
Eriophyllum pringlei

Arizona Blanketflower *Gaillardia arizonica*

Annual **herb**, 6 to 18 inches tall; **stems** erect, 1 to several, unbranched. **Leaves** basal and low on the stem, elliptical in outline, pinnately divided, 1 to 4 inches long, glandular-hairy. **Heads** solitary at the stem tips, about 1 inch across; involucral bracts in 2 to 3 series, greenish purple, lance-shaped, long-hairy at the base and along the margins; receptacle chaffy with threadlike scales; **ray flowers** 6 to 16, yellow, 3-lobed at the tip; **disk flowers** many, hairy, dull yellow. **Achenes** wedge-shaped, with long hair and a pappus of 5 to 10 papery scales.

This is an occasional plant of gravelly soils in the Sonoran Desert of Arizona, barely reaching into Nevada and Utah.

Texas Indian Blanket *Gaillardia pulchella*

Annual **herb,** 6 to 20 inches tall; **stems** erect or spreading, pubescent, solitary or more often several from a branched root crown. **Leaves** basal and alternate, elliptical, 1 to 3 inches long, sometimes toothed or lobed, pubescent with long hairs. **Heads** showy, 2 to 3 inches across, solitary at stem tips; involucral bracts in 2 series, lance-shaped, hairy, reflexed downward when and after the heads are in bloom; receptacle chaffy with threadlike scales; **ray flowers** 6 to 12, red at the base, yellow toward the deeply 3-lobed tip; **disk flowers** numerous, purplish red. **Achenes** wedge-shaped, hairy, with a pappus of 5 to 10 papery, awn-tipped scales.

The specific epithet *pulchella* (beautiful) is aptly applied to this species. The common name, Indian blanket, relates to the color pattern of the rays. Frequently this plant and *Gaillardia aristata*, the common species of less arid regions, are cultivated as ornamentals and are often called "black-eyed Susan." Texas Indian blanket grows in sandy soils of the Chihuahuan Desert, generally along roadsides.

Utah Blanketflower *Gaillardia spathulata*

Perennial **herb** from a stout taproot, 6 to 20 inches tall; **stems** usually several from a branching root crown, erect, pubescent. **Leaves** alternate, glandular-pubescent, spoon-shaped, 1 to 3 inches long, sometimes toothed or lobed. **Heads** about 1 inch across, cone-shaped, solitary at the stem tips; involucral bracts in 2 to 3 series, narrowly lance-shaped; receptacle chaffy with several bristles; **ray flowers** 7 to 10, yellow, only ¼ inch long, deeply 3-lobed; **disk flowers** numerous, yellow, hairy. **Achenes** club-shaped, yellow-hairy, with a pappus of awn-tipped scales.

This blanketflower grows in sandy, often saline soils of Utah desert regions.

Desert Sunflower *Geraea canescens*

Annual, taprooted **herb,** up to 30 inches tall, the entire plant generally clothed with soft, white hairs; **stems** solitary but often branched, particularly above the middle. **Leaves** basal and alternate, reduced in size upward on the stem, egg-shaped to lance-shaped, ½ to 4 inches long, conspicuously veined, sometimes toothed, dark green with a silvery sheen from the pubescence. **Heads** showy, about 2 inches across, solitary or more often in open clusters at the stem tip; involucral bracts in 2 to 3 series, narrowly lance-shaped, hairy; receptacle chaffy, the scales folded around the achenes; **ray flowers** 10 to 20, bright golden yellow; **disk flowers** numerous, golden yellow. **Achenes** strongly flattened, wedge-shaped, the thin edges long-hairy, with a pappus of 2 bristles.

Desert sunflower grows in sandy sites, often blanketing broad expanses of the Mojave and Sonoran Deserts. It is reported to hybridize with brittlebush.

Arizona Blanketflower
Gaillardia arizonica

Utah Blanketflower
Gaillardia spathulata

Texas Indian Blanket
Gaillardia pulchella

Desert Sunflower
Geraea canescens

Crustleaf
Glyptopleura marginata

Annual, tufted **herb** with milky juice (sap), 1 to 2 inches tall; **stems** few to many. **Leaves** densely crowded on the short stems, 1 to 2 inches long, pinnately lobed and toothed; the leaf margin is conspicuously white and hard (crusty). **Heads** showy, about 1 inch across, 1 to 3 at the tip of the short stems; involucral bracts in 2 series different in size and shape; **ray flowers** 8 to 16, cream-colored to yellowish; **disk flowers** none. **Achenes** angular, club-shaped, with a short beak tipped by a pappus of numerous bristles.

Although not particularly common, crustleaf is included in this book because it is unusual and enchanting. It grows in sandy soils of the Mojave and Great Basin Deserts.

Curly Gumweed
Grindelia squarrosa

Low, perennial **herb,** 6 to 30 inches tall; **stems** erect or spreading, usually several from a branched root crown. **Leaves** alternate, elliptical or lance-shaped, 1 to 2 inches long, generally toothed, appearing varnished. **Heads** strongly gummy (resinous), 1 to 2 inches across, in open clusters at the stem and branch tips; involucral bracts in several series, the tips rolled backward; **ray flowers** 20 to 30, yellow; **disk flowers** numerous, yellow. **Achenes** angular, hairless (glabrous), with a pappus of 2 to 4 stiff awns.

This and other desert species of *Grindelia* are said to be poisonous but are unpalatable and rarely eaten. Because of this, they benefit from overgrazing, which relaxes the competition. A related plant of the Painted Desert is **resinbush** *(Vanclevea stylosa),* a low, resinous shrub with discoid heads.

Goldenweeds/Goldenbushes
Haplopappus **species**

Traditionally, *Haplopappus* has been a large and extremely variable genus, a depository for a hodgepodge of loosely related, daisylike DYCs (damned yellow composites) sharing a few characteristics of predesignated importance. The problem has been that while there is considerable separation among many of the included species, intermediates link them together. With the aid of such powerful new tools as DNA analysis, scientists are beginning to resolve alliances among the old *Haplopappus* and to place some species in different genera—*Ericameria, Isocoma,* and *Stenotus,* for example.

Prairie Sunflower
Helianthus petiolaris

Annual **herb,** up to 2 feet tall; **stems** usually solitary but branched, made rough to the touch by short, stiff hairs. **Leaves** alternate or lowermost opposite, egg-shaped to lance-shaped, ½ to 3 inches long, generally rough-hairy. **Heads** about 2 inches across, solitary at the tip of the stem and branches; involucral bracts nearly equal in length, narrowly lance-shaped, hairy; receptacle chaffy, the scales 3-lobed and folded around the achenes; **ray flowers** 9 to 21, bright yellow; **disk flowers** numerous, dark reddish purple. **Achene** flattened, wedge-shaped, with a pappus of 2 fragile awns.

This is a wide-ranging species, primarily at home in the prairie states but ranging west into the Painted Desert, where it prefers sandy soils, often in washes.

Crustleaf
Glyptopleura marginata

Thrifty Goldenweed
Haplopappus armeroides
var. *armeroides*

Curly Gumweed *Grindelia squarrosa*   Prairie Sunflower *Helianthus petiolaris*

Cheese Bush (Burro-Bush)   *Hymenoclea salsola*

Low, rounded, pale green, extensively branched, resinous **shrub** (or **subshrub**), 2 to 4 feet tall; **stems** straw-colored; branches slender and flexuous. **Leaves** alternate, narrow and threadlike, woolly-pubescent on the underside, 1 to 2 inches long; lower leaves pinnately divided with threadlike lobes. Heads unisexual; **male** (staminate) **heads** discoid, pale yellow to translucent, borne in spikes at the tips of branches; involucral bracts persistent, whitish, fused and saucer-shaped; receptacle chaffy. **Female** (pistillate) **heads** clustered below the staminate heads, burrlike, flowers only 1 per head with no corolla. **Fruit** a 1-seeded, winged "burr," the wings actually persistent involucral bracts.

This is a common and often dominant shrub in sandy flats and washes of the Mojave and Sonoran Deserts. Aesthetically, however, it is a loser. The heads are small and nonshowy, and the plants smell bad. The common name "cheese bush" relates to the unpleasant odor of the herbage when damaged.

Hyaline Herb   *Hymenopappus filifolius*

Perennial **herb**, 6 to 24 inches tall; **stems** erect, many from a branched root crown, generally woolly-pubescent, at least below. **Leaves** basal and alternate, twice pinnately divided into threadlike segments up to 1 inch long. **Heads** discoid, ½ inch across, solitary or few at the stem tips; involucral bracts lance-shaped with papery margins, more or less equal in length; **ray flowers** none; **disk flowers** numerous, yellow. **Achenes** 4-angled, densely hairy, with a pappus of several membranaceous scales (*Hymenopappus*, "membranaceous pappus").

This is a highly variable, wide-ranging herb of many habitats. It grows in all our deserts in one form or another.

Stemless Bitterweed   *Hymenoxys acaulis*

Perennial **herb**, up to 30 inches tall; **stems** generally several from a branched root crown, erect, leafless. (A leafless stem is technically only a flower or inflorescence stalk; thus, this species [*acaulis*, "without a stem"] is stemless.) **Leaves** basal, linear, ½ to 2 inches long, usually dotted with small glands. **Heads** showy, about 2 inches across, solitary at the stem tip; involucral bracts woolly-pubescent, nearly equal in length; **ray flowers** 8 to 13, bright yellow, 3-lobed; **disk flowers** many, yellow. **Achenes** hairy, wedge-shaped, with a pappus of 5 to 7 papery, awn-tipped scales.

This is a variable species, with several recognized varieties. It grows in rocky sites in all our deserts.

Cushion Bitterweed   *Hymenoxys depressa*

Low, cushion-forming, perennial **herb**, only a few inches high; **stems** hairy, erect, several from a branched root crown. **Leaves** basal, linear to narrowly club-shaped, ¼ to 1 inch long, dotted with small glands, growing from a thatch of leaf bases from previous seasons. **Heads** about ⅔ inch across, solitary on the short stems; involucral bracts covered by long hairs, nearly equal in length; **ray flowers** 5 to 9, yellow, 3-lobed; **disk flowers** numerous, yellow. **Achenes** hairy, wedge-shaped, with a pappus of 5 to 7 papery scales.

The growth form of this handsome dwarf suggests it should be an alpine rather that desert species. Its rocky, exposed habitat, though, is similar to alpine ridges. It grows in the high deserts of central Utah.

Several additional species of *Hymenoxys* grow in North American deserts. They are characterized by yellow, daisylike heads in conjunction with gland-dotted leaves and membranaceous *(hymen-),* pointed *(-oxys)* pappus scales. Some species are known to be poisonous and some have a history of medicinal use.

Cheese Bush
Hymenoclea salsola

Cushion Bitterweed
Hymenoxys depressa

Hyaline Herb
Hymenopappus filifolius **var.** *cinereus*

Stemless Bitterweed
Hymenoxys acaulis **var.** *arizonicus*

Jimmyweed   *Isocoma wrightii (Haplopappus heterophyllus)*

Robust, resinous **subshrub**, 1 to 3 feet tall; **stems** many, woody toward the base, erect and spreading. **Leaves** alternate, linear, 1 to 3 inches long, generally arched upward, crowded on the stem. **Heads** discoid, individually small but congested into a flat-topped or dome-shaped mass at the stem tip; involucral bracts in 3 to 4 overlapping series, firm and glandular-sticky; **ray flowers** none; **disk flowers** several, yellow. **Achenes** hairy, wedge-shaped, with a pappus of numerous tan-colored bristles.

Jimmyweed seems to prefer the somewhat alkaline soils of the Chihuahuan Desert, ranging westward into southern Arizona. This and other *Isocoma* species are known to be poisonous to livestock, but are rarely eaten; thus, they can become invasive in areas where heavy grazing eliminates the competition.

White Tidytips   *Layia glandulosa*

Annual, glandular-hairy **herb**, 2 to 20 inches tall; **stems** generally solitary, sometimes branched above. **Leaves** alternate, narrowly elliptical to linear, 1 to 4 inches long, lower ones usually toothed or lobed. **Heads** solitary at the stem tips, about 1 inch across; involucral bracts nearly equal in length, glandular and long-hairy; receptacle chaffy with scales; **ray flowers** 4 to 12, white, conspicuously 3-lobed; **disk flowers** many, yellow. **Achenes** hairy, wedge-shaped, with a pappus of several flattened, feathery awns.

This little charmer is common in sandy soils of the Great Basin, ranging southward into the Mojave and Sonoran Deserts. A few other species of *Layia* grow in the deserts, some with white rays and some with yellow rays.

Rose Heath   *Leucelene ericoides*

Low, mat-forming, perennial **herb**, 2 to 6 inches high, spreading from short rhizomes plus a branching root crown; **stems** many, generally branched, glandular-hairy. **Leaves** alternate, glandular-hairy, linear to narrowly spoon-shaped, less than ½ inch long. **Heads** about ½ inch across, solitary at the tips of stems and short branches; involucral bracts in several overlapping series, narrowly lance-shaped, with a green center and white, papery margins; **ray flowers** 12 to 25, white to pinkish; **disk flowers** many, yellow. **Achenes** hairy, cylindrical, with a pappus of numerous capillary bristles.

Rose heath looks like a typical alpine cushion plant. It is comfortably at home in the desert, though, ranging from the Great Basin and Painted Deserts southward into the Chihuahuan Desert. It prefers rocky sites.

Bigelow Aster   *Machaeranthera (Aster) bigelovii*

Robust, biennial or perennial **herb**, 1 to 2 feet tall; **stems** solitary or few, branched above, clothed with short, glandular hairs. **Leaves** alternate, lance-shaped to elliptical, sharply toothed, 1 to 3 inches long. **Heads** showy, about 2 inches across, solitary at the tips of branches; involucral bracts in several overlapping series, narrowly lance-shaped, spreading outward and downward, glandular-hairy; **ray flowers** many, lavender blue; **disk flowers** numerous, yellow. **Achenes** hairy, club-shaped, with a pappus of numerous, dull white capillary bristles.

This tall aster is a handsome plant, sometimes growing in dense, colorful populations on desert mountain slopes and along canyon walls. It ranges from the deserts of Utah through Arizona and into New Mexico.

Jimmyweed
Isocoma wrightii
(Haplopappus
heterophyllus)

Rose Heath
Leucelene ericoides

White Tidytips   **Bigelow Aster**
Layia glandulosa   *Machaeranthera (Aster) bigelovii*

Hoary Aster   *Machaeranthera canescens*

Annual to biennial or short-lived perennial **herb,** 4 to 20 inches tall; **stems** usually solitary but freely branched, the branches often spreading, sometimes pubescent. **Leaves** basal (soon withering) and alternate, narrowly lance-shaped to linear, generally arched downward, toothed or not, ½ to 4 inches long. **Heads** about 1 inch across, borne in open clusters along the branches; involucral bracts in several overlapping series, linear, spreading outward and downward, glandular-sticky; **ray flowers** 12 to 25, lavender pink, narrowly elliptical; **disk flowers** numerous, yellow. **Achenes** narrowly club-shaped, densely white-hairy, with a pappus of capillary bristles.

Machaeranthera canescens is a variable complex of intergrading varieties or subspecies awaiting a definitive treatment by a competent taxonomist. It grows in many habitats and in all North American deserts except, perhaps, the Chihuahuan Desert.

Slender Goldenweed   *Machaeranthera (Haplopappus) gracilis*

Low, annual **herb,** 2 to 10 inches tall; **stems** solitary or few, generally branched, clothed with soft bristles. **Leaves** alternate, lance-shaped to elliptical, ½ to 1 inch long, toothed or lobed, the teeth or lobes bristle-tipped. **Heads** about 1 inch across, solitary at the tips of branches; involucral bracts in several overlapping series, linear, hairy and bristle-tipped; **ray flowers** 15 to 20, golden yellow; **disk flowers** numerous, yellow. **Achenes** densely pubescent, club-shaped, with a pappus of unequal capillary bristles.

Slender goldenweed is an occasional plant in sandy flats and washes of the Mojave Desert, ranging south and east into the Chihuahuan Desert.

Gumweed Aster   *Machaeranthera grindelioides*

Perennial, glandular-sticky **herb,** 4 to 12 inches high; **stems** erect and spreading, clumped. **Leaves** alternate, more or less egg-shaped, ½ to 2 inches long, with spine-tipped teeth and glandular margins. **Heads** discoid, yellow, ⅓ to ½ inch wide, solitary at the tips of the stems and branches; involucral bracts in 3 to 4 series, lance-shaped, with spreading tips, glandular-sticky. **Achenes** densely hairy, club-shaped, with a pappus of tannish capillary bristles.

As suggested by the Latin and common names, this "aster" closely resembles rayless species of gumweed *(Grindelia),* both in general appearance and in gumminess. However, the pappus consists of capillary bristles versus a few awns in *Grindelia.* Gumweed aster grows in varied habitats in the Great Basin and Painted Deserts.

Cut-Leaf Goldenweed   *Machaeranthera pinnatifida*

Perennial **herb,** 8 to 20 inches tall; **stems** clumped from a branched, woody root crown. **Leaves** alternate, elliptical in outline, 1 to 3 inches long, lower ones pinnately dissected, upper ones lobed or toothed, the lobes and teeth bristle-tipped. **Heads** ½ to 1 inch across, clustered near the tips of branches; involucral bracts in several overlapping series, narrowly lance-shaped, often glandular; **ray flowers** 20 to 30, yellow, linear; **disk flowers** yellow. **Achenes** hairy, club-shaped, with a pappus of tan capillary bristles.

This is a complex species with much variation, particularly in pubescence, ranging from hairless (glabrous) to white-woolly. It intergrades with other species, including **spiny goldenweed *(M. [Haplopappus] spinulosa),*** which differs by having spinier leaves and involucral bracts. Cut-leaf goldenweed grows in sandy and gravelly plains of the Mojave, Sonoran, and, most notably, Chihuahuan Deserts.

Hoary Aster *Machaeranthera*
canescens var. *artistata*

Slender Goldenweed *Machaeranthera*
(Haplopappus) gracilis

Gumweed Aster
Machaeranthera
grindelioides var.
grindelioides

Cut-Leaf
Goldenweed
Machaeranthera
pinnatifida

Tansy-Leaf Aster   *Machaeranthera tanacetifolia*

Annual or biennial **herb,** up to 20 inches tall; **stems** solitary or few, generally branched, glandular-hairy. **Leaves** pinnately divided (tansylike) into small, bristle-tipped segments. **Heads** showy, 2 to 3 inches across, solitary at the tips of branches; involucral bracts in several overlapping series, narrowly lance-shaped, the tips spreading outward and downward; **ray flowers** 11 to 30, bluish purple; **disk flowers** numerous, yellow. **Achenes** hairy, club-shaped, with a pappus of numerous dull, white capillary bristles.

Tansy-leaf aster is strikingly attractive and widely distributed, ranging from the Great Basin and Painted Deserts southward into the Sonoran and Chihuahuan Deserts. It prefers gravelly soils and is often abundant along roadsides.

Snake's-Head   *Malacothrix coulteri*

Annual **herb,** 3 to 20 inches tall; **stems** straw-colored, solitary but generally branched from the base. **Leaves** basal and alternate, bluish green (glaucous), up to 4 inches long, toothed or pinnately lobed; the stem leaves clasp the stem and have earlike basal lobes. **Heads** about ½ inch in diameter, solitary on short stalks along the branches; involucral bracts in several overlapping series, broadly ovate, papery with a purple to green central stripe; **ray flowers** many, lemon yellow; **disk flowers** none. **Achenes** brown, strongly ribbed, elliptical, with a pappus of numerous inner, deciduous capillary bristles and 2 to 4 outer, persistent spines.

The common name of this species relates to the roundish involucre, with its scalelike bracts. It grows in sandy soils, primarily in the Mojave Desert.

Torrey Malacothrix   *Malacothrix torreyi*

Annual **herb,** 4 to 16 inches tall; **stems** generally solitary but branched, often reddish. **Leaves** mainly basal, fleshy, bluish green (glaucous), pinnately lobed, the lobes irregularly toothed. **Heads** showy, about 2 inches across, solitary at the tips of branches; involucral bracts narrowly lance-shaped, bearing tack-shaped hairs; **ray flowers** many, bright yellow; **disk flowers** none. **Achenes** vase-shaped, brown, with an inner pappus of bristles and outer pappus of 2 to 4 teeth.

This species overlaps in distribution with yellow-saucers in the Great Basin and shares many characteristics with it, differing in having somewhat larger heads, less regularly lobed and toothed leaves, and an outer pappus of 2 to 4 persistent teeth. It grows in a greater variety of habitats, often in alkaline soils, but seldom forms dense populations.

Tansy-Leaf Aster *Machaeranthera tanacetifolia*

Snake's-Head *Malacothrix coulteri*

Torrey Malacothrix *Malacothrix torreyi*

Desert Dandelion

Malacothrix glabrata

Annual **herb** with milky juice (sap), up to 18 inches tall; **stems** few to many, erect and spreading, usually hairless (glabrous), sometimes branched. **Leaves** basal and alternate low on the stem, pinnately divided into linear segments. **Heads** showy, 1 to 2 inches across, solitary at the stem tip or on short branches; involucral bracts narrowly lance-shaped, in two series, the outer series much shorter than the inner; **ray flowers** many, in overlapping rows, bright but pale yellow, the central unopened ones typically red; **disk flowers** none. **Achenes** narrowly vase-shaped, with a pappus similar to that of snake's-head.

The species is named desert dandelion because the plant is common and prevalent. But being common does not detract from its beauty. Frequently it puts forth a spectacular display of color; not only are the plants abundant but each plant generally has several heads in bloom at the same time. It grows in sandy soils in all our deserts except the Chihuahuan Desert.

A similar species that also forms colorful populations is **yellow-saucers (Malacothrix sonchoides).** This is a bluish green (glaucous), glabrous herb, up to 15 inches tall. The leaves are mainly basal, elliptical in outline, ½ to 4 inches long, and pinnately divided, the segments toothed. The heads resemble those of desert dandelion but are somewhat smaller and lack the red "eye." The achenes are narrowly vase-shaped, with a single pappus of deciduous capillary bristles. Yellow-saucers is common in the Great Basin and Painted Deserts, ranging southward into the Mojave and Sonoran Deserts. It prefers sandy soils.

Damned Yellow Composites (DYCs)
Malacothrix and other species

Several descriptions in this book mention "DYCs," usually in a derogatory sense. The basis for the implied resentment is the combination of a multitude of species and the frequent difficulty in distinguishing among them. The continual reclassification and realignment of the groups by competent taxonomists reflects this difficulty. Another factor that promotes the pervasiveness of the yellow composites is that many of them dominate large expanses of desert landscape. Unsurpassed in the color they add to the desert, DYCs nonetheless are a problem for anyone who would ask, "What plant is that?" Another question that a thoughtful person might ask is, "Why are there so many yellow composites?" First, composites as a family have several features going for them, including a highly successful reproductive system that promotes out-crossing but generally ensures self-fertilization in the absence of pollen from another plant. There are plenty of exceptions to this generality, including the many unisexual, wind-pollinated species. Second, the head (inflorescence) of most composites is structured in a way that floral rewards are easily accessed, and accordingly there is an extremely wide variety of potential pollinators: most composites have a generalist pollination strategy. Third, yellow is a neutral color for insects, a color that all types see and read as "reward."

Of the innumerable composites that paint the deserts yellow, species of *Malacothrix* rank among the top, particularly *M. glabrata,* the desert dandelion. This DYC is as ubiquitous and colorful in the desert as the common dandelion is in our lawns, gardens, pastures, and meadows. Both welcome spring with a blaze of color.

Desert Dandelion community *Malacothrix glabrata*
Inset: Desert Dandelion   *Malacothrix glabrata*

Yellow-Saucers (*Malacothrix sonchoides*) and chenopod community
Inset: Yellow-Saucers   *Malacothrix sonchoides*

Blackfoot Daisy $\qquad$ *Melampodium leucanthemum*

Low, mound-shaped, perennial **herb,** 6 to 20 inches tall; **stems** erect, usually several from a branched root crown. **Leaves** opposite, narrowly elliptical with a prominent white midvein, sometimes toothed or lobed, 1 to 2 inches long. **Heads** showy, about 1 inch across, solitary on leafless stalks; involucral bracts in 2 sets—the outer set of 5 egg-shaped and fused at the base, cuplike, and the bracts of the inner set smaller and wrapped around the ray flower achenes; **ray flowers** 8 to 12, creamy white; **disk flowers** many, yellow. **Achenes** club-shaped, with no pappus.

This distinctive daisy grows mainly in limestone soils of the Chihuahuan Desert, ranging west into the Sonoran Desert of Arizona.

Desert-Star $\qquad$ *Monoptilon bellioides*

Prostrate annual **herb,** 1 to 3 inches high; **stems** reddish, generally branched and spreading from the base. **Leaves** in a basal rosette and in tufts beneath the flowering heads; basal leaves narrowly spoon-shaped, up to 1 inch long, covered with stiff hair; upper leaves smaller. **Heads** about ½ inch across, solitary on branch tips; involucral bracts linear, equal in length, glandular-hairy; **ray flowers** 12 to 20, white to pale lavender; **disk flowers** many, yellow. **Achenes** club-shaped, with a pappus consisting of a combination of small bristles and scales.

This wee daisy (*bellioides,* "daisylike") sometimes grows in such profusion that the desert appears to be covered with snow. It grows in sand deposits in rocky habitats of the Mojave and Sonoran Deserts. Another desert star, *Monoptilon bellidiforme,* is very similar but smaller in all aspects. It grows in the Mojave Desert and has a pappus of a single, plumose-tipped bristle.

Spanish Needle $\qquad$ *Palafoxia arida*

Annual, glandular-hairy, strong-scented and bitter-tasting **herb,** 10 to 24 inches tall; **stems** erect, freely branched. **Leaves** alternate, linear to narrowly lance-shaped, up to 5 inches long. **Heads** discoid, ⅔ inch long, solitary at the ends of branches; involucral bracts greenish purple, linear, more or less uniform in length, glandular-sticky; **ray flowers** none; **disk flowers** 10 to 30, the corolla white to pale lavender, the anther tube purple. **Achenes** hairy, narrowly quadangular, with a pappus of 4 to 6 scales.

Spanish needle grows in sandy washes of the Mojave and Sonoran Deserts. The common and Latin names honor Palafox, a Spanish general; "needle" probably relates to the needlelike achenes.

Chihuahuan Palafoxia $\qquad$ *Palafoxia sphacelata*

Annual **herb,** 12 to 30 inches tall; **stems** erect, sparingly branched, glandular-hairy above. **Leaves** alternate, lance-shaped to triangular, blades 1 to 3 inches long, bluish green (glaucous). **Heads** about ⅔ inch across, solitary at the tips of branches; involucral bracts greenish purple, linear, more or less uniform in length, glandular-sticky; **ray flowers** 4 to 6, pink to red-lavender, deeply 3-lobed; **disk flowers** pink; anthers purple. **Achenes** hairy, narrowly quadangular, with a pappus of 4 to 8 narrow scales.

This palafoxia is a frequent inhabitant in sandy flats of the Chihuahuan Desert. It is one of several red-headed species that grow in Texas.

Blackfoot Daisy
*Melampodium
leucanthemum*

Spanish Needle
Palafoxia arida

Desert-Star
Monoptilon bellioides

Chihauhuan Palafoxia
Palafoxia sphacelata

Mariola   *Parthenium incanum*

Low, white-woolly, strongly aromatic, extensively branched **shrub,** 20 to 30 inches tall. **Leaves** alternate, about ½ inch long, pinnately divided. **Heads** ¼ inch across, in clusters at the branch tips; involucral bracts in 2 series; receptacle chaffy with many scales; **ray flowers** 5, white; **disk flowers** numerous, cream-colored to yellowish. **Achenes** flattened, black, with a pappus of 2 awns.

Mariola is common and often a dominant on gravelly slopes and plains in the Chihuahuan Desert, ranging westward into Arizona and northward to Utah. Like the more famous guayule or Mexican rubber plant *(Parthenium argentatum),* which also grows in the Chihuahuan Desert, it contains extractable amounts of rubber. An aromatic herbaceous species *(P. confertum),* is also common in the Chihuahuan Desert. It resembles mariola except the pappus consists of scales.

Emory Rock-Daisy   *Perityle emoryi*

Annual, strong-scented, glandular-hairy **herb,** 8 to 20 inches tall; **stems** mainly erect, generally branched. **Leaves** alternate, leaf blades 1 to 4 inches long, nearly round to triangular in outline but variously divided, lobed and toothed. **Heads** about ⅓ inch across, solitary at the tips of stems and branches; involucral bracts narrowly lance-shaped, more or less uniform in length; **ray flowers** 6 to 12, white; **disk flowers** many, yellow. **Achenes** hairy, club-shaped but flattened, with a pappus of several small scales.

Emory rock-daisy is conspicuous in its rocky habitat, with vibrant green foliage and snow-white rays. It ranges from the Mojave Desert southward through the Sonoran Desert, growing mainly on rock outcrops and canyon walls.

Desert Fir (Pygmy Cedar)   *Peucephyllum schottii*

Aromatic, rounded, evergreen **shrub,** up to 8 feet tall; **stems** solitary but freely branched; bark gray, smooth. **Leaves** alternate, needlelike, dotted with glands, appearing varnished, crowded along the branches, about ⅓ inch long. **Heads** discoid, ½ inch long, solitary at the tips of the many branches; involucral bracts resinous-sticky, linear, in two series, the inner ones flattened, the outer ones nearly round in cross section; **ray flowers** none; **disk flowers** 12 to 18, yellow. **Achenes** blackish, stiff-hairy, narrowly wedge-shaped, with a pappus of many capillary bristles.

In the absence of flowers, this shrub could pass as a conifer: its needlelike leaves have a balsam (fir) fragrance when crushed. The generic name means "fir leaf." The species is fairly common on gravelly slopes and washes in the Mojave and Sonoran Deserts.

Painted Desert Bahia   *Platyschkuhria (Bahia) integrifolia*

Perennial **herb,** 6 to 20 inches tall; **stems** solitary to several from a woody root crown. **Leaves** basal and alternate low on the stem, reduced to bracts higher on the stem; leaf blades bluish green (glaucous), generally glandular-hairy, elliptical to narrowly diamond-shaped, 3-veined, 1 to 3 inches long. **Heads** about 1 inch across, solitary or few at the stem tip; involucral bracts elliptical, in 2 series of nearly equal length; **ray flowers** 7 to 13, yellow; **disk flowers** many, yellow. **Achenes** quadrangular, club-shaped, with a pappus of several scales.

Two or three varieties of this species have been recognized, the most common desert form appropriately placed in the variety *desertorum.* This is a Painted Desert endemic, growing in clayey or fine-sand soils, often in alkaline areas.

Mariola
Parthenium incanum

Desert Fir
Peucephyllum schottii

Emory Rock-Daisy
Perityle emoryi

Painted Desert Bahia *Platyschkuhria (Bahia) integrifolia* var. *desertorum*

Arrowweed
Pluchea sericea

Medium-size **shrub,** up to 8 feet tall; **stems** erect, straight and willowlike, densely matted with white, felty pubescence. **Leaves** alternate, narrowly elliptical, crowded on the stem, silky-pubescent, 1 to 2 inches long. **Heads** discoid, about ⅓ inch long, crowded at the tips of branches; involucral bracts broadly lance-shaped, in several overlapping series; **ray flowers** none; **disk flowers** numerous, pink to rosy purple. **Achenes** cylindrical, smooth, with a pappus of several small bristles.

Arrowweed grows near springs and along waterways, often forming dense thickets. Around Palm Springs, California, it is typically associated with the desert palm, but it has a broader range, growing along river systems in all our deserts. Indians used the straight, tough stems to make arrows.

Desert Velvet (Turtle-Back)
Psathyrotes ramosissima

Low, dome-shaped (like the back of a turtle), perennial **herb,** densely clothed with white, velvety pubescence. **Leaves** alternate, long-stalked, leaf blades ½ to 1 inch long, generally wider than long, coarsely toothed, nerves prominent and sunken. **Heads** discoid, only ¼ inch long, borne on stalks from leaf axils and surrounded by a whorl of leafy bracts; involucral bracts in two series, the outer curved downward; **ray flowers** none; **disk flowers** several, yellow. **Achenes** densely hairy, with a pappus of brownish bristles.

This distinctive plant grows in sandy flats and washes in the Mojave and Sonoran Deserts, often in association with creosote bush. When the leaves are crushed they smell like turpentine.

White-Stemmed Paperflower
Psilostrophe cooperi

Round, perennial, white-woolly **subshrub,** 1 to 2 feet tall and broad; **stems** 1 to several, woody at the base, erect and spreading, extensively branched. **Leaves** alternate, linear, ½ to 3 inches long. **Heads** many, in open clusters along the branches, about 1 inch across; involucral bracts linear, woolly-pubescent, in two series of nearly equal length; **ray flowers** 4 to 8, bright lemon yellow, 3-lobed, becoming papery and remaining on the achene until it is shed; **disk flowers** many, yellow. **Achenes** cylindrical, glandular-hairy, yellowish, with a pappus of 4 to 6 unequal, papery scales.

This is a distinctive plant with its white stems, linear leaves, and strikingly symmetrical sphere of persistent yellow flowers. It is locally abundant in the Mojave and Sonoran Deserts, growing in sandy plains and washes.

Farther east, from the Painted Desert southward into the Chihuahuan Desert, white-stemmed paperflower is replaced by **woolly paperflower (P. tagetina),** which has only 2 to 5 ray flowers and whitish achenes.

Desert Chicory
Rafnesquia neomexicana

Annual **herb** with milky juice (sap), 6 to 16 inches tall; **stems** erect, 1 to few, generally branched, bluish green (glaucous). **Leaves** mainly basal, pinnately divided, but often withering by the time the plant blooms; stem leaves smaller, irregularly divided, and clasp the stem with earlike basal lobes. **Heads** showy, 1½ inches across, solitary at the tips of branches; involucral bracts in 2 series, the inner longer and narrower; **ray flowers** 12 to 18, white to cream-colored; **disk flowers** none. **Achenes** cylindrical, beaked, with a pappus of feathery (plumose) bristles.

This engaging citizen of the desert, a distant cousin to the common chicory, grows in sandy and gravelly soils of the Mojave, Sonoran, and Chihuahuan Deserts.

Arrowweed
Pluchea sericea

White-Stemmed Paperflower
Psilostrophe cooperi

Desert Velvet *Psathyrotes ramosissima*

Desert Chicory *Rafnesquia neomexicana*

Prairie Coneflower (Mexican Hat) *Ratibida columnaris*

Perennial **herb,** 1 to 3 feet tall; **stems** erect and branched, pubescent with scattered resin dots. **Leaves** alternate, pubescent, pinnately divided into narrow segments ½ to 1 inch long. **Heads** cylindrical (columnar) 1 to 2 inches long, solitary at the tips of branches; involucral bracts linear; receptacle chaffy, the scales folded around the disk flower achenes; **ray flowers** 3 to 7, yellow, often with a reddish brown base, spreading or reflexed downward; **disk flowers** numerous, purplish brown. **Achenes** flattened, the thin edges hairy (ciliate), with a pappus of 2 teeth.

This plant is primarily a prairie species but ranges westward into the deserts in areas where drought is not too severe.

Thread-Leaf Groundsel *Senecio douglasii* var. *longilobus*

Low, rounded, white-woolly **subshrub,** 15 to 30 inches tall; **stems** several, freely branched, woody at the base. **Leaves** alternate, 1 to 4 inches long, narrowly linear (threadlike) or pinnately divided into linear segments. **Heads** about 1 inch across, clustered at the tips of branches; involucral bracts in 2 series, the outer ones short and inconspicuous, the inner ones lance-shaped with papery margins and a hairy-tufted tip; **ray flowers** 7 to 15, yellow; **disk flowers** numerous, yellow. **Achenes** cylindrical, soft-hairy, with a pappus of capillary bristles.

This and other varieties of *S. douglasii* are sometimes placed in the species *S. flaccidus.* It is a distinctive and handsome plant, with bright yellow heads and white-woolly leaves and stems. It is said to be poisonous and benefits from grazing pressure on surrounding plants. It prefers sandy soils, and ranges from the Painted Desert southward into the Chihuahuan Desert.

Great Basin Groundsel *Senecio multilobatus*

Short-lived perennial **herb,** up to 2 feet tall; **stems** erect, 1 to several, branched above. **Leaves** basal and alternate, 1 to 4 inches long, pinnately divided, sometimes woolly-pubescent, sometimes hairless (glabrous). **Heads** about ⅔ inch across, borne in flat-topped clusters at the stem tip; involucre (and **achenes**) as described above for thread-leaf groundsel; **ray flowers** 5 to 13, bright yellow; **disk flowers** numerous, yellow.

Senecio multilobatus and *S. douglasii* are only two of several desert species of *Senecio.* All have divided, lobed, or toothed leaves, yellow heads, and an involucre as described above. Great Basin groundsel likes gravelly soils and is most abundant in the Great Basin and Painted Deserts.

Annual Wire-Lettuce *Stephanomeria exigua*

Annual or biennial **herb** with milky juice (sap), 3 to 20 inches tall; **stems** erect, generally solitary but freely branched, the branches thin and wiry. **Leaves** basal and alternate, 1 to 2 inches long, once or twice pinnately divided, reduced and becoming bractlike upward on the stem. **Heads** many, about ½ inch across, involucral bracts in 2 series, the inner ones narrowly lance-shaped with a papery margin, the outer ones egg-shaped and much shorter; **ray flowers** 5 to 6, pale pink to lavender; **disk flowers** none. **Achenes** angled and rough, club-shaped, with a pappus of feathery (plumose) bristles.

This highly variable, wide-ranging, and sand-loving species grows in all North American deserts in one form or another. Several other species of *Stephanomeria* also grow in our deserts, resembling annual wire-lettuce in floral color (white, pink, or lavender) and general characteristics of the heads.

Prairie Coneflower
Ratibida columnaris

**Thread-Leaf
Groundsel** *Senecio
douglasii* var.
longilobus

Great Basin Groundsel
Senecio multilobatus

Annual Wire-Lettuce
Stephanomeria exigua

Fremont Xerasid
Syntrichopappus fremontii

Small annual **herb,** 2 to 6 inches tall, the entire plant woolly-hairy, the wool often in tufts; **stems** erect to spreading or even prostrate on the ground, generally solitary but branched. **Leaves** alternate, narrowly elliptical to spoon-shaped, often 3-lobed at the tip, ⅓ to 1 inch long. **Heads** ¼ inch across, clustered at the end of the branches; involucral bracts 5, elliptical, with papery margins; **ray flowers** generally 5, yellow, 3-lobed; **disk flowers** numerous, yellow. **Achenes** 5-angled, hairy, with a pappus of minutely barbed, capillary bristles.

This "son of the desert" *(xerasid)* grows in sandy and gravelly soils of the Mojave Desert and the Sonoran Desert in Arizona. What it lacks in size and splendor it often makes up in numbers.

Lemmon Marigold
Tagetes lemmonii

Robust, malodorous **subshrub,** up to 3 feet tall; **stems** several, woody at the base, freely branched. **Leaves** opposite, pinnately compound; leaflets narrowly lance-shaped, about 1 inch long, dotted with resin glands. **Heads** showy, 1½ inches across, solitary on leafless stalks; involucral bracts uniform in length, united into a tube, gland-dotted; **ray flowers** 7 to 12, golden yellow; **disk flowers** many, golden yellow. **Achenes** narrowly cylindrical, with a pappus of a few scales.

Although this is an attractive plant, it is difficult to appreciate up close because of its foul odor. Some people say it is poisonous. Lemmon marigold grows in the desert mountains of southern Arizona.

Horsebrush
Tetradymia species

Low, rounded, often spiny **shrub,** 1 to 3 feet tall; **stems** freely branched, white-woolly. **Leaves** alternate to clustered along the stem, narrowly elliptical to linear, often modified into stiff spines. **Heads** discoid, about ½ inch long, crowded along the ends of leafy branches; involucral bracts 4 to 6, rigid, woolly, equal in length; **ray flowers** none; **disk flowers** 4 to 8, yellow. **Achenes** hairy, angled; pappus usually of capillary bristles.

The two most common and often dominant species of horsebrush are **little-leaf horsebrush *(Tetradymia glabrata)*** and **thorny horsebrush *(T. spinosa).*** In little-leaf horsebrush the leaves of the main stem are not modified into stiff spines, and the heads are borne in dense terminal clusters. In thorny horsebrush the heads are solitary or few in leaf axils along leafy branches, and the main stem leaves become vicious spines. Both species are most abundant in the Great Basin, ranging eastward into the Painted Desert and southward into the Mojave. These and other *Tetradymia* species are poisonous to livestock, particularly sheep.

Fremont Xerasid *Syntrichopappus fremontii*

Lemmon Marigold *Tagetes lemmonii*

Thorny Horsebrush *Tetradymia spinosa*

Navajo Tea
Thelesperma subnudum

Perennial **herb,** up to 12 inches tall; **stems** erect, solitary or few. **Leaves** primarily basal, gray-pubescent, 1 to 4 inches long, divided into narrow segments; generally there are 1 to 2 pairs of opposite, nondivided leaves at the base of the stem, the stem thus almost naked ("subnude"). **Heads** showy, 1 to 2 inches across, solitary at the stem tip; involucral bracts in two series, the outer ones half as long as the inner ones, spreading, the inner ones fused half their length, nonspreading, all have papery margins; receptacle chaffy with broad, papery scales; **ray flowers** 7 to 13, bright yellow; **disk flowers** many, yellow. **Achenes** narrowly elliptical, with a pappus consisting of a toothed crown.

This is primarily a Painted Desert species, where it grows mainly in sandy flats. The stems and leaves have traditionally been brewed into a tea by Indians, thus the common name.

Parralena
Thymophylla (Dyssodia) pentachaeta

Perennial, strong-scented **herb** or **subshrub,** 4 to 8 inches high; **stems** tufted, erect, woody at the base. **Leaves** opposite, about ½ inch long, divided into stiff, linear lobes, dotted with tiny glands. **Heads** about ⅔ inch across, solitary at the branch tips; involucral bracts narrowly elliptical, gland-dotted, nearly uniform in length or with a few tiny outer ones; **ray flowers** about 13, bright yellow; **disk flowers** numerous, yellow. **Achenes** narrowly club-shaped, with a pappus of bristle-tipped scales.

This is a variable species, ranging from the Chihuahuan Desert, where it is most common and variable, north and east to the Mojave Desert. It prefers gravelly soils.

Hoary Ground-Daisy
Townsendia incana

Mat-forming, white-woolly (hoary, also *incana*) perennial **herb,** 1 to 2 inches high; **stems** generally several, clumped, from a branched root crown. **Leaves** alternate, narrowly spoon-shaped, ⅓ to 1 inch long. **Heads** showy, about 1 inch across, solitary on the short stems; involucral bracts in several overlapping series, lance-shaped, the margins papery and ciliate; **ray flowers** 13 to 30, whitish on top and purplish beneath; **disk flowers** numerous, yellow. **Achenes** flattened, with forked hairs and a pappus of capillary bristles.

This is only one of several species of *Townsendia* that grow in desert mountains. All are attractive, mat-forming, daisylike plants preferring rocky habitats. Hoary ground-daisy is a Painted Desert inhabitant. In the Great Basin it is largely replaced by *Townsendia florifer,* a somewhat taller, biennial herb.

Yellow-Head
Trichoptilium incisum

Low, annual or short-lived perennial **herb,** 2 to 8 inches high; **stems** solitary or few, wiry, spreading, unbranched. **Leaves** basal or nearly so, about 1 inch long, sharply toothed (incised), densely woolly, resin-dotted. **Heads** discoid, yellow, ⅓ inch in diameter, solitary at the stem tips; involucral bracts narrowly elliptical, nearly equal in length, glandular-woolly. **Achenes** hairy, wedge-shaped, with a pappus of 5 scales, each bearing several bristles.

Yellow-head grows in rocky habitats in the Mojave and Sonoran Deserts.

Navajo Tea
Thelesperma subnudum var. *subnudum*

Hoary Ground-Daisy
Townsendia incana

Parralena
*Thymophylla
(Dyssodia) pentachaeta*

Yellow-Head
Trichoptilium incisum

Trixis
Trixis californica

Low, mound-shaped, glandular-pubescent **shrub,** 1 to 2 feet tall; **stems** erect and spreading, extensively branched. **Leaves** alternate, narrowly lance-shaped with a conspicuous midvein, strongly glandular, 1 to 4 inches long, the margins rolled under and sometimes toothed. **Heads** narrow, about ½ inch long, in open clusters at branch tips; involucral bracts uniform in length, linear, keeled on the back; receptacle hairy; **ray flowers** none; **disk flowers** 11 to 27, 2-lipped, the outer lip resembling a ray. **Achenes** narrowly cylindrical, glandular, with a pappus of capillary bristles.

Trixis is an attractive shrub with abundant, small, bright yellow heads. Even when not in flower, the tubes formed from the persistent involucral bracts are conspicuous and flowerlike. The species is common in washes and along canyon walls of the Sonoran and Chihuahuan Deserts.

Golden Crownbeard
Verbesina encelioides

Robust, unpleasantly fragrant, annual **herb,** up to 40 inches tall; **stems** erect, solitary or few, densely short-hairy. **Leaves** opposite low on the stem, alternate above; blades 1 to 4 inches long, lance-shaped, toothed, hairy beneath. **Heads** showy, about 2 inches across, solitary at the tip of the stem and branches; involucral bracts nearly equal in length, narrowly lance-shaped; receptacle chaffy, each scale folded around an achene; **ray flowers** 12 to 15, golden yellow, 3-lobed; **disk flowers** numerous, brownish yellow. **Achenes** flattened, hairy, with a pappus of 2 awns.

This is a handsome plant, with bright golden flowers, attractively sculpted leaves, and grayish herbage. It is poisonous but unpalatable, because of its taste and smell, and invades areas where grazing pressure is high. It prefers deep, periodically moist soils and is found in all our deserts, often in disturbed sites.

Parish Goldeneye
Viguiera parishii

Low, dense **shrub** clothed with short, stiff hair, 1 to 2 feet tall; **stems** spreading, extensively branched. **Leaves** mainly opposite, a few upper, reduced leaves alternate; blades 1 to 2 inches long, triangular, conspicuously veined, toothed or not. **Heads** showy, about 2 inches across, solitary at the tips of branches; involucral bracts in two unequal series, narrowly elliptical to lance-shaped; receptacle chaffy, each scale folded around an achene; **ray flowers** 7 to 15, golden yellow; **disk flowers** numerous, brownish yellow. **Achenes** somewhat flattened, hairy, elliptical, with a pappus of 2 awns.

Parish goldeneye grows on rocky slopes and gravelly plains of the Mojave and Sonoran Deserts. It is most abundant in the Yuma Desert area of southeast Arizona.

In the Chihuahuan Desert, Parish goldeneye is replaced by **resinbush (*Viguiera stenoloba),*** a dense, resinous shrub with a varnished appearance. The lower leaves are opposite and pinnately divided into narrow segments, 1 to 2 inches long. The upper leaves are linear and undivided. The heads, 1 to 2 inches across, are solitary on the branches. The involucral bracts are in three overlapping series, and the receptacle is chaffy, each scale folded around an achene. The heads have 12 bright yellow ray flowers and numerous dull yellow disk flowers. The achenes have no pappus. Resinbush is common on the upper bajadas (slopes) of the Chihuahuan Desert, where it is sometimes a conspicuous dominant. It flowers over an extended period of time, but the older heads give the plants a ragged, unattractive look.

Trixis
Trixis californica

Resinbush
Viguiera stenoloba

Golden Crownbeard *Verbesina encelioides*   **Parish Goldeneye** *Viguiera parishii*

Rough Mule's-Ears
Wyethia scabra

Robust, perennial **herb,** 1 to 2 feet tall; **stems** several, clumped, stiffly erect, covered with short, stiff (scabrous) hairs. **Leaves** alternate, scabrous, narrowly elliptical with a prominent midvein, 2 to 6 inches long. **Heads** at least 3 inches across, solitary at the stem tips; involucral bracts in 3 overlapping series, narrowly lance-shaped; receptacle chaffy, the scales folded; **ray flowers** 10 to 23, bright yellow; **disk flowers** numerous, yellow. **Achenes** quadrangular, hairless, with a pappus consisting of a crown.

If flower size (head size in this species) and color are the determinants of beauty, this is one of our most beautiful desert wildflowers. On the other hand, it is just another, though oversized, DYC. Its center of distribution is the Painted Desert, where it grows in sandy plains.

Snakeweeds
Xanthocephalum (Gutierrezia) **species**

Low, mound-shaped, extensively branched **subshrubs** or **herbs. Leaves** alternate, narrow, often threadlike, resinous-sticky. **Heads** small, solitary or in leafy clusters at the ends of branches; involucral bracts in overlapping series, resinous; **ray flowers** 1 to 13, yellow; **disk flowers** many, yellow. **Achenes** white-hairy, elliptical, with a pappus of several short scales.

Snakeweeds are often dominant over broad desert expanses, particularly in areas with a history of heavy grazing; the plants are toxic and unpalatable. They resemble small rabbitbrushes, differing in that the involucral bracts are not in vertical rows and the pappus consists of scales rather than capillary bristles.

In the Chihuahuan Desert, the two most common species are **annual** and **Texas snakeweed (X. dracunculoides** and **X. texanum).** Both are widespread, erect, branched annuals that prefer gravelly soils, often in disturbed areas, such as along roadsides. In other deserts the most common species are **small-headed broomweed (X. microcephalum)** and **matchbrush (X. sarothrae),** both mound-shaped subshrubs. The former has tiny heads (*micro,* "tiny"; *cephalum,* "head"), with only a few overlapping involucral bracts, 1 to 2 ray flowers, and 1 to 3 disk flowers. Matchbrush has heads about ⅓ inch across, clustered at the tips of branches, 2 to 3 series of involucral bracts, 3 to 7 ray flowers, and 3 to 8 disk flowers.

Mojave Woody Aster
Xylorhiza tortifolia

Low, perennial **subshrub,** 8 to 20 inches tall; **stems** erect and spreading, clustered from a branched root crown, glandular-hairy, woody at the base. **Leaves** alternate, narrowly elliptical to lance-shaped, glandular-hairy, 1 to 4 inches long, generally with spine-tipped teeth and a spiny tip. **Heads** large and showy, about 3 inches across, solitary at the stem tips; involucral bracts in several series, narrowly lance-shaped, glandular-hairy; **ray flowers** many, lavender blue to white; **disk flowers** numerous, yellow. **Achenes** narrowly club-shaped, hairy, with a pappus of capillary bristles.

This is a strikingly attractive "aster," and the fact that it often grows alone in a desolate setting, such as desert pavement, adds to its beauty. It ranges from its namesake desert, the Mojave, into the Sonoran Desert.

Rough Mule's-Ears *Wyethia scabra* var. *scabra*

Small-Headed Broomweed *Xanthocephalum (Gutierrezia) microcephalum*

Mojave Woody Aster *Xylorhiza tortifolia*

Cisco Woody Aster
Xylorhiza venusta

Perennial **herb** or **subshrub,** 6 to 20 inches tall, clothed with short, white hair; **stems** erect, few to many from a branched, woody root crown. **Leaves** alternate but restricted to the lower half of the stem, elliptical, 1 to 4 inches long, neither toothed nor lobed. **Heads** large and showy, about 2 inches across, solitary at the stem tips; involucral bracts in several overlapping series, narrowly lance-shaped, pubescent; **ray flowers** 12 or more, white to purplish; **disk flowers** numerous, yellow. **Achenes** narrowly club-shaped, hairy, with a pappus of numerous capillary bristles.

Cisco woody aster is endemic to the Painted Desert. It grows, often in abundance, in wind-blown, clayey or sandy alkaline soils rich in selenium, generally in association with *Atriplex* species. This is a hostile world, where only the toughest survive.

Desert Zinnia
Zinnia acerosa

Low, mound-shaped **subshrub,** 4 to 8 inches tall; **stems** woody at the base, densely clustered and freely branched, generally pubescent. **Leaves** opposite, needle-shaped (acerose), about 1 inch long, usually stiffly hairy. **Heads** 1 inch across, in leafy clusters at the stem tips; involucral bracts elliptical, in overlapping series, the margins papery; receptacle chaffy, the scales folded around the achenes; **ray flowers** 3 to 6, white, becoming papery and persisting on the achenes until they are mature; **disk flowers** few, yellow to brownish. **Achenes** triangular, wedge-shaped, hairy, with a pappus of 2 to 3 awns.

This is a locally abundant and attractive plant in spite of the fact that the persistent rays become discolored and look "tired" as the heads age. Its center of distribution is the Chihuahuan Desert, ranging westward into Arizona. It prefers limestone soils. A second species with a similar distribution and habitat preference is **showy zinnia *(Zinnia grandiflora),*** which has showy bright yellow flowers but is less noticeable than desert zinnia because it is just another DYC. With the exception of flower color, it shares the characteristics of desert zinnia.

Cisco Woody Aster *Xylorhiza venusta*

Desert Zinnia *Zinnia acerosa*

Showy Zinnia *Zinnia grandiflora*

TAMARISK FAMILY   Tamaricaceae

In North America, this family is represented by a single genus, *Tamarix,* with four species, all introduced as ornamentals. They are large shrubs with small, overlapping, scalelike leaves borne on jointed twigs. The stems are shiny green to whitish, and hairless (glabrous). The flowers are small and densely clustered in narrow, pinkish spikes. Generally, the flowers have five sepals, five petals, and five stamens. The ovary is superior and matures into a capsule with small, hairy-tufted, wind-dispersed seeds.

The species have found the desert environment of North America much to their liking and have become noxious weeds. They grow along waterways, lakeshores, and areas where the water table is near the surface. In the deserts, they frequently lower the water table because of their dense growth and excessive water absorption. They also grow in and probably prefer alkaline soils, excreting excess salt from salt glands scattered among the leaves. Because of this, together with the cedarlike leaf shape and arrangement, the most common species *(Tamarix ramosissima)* is sometimes called **salt cedar.** The most frequently used common name, which applies to all species, is **tamarisk**.

UNICORN-PLANT FAMILY   Martyniaceae

Unicorn-plants comprise a small family, with only a few species of the genus *Proboscidea* growing in North American deserts. This genus and the family in general are characterized by an unusual fruit: an elliptical, 2- to 4-inch, single-compartmented, many-seeded capsule with a leathery or fleshy outer wall, variously sculpted or spiny, and a woody inner wall. The outer wall eventually sloughs away. The persistent style, which is longer than the ovary, curves inward (like the horn of a unicorn?), and eventually splits to form two horns or claws, which remain attached to the capsule. The flowers, too, are large, bilaterally symmetrical, and showy. The petals (corolla) are fused into a tube with five lobes, the lower one much the largest and most colorful. The flowers have four stamens.

Our two most common species are **desert unicorn-plant *(Proboscidea althaeifolia)*** and **common unicorn-plant *(P. louisianica).*** The former is an uncommon perennial herb with a bright yellow corolla marked with maroon stripes on the lower lobe. It grows in sandy soils of the Sonoran and Chihuahuan Deserts. Common unicorn-plant has dull white to reddish violet flowers, up to 2 inches long. It is less drought tolerant, growing in relatively moist sites, most often along roadsides and other disturbed areas. It is uncommon west of Texas.

Tamarisk *Tamarix ramosissima*

Common Unicorn-Plant *Proboscidea louisianica*

VERVAIN FAMILY Verbenaceae

Verbenaceae is a large, primarily tropical family, with species ranging from annual herbs to trees, such as teak. Many species are cultivated as ornamentals; some are near-cosmopolitan weeds; a few grow in North American deserts. The vervains are classified as close allies of mints, and they share many mint characteristics: opposite leaves, which are generally toothed or lobed; fused and often bilaterally symmetrical petals (corollas); and an ovary that divides into four, or sometimes fewer, 1-seeded nutlets.

Common Bee Bush *Aloysia gratissima*

Medium-size **shrub,** 3 to 8 feet tall; **stems** thin, stiff, freely branched, the branches generally spine-tipped. **Leaves** opposite, elliptical, entire (neither toothed nor lobed), densely pubescent, at least on the lower surface, ¼ to 1 inch long. **Flowers** small, only about ¼ inch long, pleasantly fragrant, borne in opposite spikes from leaf axils; sepals fused with 4 lobes; corolla slightly bilaterally symmetrical, fused into a narrow tube with 4 to 5 lobes; stamens 4 in two sizes, derived from the corolla tube. **Fruit** a pair of 1-seeded nutlets.

As the common name suggests, this shrub is very attractive to bees, with its strong vanilla odor and rich nectar reward. It grows among rocks in the Chihuahuan Desert. In the Sonoran Desert it is replaced by **oreganillo** *(Aloysia wrightii),* which has woolly, toothed leaves and even smaller flowers. Oreganillo also grows in Texas.

Southwestern Verbena *Verbena gooddingii*

Perennial **herb,** 4 to 18 inches tall; **stems** erect to spreading, covered with soft hair, few to several from a branched root crown, generally branched. **Leaves** opposite, dissected and toothed, clothed with tangled, white hairs, ½ to 2 inches long. **Flowers** showy, more or less radially symmetrical, about ½ inch long, borne in dense spikes at the branch tips; sepals (calyx) pubescent, fused with 5 teeth; corolla pale lavender blue, fused into a narrow tube with 5 spreading lobes. **Fruit** four 1-seeded, elliptical nutlets.

This is probably the most widespread and abundant of desert verbenas, often found in association with creosote bush on gravelly and sandy soils. It grows in the Mojave, Sonoran, and Chihuahuan Deserts.

Common Bee Bush *Aloysia gratissima*
Southwestern Verbena *Verbena gooddingii*
Inset: Southwestern Verbena *Verbena gooddingii*

Pinleaf Vervain
Verbena perennis

Perennial **herb,** 12 to 15 inches tall; **stems** stiffly erect, narrow, tufted and broomlike, sparingly branched. **Leaves** opposite, narrowly elliptical to linear (pinlike) with the margins rolled under, mainly neither lobed nor toothed (entire), about 1 inch long. **Flowers** slightly bilaterally symmetrical, about ⅓ inch long, borne in narrow, open spikes at the tips of stems and branches; calyx pubescent, fused with 5 short lobes; corolla deep lavender blue, fused into a narrow tube with 5 spreading lobes, the lower somewhat the largest. **Fruit** four 1-seeded, elliptical nutlets.

Populations of pinleaf vervain are strikingly attractive but not particularly abundant. The species grows on less arid desert slopes of Texas, ranging west into Arizona. **Hillside vervain (*Verbena neomexicana*)** is a closely related species with a broader range, particularly in the Sonoran Desert, and similar habitat preference—gravelly desert mountain slopes (hillsides). This extremely variable, glandular-hairy species has somewhat smaller flowers and narrower spikes than pinleaf vervain, with leaves pinnately divided.

Desert Verbena
Verbena wrightii

Perennial **herb,** 8 to 20 inches tall; **stems** erect and spreading, few to many from a branched root crown, generally clothed with soft hairs. **Leaves** opposite, 1 to 2 inches long, 2 or 3 times pinnately divided into narrow, pubescent segments. **Flowers** showy, ½ inch long, slightly bilaterally symmetrical, borne in a congested spike at the stem tips; calyx densely glandular-hairy, fused with 5 unequal, short lobes; corolla pink to vibrant magenta, fused into a narrow tube with 5 spreading lobes, the lower generally heart-shaped and larger than the others. **Fruit** four 1-seeded nutlets.

This is arguably the most beautiful of several desert verbenas. It grows in gravelly soils of washes and slopes in the Chihuahuan Desert and Sonoran Desert of Arizona.

WATERLEAF FAMILY
Hydrophyllaceae

Hydrophyllaceae is one of those families where most characteristics are qualified with "generally": plants generally herbaceous and generally clothed with long hair; leaves generally alternate and generally compound; inflorescence generally coiled (scorpioid); flower parts generally in fives and generally radially symmetrical; stamens generally extending well beyond the mouth of the corolla. Unqualified characteristics include fused petals (corolla) and capsular fruit with the seeds attached to the outer wall (parietal placentation). Most desert species are annuals.

Whispering Bells
Emmenanthe penduliflora

Annual, glandular-sticky **herb,** 8 to 24 inches tall; **stems** erect, branched above. **Leaves** alternate, pinnately divided, ½ to 4 inches long. **Flowers** pendulous, about ½ inch long, borne in a coiled raceme that straightens out as the fruits mature; sepals 5, dark green, egg-shaped; corolla generally pale yellow, bell-shaped, with 5 short lobes, delicate and soon withering but persistent as the ovary matures; stamens included within the corolla tube. **Fruit** an elliptical, somewhat flattened, many-seeded capsule.

This plant grows along gravelly foothills of the Mojave and Sonoran Deserts. The seeds apparently are stimulated to germinate by heat, since the plants are more prominent in burned-over areas.

Pinleaf Vervain
Verbena perennis

Desert Verbena
Verbena wrightii

Hillside Vervain   **Whispering Bells** *Emmenanthe*
Verbena neomexicana   *penduliflora* var. *penduliflora*

Desert Mat
Nama demissum

Low, mat-forming, annual **herb,** 1 to 6 inches high; **stems** prostrate, forked (dichotomously branched), generally densely hairy. **Leaves** alternate but clustered at the base of the stem and below the flowers, linear to elliptical, pubescent, ½ to 2 inches long; leaf margin rolled under. **Flowers** ⅓ to ½ inch long and across, solitary or clustered at the tips of branches; sepals 5, narrowly lance-shaped; corolla pink to purplish, funnel-shaped, with a narrow tube and 5 spreading lobes; stamens included within the corolla tube. **Fruit** an elliptical, many-seeded capsule.

Like most annuals, desert mat responds to precipitation pulses. In particularly moist years the plants are relatively robust, have many flowers, and often form large, colorful populations. In dry years the plants are few and far between and may bear a single flower. The plants grow on clayey and sandy soils of the Great Basin, Mojave, and Sonoran Deserts.

Desert mat is a variable species, and its characteristics overlap with those of other namas, particularly **Great Basin nama** *(Nama aretioides).* These two desert beauties are separated by their styles. In desert mat the two styles are nonfused; in Great Basin nama, the styles are fused half their length. The two species grow in similar habitats and overlap in range.

In the Chihuahuan Desert, these two namas are replaced by **Havard nama** *(Nama havardii),* an endemic to the Big Bend region of western Texas. This is a densely hairy, annual herb, 6 to 15 inches tall, with erect stems that are extensively branched from the base. The flowers are pink to lavender or occasionally white, ⅓ to ½ inch long, and clustered along the tips of the many branches. It grows along desert washes and gravelly slopes.

Baby Blue-Eyes
Nemophila menziesii

Annual **herb,** 4 to 15 inches tall; **stems** erect, solitary, sometimes branched above, clothed with soft, white hair. **Leaves** opposite, ½ to 2 inches long, pinnately compound, the leaflets narrow, densely pubescent. **Flowers** showy, about 1 inch across, solitary at stem and branch tips; sepals 5, hairy, lance-shaped with spurlike appendages at their base; corolla sky blue and bowl-shaped, with a white center; stamens positioned above the corolla tube. **Fruit** an egg-shaped, many-seeded capsule.

This is a beautiful and highly variable species. It grows in the less droughty, more meadowlike regions of the Mojave and Sonoran Deserts, extending upward into more mesic biomes.

Desert Mat *Nama demissum*   Baby Blue-Eyes *Nemophila menziesii*

Great Basin Nama
Nama aretioides var.
multiflora

Havard Nama
Nama havardii

PHACELIAS
Phacelia species

Annual plants constitute a greater proportion of the desert flora than of any other biome, and *Phacelia* contributes more than its share of these annuals. In most phacelias the flowers are blue to purple and in coiled (scorpioid) racemes, which uncoil as the flowers mature. Generally the stamens extend well beyond the fused corolla. The plants are usually hairy, often glandular; the leaves range from toothed to divided.

Probably the most common, widespread, and variable species is **notch-leaved phacelia *(P. crenulata)*** *(cren,* "notched"). The plants are glandular-hairy and vary from a few inches to 2 feet tall, sometimes taller when growing up through shrubs, such as creosote bush. The stems are erect but branches may be widely spreading, giving the plants a bushy appearance. Leaf shape varies from nearly round to narrowly elliptical, and the blades vary from merely toothed or irregularly lobed to pinnately divided. The flowers are blue to purple with a white throat. One or more varieties grow in all our deserts, usually in sandy soils.

Caltha-Leaved Phacelia
Phacelia calthifolia

Succulent, annual **herb,** 4 to 15 inches tall; **stems** erect or spreading, sometimes branched, covered with stalked glands. **Leaves** mainly basal, blades nearly round, ½ to 2 inches long, toothed. **Flowers** ⅓ to ½ inch long and across, borne in coiled racemes; sepals 5, linear, glandular-hairy; corolla violet to purple, funnel-shaped; stamens extending well beyond the corolla.

This species grows in sandy flats of the Mojave Desert.

Lace-Leaf Phacelia
Phacelia distans

Annual **herb,** 6 to 30 inches tall; **stems** erect to spreading, generally branched from the base, glandular-hairy. **Leaves** alternate, 1 to 4 inches long, once or twice pinnately compound, the narrow segments usually further toothed. **Flowers** ⅓ inch long, many, in long, coiled spikes; sepals 5, linear, densely hairy and glandular; corolla blue to purplish, funnel-shaped; stamens extending well beyond the corolla. **Fruit** a roundish, pubescent, few-seeded capsule.

This is a common species on gravelly slopes of the Mojave Desert. It closely resembles and may be confused with **tansy-leaf phacelia *(P. tanacetifolia),*** which also grows in the Mojave Desert. The two species are separated by their corollas and fruits. The corolla of tansy-leaf phacelia is more or less persistent around the maturing ovary, and the fruit is egg-shaped rather than round.

Notch-Leaved Phacelia
Phacelia crenulata var. *ambigua*

Caltha-Leaved Phacelia
Phacelia calthifolia

Notch-Leaved Phacelia
Phacelia crenulata var. *crenulata*

Lace-Leaf Phacelia
Phacelia distans

Bluebell Phacelia *Phacelia campanularia*

Annual **herb,** 6 to 20 inches tall; **stems** erect, sometimes branched above, covered by stalked glands, particularly in the inflorescence. **Leaves** alternate; leaf blade nearly round, conspicuously veined, coarsely toothed, about as long as the leaf stalk (petiole). **Flowers** an inch or more long, borne in a coiled raceme that straightens out as the flowers mature; sepals 5, narrowly elliptical, glandular-hairy; corolla deep blue to purple, bell-shaped, with 5 lobes; stamens about as long as the corolla lobes. **Fruit** an egg-shaped, glandular, many-seeded capsule.

This is our most attractive phacelia. The flowers are beautiful and bear a striking resemblance to Canterbury bells of the genus *Campanula;* the species is sometimes called "wild Canterbury bell." It grows in gravelly plains of the Mojave and Sonoran Deserts.

Fremont Phacelia *Phacelia fremontii*

Low annual **herb,** 2 to 10 inches tall; **stems** solitary or few, generally not branched, sparsely pubescent to glandular-hairy above. **Leaves** basal and alternate, pinnately divided, elliptical, 1 to 3 inches long. **Flowers** showy, about ½ inch long and across, few to many in coiled racemes; sepals 5, linear to narrowly elliptical, pubescent; corolla pale lavender with a yellow throat, funnel-shaped with 5 spreading lobes; stamens not extending beyond the corolla tube. **Fruit** an egg-shaped, pubescent, many-seeded capsule.

The pale lavender flowers with a yellow throat and short stamens are unusual among phacelias, making the species easy to recognize. It grows in sandy or gravelly soils of the Great Basin, Mojave, and Sonoran Deserts, often in great abundance in moist springs.

Robust Phacelia *Phacelia robusta*

Robust annual or biennial, glandular-sticky **herb,** up to 2 feet tall; **stems** erect, 1 to several, mainly unbranched. **Leaves** basal and alternate, triangular, coarsely toothed to shallowly lobed, 1 to 6 inches long and nearly as wide. **Flowers** ¼ to ⅓ inch long and wide, numerous in dense, coiled spikes; sepals 5, elliptical, glandular; corolla pale pinkish lavender to nearly white, funnel-shaped; stamens extending well beyond the corolla. **Fruit** a roundish, pubescent, 4-seeded capsule.

This is an occasional plant of gravelly and rocky areas in the foothills of the Chihuahuan Desert. Other phacelias that grow in the same habitat are similar and often difficult to distinguish.

Round-Leaf Phacelia *Phacelia rotundifolia*

Low, rather succulent, annual **herb,** 2 to 8 inches high; **stems** erect to prostrate, generally branched from the base, glandular-hairy. **Leaves** basal and alternate, roundish (rotund) to broadly heart-shaped, coarsely toothed, ½ to 2 inches long and wide, the leaf blade about as long as the leaf stalk (petiole). **Flowers** only ¼ inch long, few to many in coiled racemes; sepals 5, linear to narrowly elliptical, densely glandular-hairy; corolla white or pale lavender, bell-shaped; stamens not extending beyond the corolla. **Fruit** an elliptical, pubescent, many-seeded capsule.

With its roundish leaves and white flowers, this species is one of the most distinctive of the many desert phacelias. It grows in rocky habitats, often on limestone outcrops and primarily in the Mojave Desert.

Bluebell Phacelia
Phacelia campanularia

Robust Phacelia
Phacelia robusta

Fremont Phacelia *Phacelia fremontii*   **Round-Leaf Phacelia** *Phacelia rotundifolia*

Key to Identifying North American Desert Wildflowers to Family

An identification key may frustrate the botanical novice, but familiarity with the key and with plant structures in general should resolve most difficulties. Knowledge of plant structures can be supplemented by referring to the descriptive illustrations and glossary.

This key is dichotomous, or two-branched: at every numbered pair in the key, the user has two mutually exclusive choices, *a* or *b*. To identify a plant to family, start at the beginning of the key and always progress forward (never backward). Choose between the two descriptions (*a* and *b*) in each numerical set and go on to the next two choices until your choice refers you to a family and page number, where the species of that family are pictured and described in the text.

A few reminders to help you use the key: always choose between *a* and *b* in the same numbered pair; read the descriptions for *a* and *b* carefully before making a choice; after choosing between *a* and *b* proceed to the next numerical dichotomy until the family has been identified; qualifying words, such as *mainly, often, usually,* or *generally,* mean what they say and should not be ignored.

1a. Plants reproducing by spores rather than seeds; leaves large, compound and all basal; no flowers produced .... **Fern family (Polypodiaceae) page 78**
1b. Plants reproducing by seeds; leaves various—sometimes compound, sometimes not; flowers *usually* produced 2

2a. Large shrubs or small trees with scalelike leaves; no flowers produced; fruit berrylike, green to purplish ....
.... **Cypress family (Cupressaceae, junipers) page 64**
2b. Plants not sharing the same combination of characters as above 3

3a. Leafless, green shrubs with stiffly erect and jointed, broomlike branches; no flowers produced; plants unisexual; seeds borne in cones ....
.... **Ephedra family (Ephedraceae) page 68**
3b. Plants having green leaves *or* otherwise not as above 4

4a. Nongreen, orange to yellow parasitic vine with threadlike stems ....
.... **Dodder family (Cuscutaceae) page 182**
4b. Plants green or otherwise not as above 5

5a. Parasite on desert shrubs; leaves scalelike in 4 rows; flowers unisexual and minute; fruit a berry ....
.... **Mistletoe family (Viscaceae, desert mistletoe) page 182**
5b. Plants not sharing the same combination of characters as above................... 6

6a. Plants spiny and leafless, thick and succulent, round and unbranched or branches in flat or cylindrical segments; flowers large and showy ....
.... **Cactus family (Cactaceae) page 40**
6b. Plants not spiny or otherwise not as above.. 7

7a. Flowers densely congested into heads (the heads sometimes tiny and congested) surrounded by greenish bracts; heads sunflower-like or daisylike (with outer ray flowers and inner disk flowers), dandelion-like (with only ray flowers), or rabbitbrush-like (with only disk flowers). See the illustrations. ....
.... **Sunflower family (Asteraceae) page 236**
7b. Flowers not in heads or if so, the heads not surrounded by bracts and resembling a single flower as described above 8

8a. Trees or shrubs greater than 6 feet tall (shrubs that vary in height from greater than 6 feet to smaller than 6 feet may be keyed both ways) 9
8b. Herbs, subshrubs, vines, or shrubs less than 6 feet tall 30

9a. Stems jointed; leaves scalelike; flowers individually tiny, pinkish, and borne in narrow, elongate clusters ...... **Tamarisk family (Tamaricaceae) page 296**
9b. Plants not sharing the same combination of characters as above................. 10

10a. Trees with palmately divided, fanlike leaves that are more than 3 feet long and equally wide .... **Palm family (Arecaceae, desert palm) page 202**
10b. Leaves much smaller and rarely fanlike 11

11a. Flowers borne in heads or dense spikes with stamens conspicuously extended; leaves twice pinnate; plants generally spiny; fruit a pod ....
.... **Legume family (Fabaceae, acacias and mesquite) page 118**
11b. Plants not sharing the same combination of characters as above................ 12

12a. Flowers radially symmetrical with 3 sepals and 3 petals, white to greenish; leaves large, more or less swordlike, and often in a basal rosette ....
.... **Lily family (Liliaceae, yuccas, agaves, etc.) page 150**
12b. Flowers not *both* white and with flower parts in threes; leaves not *both* large and swordlike 13

13a. Flowers small and nonshowy, sometimes in catkins, usually with no petals, mostly unisexual (fruits and/or bracts may be enlarged and colorful); plants *often* spiny 14
13b. Flowers individually showy or in showy inflorescences, mostly bisexual; plants spiny or not 19

14a. Leaves compound with 3 to several leaflets; fruit a 1-seeded berry (drupe); plants not spiny .... **Sumac family (Anacardiaceae) page 234**
14b. Leaves simple though *often* lobed; fruit various; plants *often* spiny 15

15a. Fruit a 3-winged, capsule; leaves narrowly elliptical to resinous; plants not spiny ....**Soapberry family (Sapindaceae, hop bush) page 228**
15b. Fruit a 1-seeded achene, drupe, or acorn; leaves various; plants *often* spiny   16

16a. Fruit an acorn, leaves have spiny margin; male flowers in catkins ....
.... **Oak (Beech) family (Fagaceae) page 198**
16b. Fruit an achene or drupe; plants otherwise not as above 17

17a. Fruit a drupe; plants spiny and often hairy but not scaly ....
...... **Buckthorn family (Rhamnaceae, condalia, gray-thorn) page 34**
17b. Fruit an achene; plants spiny or not, often covered with grayish or silvery scales 18

18a. Flowers with a tubular hypanthium; stamens 10 to 20; plants not scaly ....
.... **Rose family (Rosaceae, mountain mahogany) page 224**
18b. Flowers lacking a hypanthium; stamens 5; plants generally scaly ....
....**Goosefoot family (Chenopodiaceae) page 104**

19a. Flowers clearly bilaterally symmetrical; petals *usually* fused 20
19b. Flowers radially symmetrical or nearly so; petals *usually* not fused 25

20a. Flowers sweetpealike with an upper banner, 2 wing petals and a keel; stamens hidden within the keel; sepals fused; fruit *usually* a 1-chambered pod............
.... **Legume family (Fabaceae) page 118**
20b. Flowers not sweetpealike; stamens generally exposed; sepals fused or not; fruit various 21

21a. Ovary 2-lobed or 4-lobed, maturing into two or four 1-seeded nutlets; plants strongly aromatic; leaves opposite 22
21b. Ovary not 4-lobed, maturing into a few- to many-seeded capsule; plants not particularly aromatic; leaves alternate or opposite 23

22a. Ovary shallowly 2-lobed; nutlets 2; flowers white ....
.... **Vervain family (Verbenaceae, bee-bush) page 298**
22b. Ovary deeply 4-lobed; nutlets 4; flowers usually not white ....
.... **Mint family (Lamiaceae) page 178**

23a. Leaves linear and several inches long or pinnately compound; fruit narrowly cylindrical, several inches long. ....
.... **Bignonia family (Bignoniaceae) page 28**
23b. Leaves and fruit not as above 24

24a. Flowers red; seeds 1 to 4 per capsule; stamens 2 ....
.... **Acanthus family (Acanthaceae) page 24**
24b. Flowers lavender to blue or yellow; seeds many per capsule; stamens 4 ....
.... **Figwort family (Scrophulariaceae) page 82**

25a. Petals fused, corolla tubular or funnel-shaped; stamens borne on the corolla
tube 26
25b. Petals not fused; stamens borne on the receptacle or hypanthium 27

26a. Stems unbranched, canelike, and spiny; flowers bright red to orange, tubular,
about 1 inch long. ....
.... **Ocotillo family (Fouquieriaceae, ocotillo) page 200**
26b. Plants generally spiny but otherwise not as above ....
.... **Nightshade family (Solonaceae) page 192**

27a. Flowers whitish; stamens numerous—more than 10; leaves merely lobed ....
.... **Rose family (Rosaceae) page 224**
27b. Flowers yellow; stamens 10 or fewer; leaves compound 28

28a. Flower parts in threes: 6 sepals, 6 petals, and 6 stamens, each in two sets of
three; leaflets spiny along the margins; fruit a berry ....
.... **Barberry family (Berberidaceae) page 26**
28b. Flower parts in fives; leaflets not spiny; fruit various 29

29a. Leaves opposite; leaflets 2; fruit a roundish, white-woolly capsule ....
.... **Caltrop family (Zygophyllaceae, creosote bush) page 58**
29b. Leaves alternate; leaflets 3 to many; fruit an elongate pod ....
.... **Legume family (Fabaceae, palo verdes, etc.) page 118**

30a. Grasslike herbs with hollow, joined stems and long, narrow leaves with parallel
veins; flowers associated with bracts, small and not obvious ....
.... **Grass family (Poaceae) page 112**
30b. Stems and leaves *not both* as above; flowers *usually* obvious when present... 31

31a. Flower parts in threes: 3 sepals, 3 petals (sepals and petals often similar in color
and shape), and 6 stamens, showy; leaves mainly basal, linear or narrowly ......
lance-shaped, with parallel veins .... **Lily family (Liliaceae) page 150**
31b. Flower parts not in threes, or if so not showy and/or leaves not as above (but
see Polygonaceae) 32

32a. Petals none or indistinct from sepals; flowers *usually* not showy, often
unisexual (but see Euphorbiaceae) 33
32b. Petals and sepals present *and* petals distinct from sepals (in Nyctaginaceae,
keyed here, there are no petals but the sepals are petal-like and are surrounded by bracts resembling sepals); flowers usually bisexual 40

33a. Plants generally with milky juice (sap); sepals and petals none but inflorescence usually surrounded by colorful, petaloid bracts; fruit a 3-lobed capsule .... **Spurge family (Euphorbiaceae) page 230**
33b. Plants lacking milky juice; inflorescence not surrounded by petaloid bracts; fruit not a 3-lobed capsule 34

34a. Stamens 10 or more 35
34b. Stamens fewer than 10 36

35a. Shrubs; leaves opposite (blackbrush) or alternate (mountain mahogany) .... **Rose family (Rosaceae) page 224**
35b. Succulent herbs; leaves opposite .... **Fig Marigold family (Aizoaceae) page 80**

36a. Perianth segments 6 in two sets of 3; stamen 6 or 9; fruit a 1-seeded achene; plants not spiny; leaves basal or alternate .... **Buckwheat family (Polygonaceae) page 36**
36b. Plants not sharing the same combination of characters as above 37

37a. Leaves alternate; plants often spiny 38
37b. Leaves opposite; plants not spiny 39

38a. Fruit a drupe; flowers bisexual .... **Buckthorn family (Rhamnaceae, *Condalia*) page 34**
38b. Fruit an achene (utricle); flowers usually unisexual .... **Goosefoot family (Chenopodiaceae) page 104**

39a. Evergreen shrubs with unisexual flowers .... **Jojoba family (Simmondsiaceae, jojoba) page 116**
39b. Herbs or subshrubs with bisexual flowers .... **Amaranth family (Amaranthaceae, honey-sweet) page 26**

40a. Petals fused, at least at the base, separating from the receptacle as a unit; stamens 2 to 5 (rarely 10), usually borne on the corolla tube 41
40b. Petals separate or if fused then not separating from the receptacle as a unit and stamens more than 5 and usually borne on the receptacle 61

41a. Flowers bilaterally symmetrical 42
41b. Flowers radially symmetrical 47

42a. Fruit consisting of two or four 1-seeded nutlets; leaves opposite; plants usually having a strong sage odor 43
42b. Fruit a capsule with few to many seeds; leaves opposite or alternate; plants not sagey 44

43a. Ovary deeply 4-lobed, style arising from the base of the lobes ....
.... **Mint family (Lamiaceae) page 178**
43b. Ovary not or only slightly 4-lobed, style arising from the top of the ovary ....
.... **Vervain family (Verbenaceae) page 298**

44a. Shrubs with large yellow flowers ....
.... **Bignonia family (Bignoniaceae, trumpet flower) page 28**
44b. Herbs or if shrubs, flowers not yellow 45

45a. Capsule more than 2 inches long, tipped with a hooked beak ....
.... **Unicorn-plant family (Martyniaceae) page 296**
45b. Capsule much shorter, not beaked 46

46a. Stamens 2; seeds 4 per capsule; shrubs with red flowers ....
.... **Acanthus family (Acanthaceae) page 24**
46b. Stamens 4 to 5; seeds generally several; plants various but not shrubs with red
flowers .... **Figwort family (Scrophulariaceae) page 82**

47a. Ovary inferior; flowers *generally* congested in heads surrounded by bracts 48
47b. Ovary superior; inflorescence generally not as above 50

48a. Flowers in heads; sepals absent or modified into bristles or scales ....
.... **Sunflower family (Asteraceae) page 236**
48b. Flowers not in heads; sepals 4 to 5, not modified 49

49a. Leaves opposite; plants not viny ..... **Madder family (Rubiaceae) page 170**
49b. Leaves alternate; plant generally viny ....
.... **Gourd family (Cucurbitaceae) page 112**

50a. Stamens 10; pistils 5; plants succulent ....
.... **Stonecrop family (Crassulaceae, live-forevers) page 223**
50b. Stamens 2 to 5; pistils generally 1 to 2; plants usually not succulent 51

51a. Plants with milky juice; pistils 2, united by their styles or stigmas 52
51b. Plants lacking milky juice; pistil 1 53

52a. Leaves opposite; flowers in umbels; anthers ornate ....
.... **Milkweed family (Asclepiadaceae) page 174**
52b. Leaves alternate; flowers in panicles; anthers not ornate ....
.... **Dogbane family (Apocynaceae, blue-star) page 66**

53a. Ovary with 1 compartment and 1 seed; style and stigma 1; leaves generally
opposite with the paired leaves unequal in size ....
.... **Four-O'clock family (Nyctaginaceae) page 100**
53b. Plants varied but not sharing the same combination of characters ....
as above 54

54a. Flowers small in a narrow spike; leaves basal, linear, and parallel veined .... **Plantain family (Plantaginaceae) page 218**
54b. Inflorescence and leaves not *both* as above 55

55a. Ovary 4-lobed; fruit consisting of four 1-seeded nutlets; inflorescence generally a coiled raceme; plants usually stiff-hairy .... **Borage family (Boraginaceae) page 30**
55b. Ovary not 4-lobed; fruit other than 4 nutlets; inflorescence and pubescence various though usually not as above (but see waterleaf family) 56

56a. Stamens 2; leaves opposite .... **Olive family (Oleaceae) page 200**
56b. Stamens 4 to 5; leaves various 57

57a. Leaves opposite; style and stigma 1; flowers blue or red .... **Figwort family (Scrophulariaceae, penstemons) page 82**
57b. Leaves alternate *or* styles 3-branched (stigmas 3); flower color various 58

58a. Stigmas 3; ovary with 3 compartments; leaves often opposite .... **Phlox family (Polemoniaceae) page 206**
58b. Stigmas 1 or 2; ovary with 1 or 2 compartments; leaves alternate 59

59a. Ovary with 1 compartment; inflorescence generally a coiled raceme .... **Waterleaf family (Hydrophylaceae) page 300**
59b. Ovary with 2 or 3 compartments; inflorescence not a coiled raceme 60

60a. Stigma 1; fruit a berry or capsule .... **Nightshade family (Solonaceae) page 192**
60b. Stigmas 2; fruit a capsule .... **Morning-Glory family (Convolvulaceae, evolvulus) page 182**

61a. Flowers bilaterally symmetrical 62
61b. Flowers radially symmetrical 68

62a. Low, spiny shrubs, less than 3 feet tall; flowers lavender to reddish purple; fruit a roundish and spiny nut .... **Ratany family (Kramariaceae) page 222**
62b. Plants not sharing the same combination of characteristics as above 63

63a. Stamens more than 10; sepals showy and with a single spur .... **Buttercup family (Ranunculaceae, larkspur) page 40**
63b. Stamens 10 or fewer; sepals not both showy and spurred 64

64a. Petals 3, the lower 2 forming a keel; stamens 8; leaves simple .... **Milkwort family (Polygalaceae) page 178**
64b. Petals 4 or 5; stamens usually other than 8; leaves often compound 65

65a. Flowers sweetpealike, rarely yellow; stamens generally 10 .... **Legume family (Fabaceae) page 118**
65b. Flowers not sweetpealike, usually yellow; stamens 6 to 10 66

66a. Petals 5; stamens 10 (some often sterile and reduced) ....
.... **Legume family (Fabaceae) page 118**
66b. Petals 4; stamens 6 or 8 67

67a. Flowers strongly bilaterally symmetrical; stamens 6 in two sets of 3................
.... **Poppy family (Papaveraceae, Fumeriaceae) page 218**
67b. Flowers weakly bilaterally symmetrical; stamens 8.......................................
.... **Evening-Primrose family (Onagraceae) page 70**

68a. Stamens many, far more than 10.. 69
68b. Stamens 10 or fewer (but see Capparaceae, Polanisia) 74

69a. Inflorescence a head or dense spike; spiny shrub with pinnately compound
leaves .... **Legume family (Fabaceae) page 118**
69b. Plants not sharing the combination of characters above 70

70a. Ovary inferior; white-stemmed plants with sandpapery leaves ....
.... **Loasa family (Loasaceae) page 166**
70b. Ovary superior; plants otherwise not as above 71

71a. Stamens (filaments) fused at the base forming a tube around the style; flowers
often orange or orangeish .... **Mallow family (Malvaceae) page 172**
71b. Stamens not fused into a tube; flowers *usually* not orange 72

72a. Shrubs; petals 5 .... **Rose family (Rosaceae) page 224**
72b. Herbs; petals *usually* 4 or 6 73

73a. Petals 5; plants succulent .... **Purslane family (Portulacaceae) page 80**
73b. Petals 4 or 6; plants not succulent. ....
.... **Poppy family (Papaveraceae) page 218**

74a. Flower parts in fours: 4 sepals and 4 petals 75
74b. Flower parts in fives: 5 sepals and 5 petals 79

75a. Plants covered with vicious spines; flowers white ....
.... **Allthorn family (Koeberliniaceae) page 24**
75b. Plants not spiny; flower color various 76

76a. Ovary inferior; stamens 8; fruit a many-seeded capsule ....
.... **Evening-Primrose family (Onagraceae) page 70**
76b. Ovary superior; stamens 6 *or* if 8, fruit 2-seeded and deeply lobed 77

77a. Broomlike, more or less leafless, resinous-sticky shrubs with purple flowers
and deeply lobed fruits ....
.... **Rue family (Rutaceae, turpentine broom) page 228**
77b. Plants not as above 78

78a. Leaves palmately compound with 3 to several leaflets; stamens extending well beyond the petals .... **Caper family (Capparaceae) page 62**

78b. Leaves simple or pinnately compound; stamens usually not extended beyond the petals .... **Mustard family (Brassicaceae) page 184**

79a. Leaves simple, alternate; styles 5 .... **Flax family (Linaceae) page 98**

79b. Leaves compound, often not alternate; styles 1 or 2 80

80a. Flowers borne in umbels; leaves divided and carrotlike ....
.... **Parsley family (Apiaceae) page 204**

80b. Flowers not borne in umbels; leaves pinnately compound, not carrotlike 81

81a. Flowers pink; style becoming long and beaklike ....
.... **Geranium family (Geraniaceae, filaree) page 104**

81b. Flowers yellow (purple in fagonia); style not beaklike or if so, flowers purple and leaflets spine-tipped 82

82a. Leaves opposite; leaflets 2 to 3 ....
.... **Caltrop family (Zygophyllaceae) page 58**

82b. Leaves alternate; leaflets more than 3 ....
.... **Legume family (Fabaceae) page 118**

Plant Anatomy Illustrations

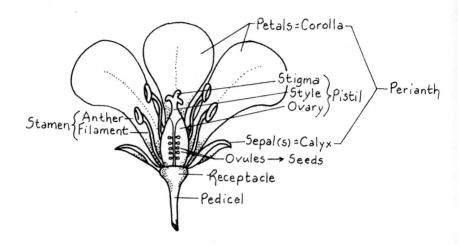

Diagramatic Sketch

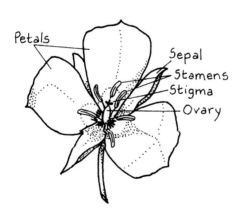

Representative: *Calochortus Kennedyi*

HYPOGYNOUS FLOWER (flower with superior ovary)

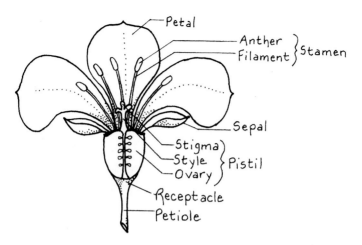

Diagramatic Sketch

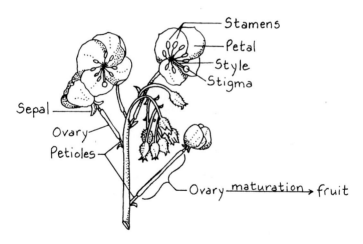

Representative: *Camissonia brevipes*

Epigynous Flower (flower with inferior ovary)

Radially Symmetrical Flowers

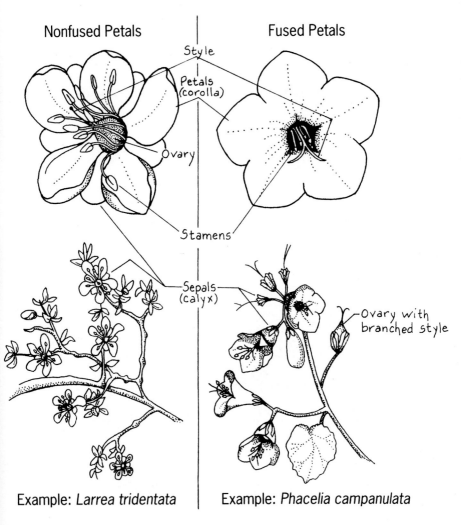

Nonfused Petals

Fused Petals

Style

Petals
(corolla)

Ovary

Stamens

Sepals
(calyx)

Ovary with
branched style

Example: *Larrea tridentata*

Example: *Phacelia campanulata*

FLOWER SHAPE

Bilaterally Symmetrical Flowers

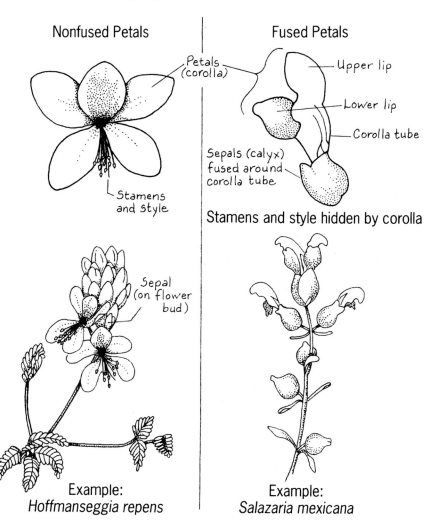

Nonfused Petals

Fused Petals

Petals (corolla)

Upper lip

Lower lip

Corolla tube

Sepals (calyx) fused around corolla tube

Stamens and style

Stamens and style hidden by corolla

Sepal (on flower bud)

Example: *Hoffmanseggia repens*

Example: *Salazaria mexicana*

FLOWER SHAPE

Spike: flowers non-stalked, sessile

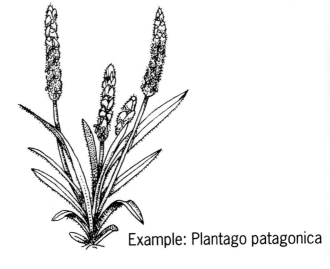

Example: Plantago patagonica

Raceme: flowers stalked, pedicellate

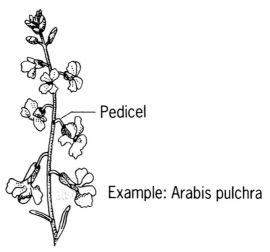

— Pedicel

Example: Arabis pulchra

INFLORESCENCE TYPES

Scorpioid Cyme: a coiled raceme or spike

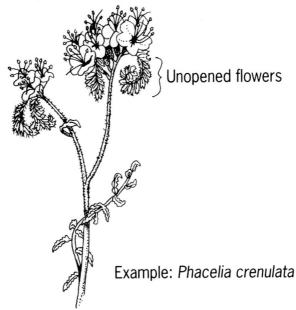

} Unopened flowers

Example: *Phacelia crenulata*

Panicle: a branched raceme

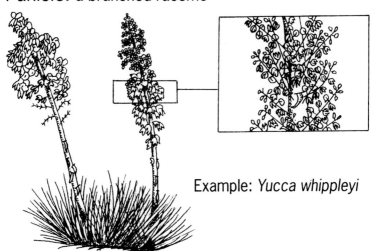

Example: *Yucca whippleyi*

INFLORESCENCE TYPES

Simple Umbel: several flowers borne from a single node

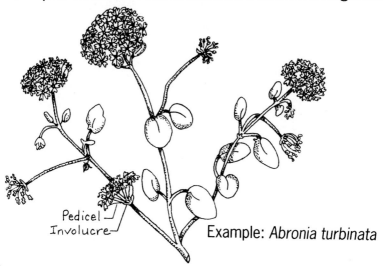

Pedicel
Involucre

Example: *Abronia turbinata*

Compound Umbel: inflorescence of primary and secondary umbels (umbels in umbels)

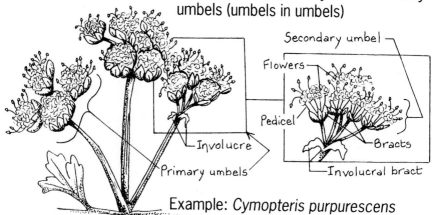

Secondary umbel

Flowers

Pedicel

Bracts

Involucre

Involucral bract

Primary umbels

Example: *Cymopteris purpurescens*

INFLORESCENCE TYPES

Head

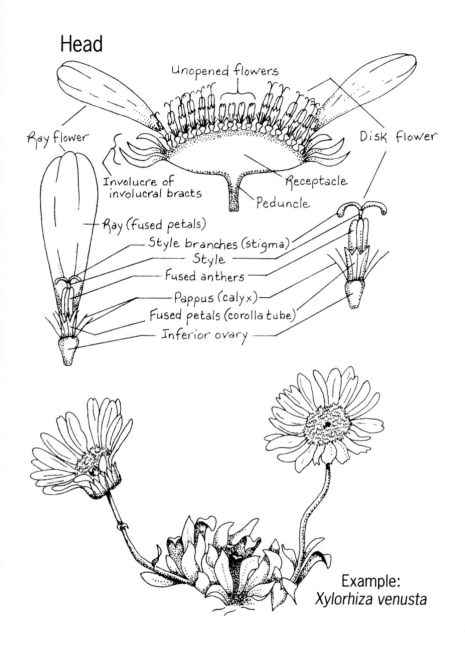

Unopened flowers

Ray flower

Disk flower

Involucre of
involucral bracts

Receptacle

Peduncle

Ray (fused petals)
Style branches (stigma)
Style
Fused anthers
Pappus (calyx)
Fused petals (corolla tube)
Inferior ovary

Example:
Xylorhiza venusta

INFLORESCENCE TYPES

Entire (smooth margin)

Representative: *Platyschkuhria integrifolia*

Toothed

Representative: *Ambrosia deltoides*

Pinnately Lobed/Divided

Representative: *Mentzelia veatchiana*

Palmately Lobed/Divided

Representative: *Sphaeralcea ambigua*

LEAF TYPE/SHAPE

Pinnately Compound

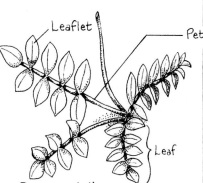

Leaflet

Petiole

Leaf

Representative:
Astragalus amphioxis

Bipinnately Compound

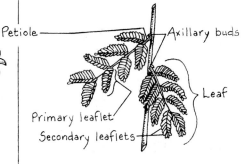

Axillary buds

Primary leaflet

Secondary leaflets

Leaf

Representative:
Calliandra eriophylla

Palmately Compound

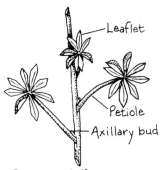

Leaflet

Petiole

Axillary bud

Representative:
Lupinus arizonicus

Dissected

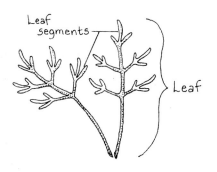

Leaf segments

Leaf

Representative:
Eschscholzia glyptosperma

LEAF TYPE/SHAPE

Alternate

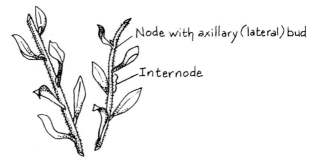

Node with axillary (lateral) bud

Internode

Representative: *Cryptantha confertifolia*

Opposite

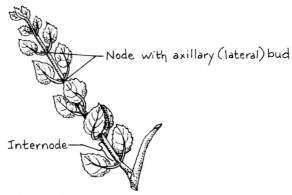

Node with axillary (lateral) bud

Internode

Representative: *Hyptis emoryi*

Basal

Representative: *Gilia subnuda*

LEAF ARRANGEMENT (POSITION)

Glossary

achene. A small, hard, one-seeded, indehiscent fruit that functions as a single seed.

alkaline. Basic as opposed to acidic; high pH.

alkaloid. A toxic nitrogen-containing substance. Plants produce many different alkaloids that serve a defensive role, being poisonous to animals.

alternate. As applied to leaves, not opposite: one leaf per node.

annual. A plant that lives only one year; growing from seed and producing seed in one year.

anther. The part of the stamen (male sex organ) that produces the pollen.

appendage. An attached part.

areole. A structure on cacti that bears spines or glochids or both.

awn. A bristlelike appendage, typically borne at the tip of some plant part.

axil (axillary). The upper angle formed by a leaf with the stem.

bajada. Slope; the upper bajadas are the upper slopes of a particular desert.

banner. Upper petal of a legume flower.

bark. Outer layer of a woody stem.

basal. As applied to leaves, at the base of the stem; at or near ground level.

beak. A prolonged, typically narrowed tip of some structure, such as a fruit.

berry. A fleshy fruit, typically with several seeds.

biennial. A plant that lives two years, the first year producing leaves and a thick taproot, the second year developing an erect stem with flowers.

bilaterally symmetrical. Relating to a flower, with similar left and right sides; mirror images can be produced by dividing the flower in a vertical plane; one (or more) of the petals and/or sepals is (are) unlike the others.

bladdery. Thin (papery) and inflated.

blade. The flat part of a leaf or petal.

bract. A small, modified, often pigmented leaf typically situated at the base of a flower or flower cluster.

bracteate. Having bracts.

bulb. A thickened, fleshy structure that typically forms belowground and functions in food storage and reproduction (as an onion bulb).

calyx. A collective term for all the sepals.

calyx lobe. One of the nonfused parts of a fused calyx.

calyx tube. The tube of a fused calyx.

capillary. Hairlike; very fine and slender.

capsule. A fruit that dries and splits open at maturity, shedding its seeds; typically it contains two or more compartments.

chaff. The thin scales on the receptacle of heads in composites.

community. A group of plants living together in a given habitat.

compound. Having two or more parts, such as compound leaves.

corolla. A collective term for a flower's petals.

cushion. A growth habit of some plants; dense and low in stature, resembling a cushion.

cylindrical. Elongate and circular in cross section.

deciduous. Falling away, as leaves falling at the end of the growing season or during periods of drought (drought deciduous).

dichotomous. Forked in more or less similar pairs.

discoid. Having only disk flowers, no ray flowers.

disk flower. One of the central flowers on the head of a sunflower, daisy, or similar plant; a tubular-shaped flower typically with 5 teeth or lobes and lacking a ray (flattened extension).

dissemination. The act of spreading or scattering, such as seeds or pollen by the wind.

divided. Separated to the base (or to the midvein in a leaf).

dominant. One of the most important plants of a given community because of numbers or size, or both; a plant that has a major effect on other plants of the community.

elliptical. Longer than wide with similar ends (not egg-shaped); a squashed circle.

elongate. Much longer than wide.

endemic. Restricted to a particular geographic area.

entire. As applied to a leaf, the margin smoothly continuous, neither toothed nor lobed.

filament. The threadlike stalk of an anther.

fleshy. Thick and succulent, juicy.

flexuous. Limber, easily bent.

follicle. A dry, podlike fruit with a single compartment that splits open at maturity.

frond. The leaf of a fern.

fruit. The ripened ovary with its seed(s).

glabrous. Without hairs.

glandular. Having glands that secrete resinous, often sticky material.

glaucous. Having a pale color, such as blue-green in leaves.

glochid. A small, usually barbed hair or bristle.

grasp. To appear to grasp the stem, as with some leaf blades that partly or totally encircle the stem.

habit. General appearance of a plant.

habitat. The home of a given plant, unique in having a particular set of environmental conditions.

head. A dense cluster of flowers that lack stalks; the inflorescence of a composite or member of the sunflower family.

herb. A plant lacking a hard, woody stem.

hypanthium. A cup-shaped or tubular structure from which the calyx, corolla, and stamens are borne.

indehiscent. Not splitting open at maturity.

inferior. As related to an ovary, the flower parts borne on (above) the ovary or, conversely, the ovary borne below (and inferior to) the flower parts.

inflorescence. A flower cluster.

involucral bract. One of the bracts (reduced leaves) surrounding a flower head in the sunflower family, or below the umbrella-like inflorescence of the parsley family.

involucre. A whorl of bracts surrounding an inflorescence, such as the head of a composite.

keel. The two lower, more or less united, keel-shaped petals of the legume family.

leaflet. One of the leaflike segments of a compound leaf.

linear. Long and very narrow, with parallel sides.

lip. One of two segments (upper or lower) of a bilaterally symmetrical corolla.

lobed. As applied to a leaf, cut or dissected (but not all the way to the midvein of the leaf).

mat-forming. Low, dense, and spreading horizontally; resembling a mat or carpet.

nodding. As related to a flower, hanging with the face of the flower downward.

node. A joint on a stem, the point where the leaves are borne.

nutlet. A hard-shelled, one-seeded fruit, one of four in the borage and mint families; a small nut.

oblong. Longer than wide.

opposite. As related to leaves, paired at the nodes; two leaves per node.

ovary. The seed-containing part of the flower that matures into a fruit.

palmate. Shaped like the palm of the hand with extended fingers.

palmately compound or **divided.** As applied to leaves, divided to the midvein, so the leaflets are borne at the same point and spread out like fingers.

panicle. A branched raceme.

pappus. Bristlelike or scalelike appendages borne on the ovary/fruit of members of the sunflower family; modified sepals. The pappus often functions in seed dispersal.

parasite. A plant growing on and deriving nourishment from another living plant.

pedicel. The stalk of a flower or fruit.

peduncle. The stalk of an inflorescence.

perennial. A plant that lives more than two years; it may die down to the roots each year but sprouts up the next.

perianth. A collective term for the calyx and corolla, used especially when they are alike.

petal. One of the segments of the inner whorl of flower parts, usually colored or showy.

petiole. Leaf stalk.

pinnate. Featherlike, with a central axis and perpendicular projections; typically applied to a leaf.

pinnately compound or **divided.** As applied to leaves, divided to the midvein, with the leaflets or leaf segments arranged on both sides of the extended axis of the petiole.

pistil. The central (female) part of the flower, containing the ovary, style, and stigma.

pistillate. Term applied to a unisexual, female flower; flower having a pistil but no stamens.

pod. A dry, dehiscent fruit, especially of the legume family.

pubescence. General term for hairiness or woolliness.

pubescent. Covered with hair.

raceme. An elongate, unbranched flower cluster, each flower having a stalk or pedicel.

radially symmetrical. Relating to a flower, star-shaped; the petals all similar in shape and size and sepals all similar to each other.

ray. The bladelike extension of a ray flower.

ray flower. One of the outer flowers of a sunflower, daisy, or similar plant, which has a flattened, elongate, colorful extension.

receptacle. The tip of a flowering stalk (petiole) on which the parts of a flower are borne.

rhizome. An underground stem that produces roots and upright branches (stems); an organ by which plants (such as quack grass and Canada thistle) spread.

root crown. The juncture between the root and stem; the crown of the root.

rosette. A cluster or whorl of leaves arising at or near ground level.

saline. Salty, having sodium salts, potassium salts, or other alkali salts.

scale. A thin, papery bract.

sepal. One of the bractlike segments of the outer whorl of flower parts, usually green.

shrub. A woody plant that branches at or near ground level.

spike. An elongate flower cluster with nonstalked flowers.

spur. A hollow extension of a petal or sepal, often containing nectar.

stamen. The male part of the flower consisting of the filament and anther.

staminate. Term applied to a unisexual male flower; flower having stamens but no pistil.

stellate. Star-shaped.

steppe. A nonforested region dominated by grasses and low shrubs.

stigma. The pollen-receptive part of a pistil.

stipule. Leaflike or bractlike appendage at the base of the petioles of some leaves. Stipules normally come in pairs and may be modified into spines.

stomate. A pore in leaves and green stems through which carbon dioxide is absorbed for photosynthesis.

style. The narrow portion of the pistil, connecting the ovary with the pollen-receptive stigma.

subshrub. A plant with stems woody at the base and herbaceous above.

succulent. Soft and juicy; filled with water.

superior. As applied to an ovary, the flower parts borne on the receptacle below the ovary; conversely, the ovary above (superior) to the other flower parts.

taproot. An elongate, unbranched, vertical root, like a carrot.

transpiration. Evaporation of water from plants, especially through stomates.

tubercle. A small prominence, such as on cacti stems.

umbel. An umbrella-shaped flower cluster or inflorescence.

unisexual. Flowers (or plants) of one sex, either staminate (male) or pistillate (female).

whorl. A group of three or more leaves, flowers, or petals radiating from a single point, such as from a node.

wing. A thin extension of an organ (seed, fruit, stem). One of a pair of lateral petals in a flower of the legume family.

woodland. An area dominated by widely spaced trees of low stature, savanna-like.

Selected References

Benson, Lyman, and Robert Darrow. 1981. *Trees and Shrubs of the Southwestern Deserts.* Tucson: University of Arizona Press.

Brown, G. W., ed. 1968 and 1974. *Desert Biology,* vols. 1 and 2. New York: Academic Press.

Correll, Donovan S., and Marshall C. Johnston. 1970. *Manual of the Vascular Plants of Texas.* Renner, Texas: Texas Research Foundation.

Evenari, Michael, Imanuel Noy-Meir, and David Goodall, eds. 1985. *Hot Deserts and Arid Shrublands. Ecosystems of the World,* vol. 12A. New York: Elsevier Press.

Hickman, James, ed. 1993. *Higher Plants of California: The Jepson Manual.* Berkeley: University of California Press.

Jaeger, Edmund. 1974. *Desert Wild Flowers.* Stanford: Stanford University Press.

———. 1974. *The North American Deserts.* Stanford: Stanford University Press.

Kearney, Thomas J., and Robert H. Peebles. 1964. *Arizona Flora.* Berkeley: University of California Press.

Larson, Peggy, and Lane Larson. 1977. *The Deserts of the Southwest.* A Sierra Club Naturalist Guide. San Francisco: Sierra Club Books.

Mozingo, Hugh. 1987. *Shrubs of the Great Basin: A Natural History.* Las Vegas: University of Nevada Press.

Nabhan, Gary P. 1982. *The Desert Smells Like Rain.* San Francisco: North Point Press.

———. 1989. *Enduring Seeds: Native American Agriculture and Wild Plant Conservation.* San Francisco: North Point Press.

Wells, Stephen, and Donald Haragan, eds. 1983. *Origin and Evolution of Deserts.* Albuquerque: University of New Mexico Press.

Welsh, Stanley L., Duane Atwood, Sherel Goodrich, and Larry Higgins. 1987. *A Utah Flora.* Provo, Utah: Brigham Young University Press.

West, Neil E., ed. 1983. *Temperate Deserts and Semi-Deserts. Ecosystems of the World,* vol. 5. New York: Elsevier Press.

Index

Grass family, 112–17
grassland communities, 10, 15, 19, 21, 113–15, 162
gravel ghost, 244–45
Grayia spinosa, 12, 18, 110–11, 224
graythorn, 34–35
greasewood, 8, 9, 12, 18, 32, 110–11
green-eyes, 246–47
Grindelia species, 272
    squarrosa, 266–67
ground-cherry, 192, 196–99
    lobed, 198–99
    thick-leaf, 196–97
ground-daisy, hoary, 288–89
groundsel, Great Basin, 284–85
    thread-leaf, 284–85
ground-thorn, 200–201
guayule, 22, 280
gumweed, 266, 272
    curly, 266–67
Gutierrezia species, 252

Haplopappus species, 266–67
    armerioides, 267
    gracilis, 272–73
    heterophyllus, 270–71
    linearifolia, 258–59
    spinulosa, 272
hazel, wild, 116
hedgehog cactus, 20, 46–47
    Engelmann, 46–47
    Fendler, 46–47
hedyotis, needle-leaf, 170–71
Hedyotis acerosa, 170–71
Helianthus petiolaris, 266–67
heliotrope, Gregg's, 32
    salt, 32–33
Heliotropium curvassavicum, 32–33
    greggii, 32
Hesperocallis undulata, 158–59
Hilaria jamesii, 15, 116–17
    mutica, 116
    rigida, 16, 116
Hoffmanseggia repens, 132–33
holly, desert, 16, 104–5
honeysuckle, desert, 24–25
honeysweet, 26–27
hop bush, 228–29
hopsage, 12, 18, 110–11, 224
horsebrush, 12, 286–87
    little-leaf, 286
    thorny, 18, 286–87
horse crippler, 44–45

Houstonia acerosa, 170–71
huisache, 118–19
hyacinth, desert, 156–57
    few-flowered, 156–57
    small-flowered, 154–55
hyaline herb, 268–69
Hybiscus coulteri, 172–73
Hydrophyllaceae, 300–307
Hymenoclea salsola, 16, 268–69
Hymenopappus filifolius, 268–69
Hymenoxys acaulis, 268–69
    depressa, 268–69
Hyptis emoryi, 178–79

Ibervillea tenuisecta, 112–13
incienso, 256
Indian blanket, Texas, 264–65
Indian mallow, 172
Indian ricegrass, 15, 116–17
indigobush, 142–47
    broom, 146–47
    Fremont, 144–45
    mesa, 144–45
    Mojave, 142–43
    Nevada, 142–43
    white, 142–43
Ipomopsis longiflora, 210–11
ironwood, 18, 140–41
Isocoma species, 266, 270
    wrightii, 270–71
Isomeris arborea, 64–65

jimmyweed, 270–71
jimsonweed, 194–95
jojoba, 116–17
jojoba family, 116–17
Joshua tree, 160–61; plants associated with, 16, 17, 60, 64, 74, 86, 224
juniper, 17, 64–67, 160, 162. *See also* piñon-juniper community
Juniperus species, 64–67
    osteosperma, 65
Justicia californica, 24–25

Keckiella antirrhinoides, 86–87
Koeberliniaceae, 24–25
Koeberlinia spinosa, 22
Krameria species, 16, 222
    erecta, 222
    grayi, 222–23
    parvifolia, 222–23
Krameriaceae, 222–23

Ronald J. Taylor in Joshua Tree National Park
—Gloria Taylor photo

About the Author

Ronald J. Taylor is a retired professor of botany and plant ecology at Western Washington University. A field trip to the Great Basin and Mojave Deserts as an undergraduate sparked his interest in desert plants, and his research and teaching provided him with many opportunities to study and photograph the plants of the desert. The author of numerous scientific and popular articles and books, Taylor has written three other Mountain Press titles: *Northwest Weeds* (1990), *Sagebrush Country* (1992), and *Mountain Plants of the Pacific Northwest* (1995, with George W. Douglas).

We encourage you to patronize your local bookstores. Most stores will order any title that they do not stock. You may also order directly from Mountain Press by mail, using the order form provided below or by calling our toll-free number and using your Visa or MasterCard. We will gladly send you a complete catalog upon request.

Some other Natural History titles of interest:

_____A Guide to Rock Art Sites Southern California and Southern Nevada	$20.00
_____Alpine Wildflowers of the Rocky Mountains	$14.00
_____Beachcombing the Atlantic Coast	$15.00
_____Birds of the Central Rockies	$14.00
_____Birds of the Northern Rockies	$12.00
_____Birds of the Pacific Northwest Mountains	$14.00
_____Coastal Wildflowers of the Pacific Northwest	$14.00
_____Edible and Medicinal Plants of the West	$21.00
_____Graced by Pines The Ponderosa Pine in the American West	$10.00
_____Hollows, Peepers, and Highlanders An Appalachian Mountain Ecology	$14.00
_____An Introduction to Northern California Birds	$14.00
_____An Introduction to Southern California Birds	$14.00
_____The Lochsa Story Land Ethics in the Bitterroot Mountains	$20.00
_____Mammals of the Central Rockies	$14.00
_____Mammals of the Northern Rockies	$12.00
_____Mountain Plants of the Pacific Northwest	$20.00
_____New England's Mountain Flowers	$17.00
_____Northwest Weeds The Ugly and Beautiful Villains of Fields, Gardens, and Roadsides	$14.00
_____OWLS Whoo are they?	$12.00
_____Plants of Waterton-Glacier National Parks and the Northern Rockies	$12.00
_____Roadside Plants of Southern California	$15.00
_____Sagebrush Country A Wildflower Sanctuary	$14.00
_____Watchable Birds of the Southwest	$14.00

Please include $3.00 per order to cover shipping and handling.

Send the books marked above. I enclose $_____

Name_____

Address_____

City_____State_____Zip_____

☐ Payment enclosed (check or money order in U.S. funds)

Bill my: ☐ VISA   ☐ MasterCard   Expiration Date:_____

Card No._____

Signature _____

Mountain Press Publishing Company
P.O. Box 2399 • Missoula, MT 59806
Order Toll Free 1-800-234-5308
Have your Visa or MasterCard ready.

Salt-tolerant greasewood growing in a salt flat (playa)

Painted Desert wildflowers

forms. Spines are the most obvious but do not protect against insects, the largest group of herbivores. More general defense strategies include bad taste, pungent odor, nutrient-poor tissue, and poisonous compounds. The latter are directed primarily toward insects and vary considerably in type, specificity, and effect. Production of defensive chemicals by plants requires a great deal of energy but is cost effective given the alternative. Many plants produce two or more types of protective compounds. For example, creosote bush produces resins and phenolics. The resins are produced and concentrated in the epidermis of mature leaves, making them nonpalatable to nearly all animals, from insects to cows. The young, nonresinous leaves are protected by phenolic compounds, which can be more easily produced than resins. As the resins accumulate and the toxic phenolics are no longer necessary, their production decreases about tenfold and energy is conserved.

DESERT ECOSYSTEMS UNDER SEIGE

By the mid-nineteenth century, the disruption and destruction of North American desert ecosystems had begun and has continued at an ever-increasing rate. The live-stock industry, both cattle and sheep, was the first to have a major impact on desert ecosystems. Although the number of sheep raised in the desert has been on the decline this century, the cattle industry has remained more or less stable. While much controversy surrounds the effects of grazing pressure, desert ecology no doubt has been compromised. The rich and varied habitats around ponds and along streams have been destroyed where cattle concentrate to drink; trampling has led to compaction of the soil, reducing water permeability and increasing runoff; disruption of the desert crust has allowed invasive weeds to become established more readily; plant communities have become altered with replacement of palatable species, such as grasses, by nonpalatable species, such as creosote bush and mesquite. Large areas have been cleared by burning and "chaining" to increase the grazing value. In some areas with a history of heavy grazing, prickly-pear cacti and introduced annual grasses have replaced most of the native plants.

But the threats to the desert ecosystem go far beyond the livestock industry. Deserts have long been treated as wastelands, places to dump garbage. They have become playgrounds for off-road vehicles and various recreational activities with little or no regard for the ecology. Most of the large desert trees have been cut for fence posts or lumber. In recent years, desert areas have experienced the highest growth rate in the United States. Urban sprawl has attacked the desert like a disease, linking the scattered towns and cities. To quench the terrible thirst of this burgeoning population, the nonrenewable desert aquifers, fossil remnants of the Ice Age, are being depleted at alarming rates. Mining activities have left deep and lasting scars. Much of the desert has been "reclaimed" for agriculture in areas where irrigational water is available. However, some of these cultivated lands have now been abandoned because of limited water supplies, rising operational costs, and/or salt accumulation in the soil. These abandoned lands are reverting back to desert but in a very altered state.

Perhaps the greatest threat to the integrity of desert ecosystems is the invasion of exotic plants, weeds. These opportunists take advantage of disturbed areas, and some are sufficiently competitive to displace native species. Shrubs that use water stores of greater depths are not competitively displaced, but herbaceous plants, especially annuals, are. The sad result is that famous desert blooms are becoming less and less spectacular, and the change most likely is nonreversible. Also of concern is the fact that weeds, particularly grasses, grow in profusion in moist years, filling the spaces between shrubs and creating a significant fire hazard. Most desert shrubs are not adapted to fire and are easily killed, greatly altering the structure of the desert ecosystem. The worst of these aliens are Mediterranean grass (*Schismus* species), annual grasses introduced from the Mediterranean region; annual brome grasses (*Bromus* species), mainly introductions from Eurasia; filaree or storksbill (*Erodium cicutarium*), also introduced from Eurasia; and a few mustards, notably tansy mustards (*Descurania* species) and tumble mustard (*Sisymbrium altisimum*). So, while the displaced native plants will probably never reclaim the desert where weeds have become established, the weeds' further invasion can be slowed—if not stopped—by progressive management. The recent establishing of a 7.5-million-acre desert wilderness under the California Desert Protection Act is a major step in the right direction. But it is only one